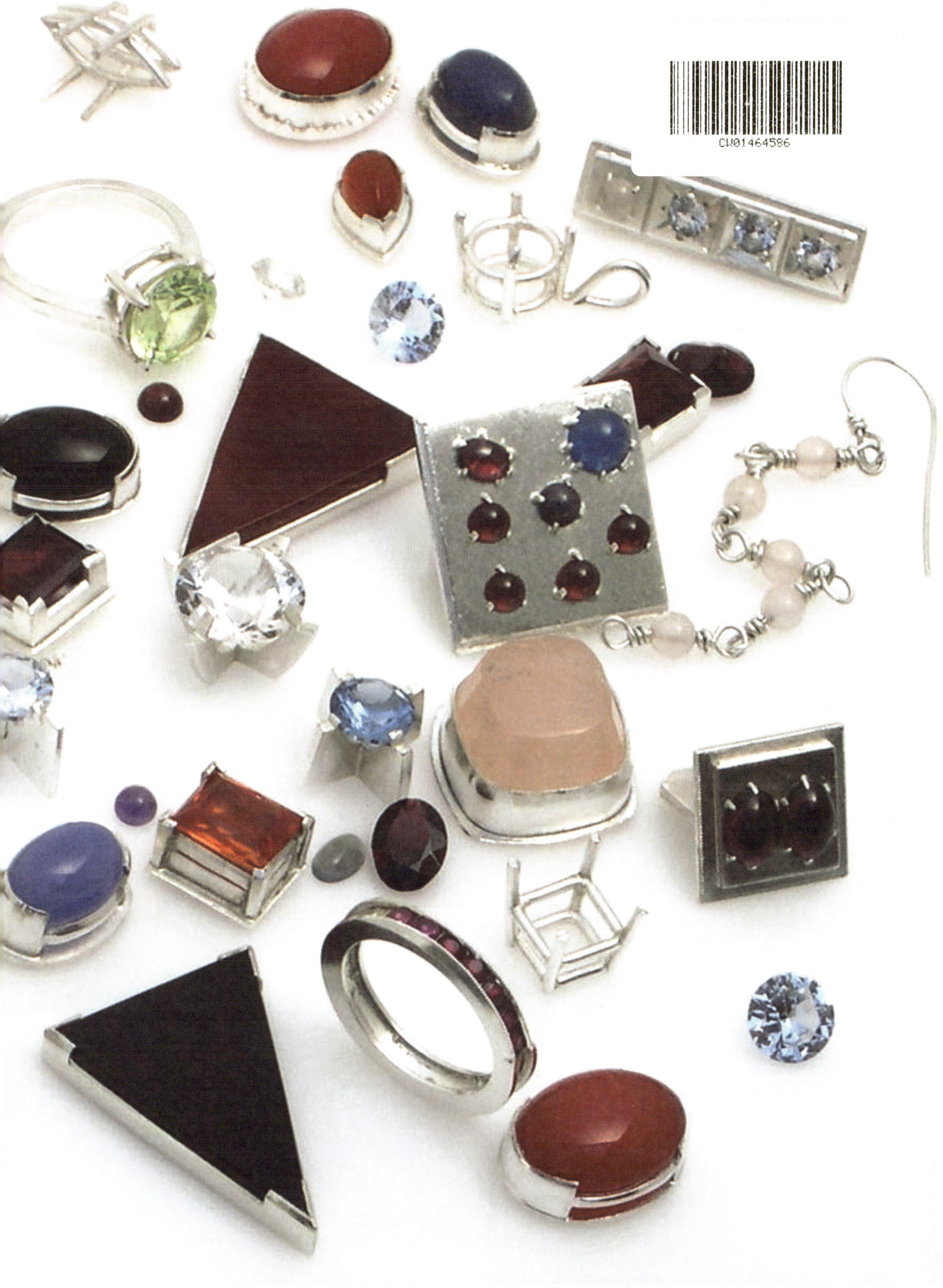

Creative
Stonesetting

Creative
Stonesetting

A&C BLACK PUBLISHERS

LONDON

A&CB

First published in Great Britain in 2008 by
A & C Black Publishers Limited
38 Soho Square
London W1D 3HB
www.acblack.com

ISBN 978-1-4081-0945-8

Copyright 2008

CIP Catalogue records for this book are
available from the British Library and
the U.S. Library of Congress.

This book is produced using paper that is made from
wood grown in managed, sustainable forests. It is
natural, renewable and recyclable. The logging and
manufacturing processes conform to the environmental
regulations of the country of origin.

Printed in Hong Kong

Drawings	John Cogswell
Book design	Tim McCreight
Editing	Tim McCreight
	Abby Johnston
Proofreading	Lois K. Edwards
Index	Jamie Kingman-Rice

Designs of all the jewelry shown in this
book belong to the artists.

Preceding page
William Richey, Ring
Platinum, gold, diamonds, topaz

Endpapers
Selection of settings made by the author.

Ronna Lugosch | Ring
Yellow and white diamonds,
18k yellow gold, platinum.
Photo: Ronn Orenstein

CREATIVE
STONESETTING

Susan Jo Klein | Munsteiner Necklace
18k gold, carved amethyst, brown diamond. Center link, 4"

photo: Peter Groesbeck

Acknowledgements

I wish to thank my incredible wife, Barbara, for her unwavering support and assistance with this project (as well as a much-needed kick in the butt on more than one occasion). I cannot even begin to thank Tim McCreight enough for his oft-tested patience, understanding, and encouragement. Thanks to Barbara Kuhlman (now deceased, but always in my heart) for helping me to start down the path of this life I so love, to my wonderful teacher, mentor, and friend, Kurt Matzdorf, for believing in me, inspiring me and sharing all he knew with me. Thanks to Bob Ebendorf for his inspiration and support, and for introducing me to the workshop circuit. Finally, thank you, thank you, thank you to all of the incredible students, both college and workshop, with whom I have trial-tested all of this material over the past three decades. We have all worked hard and played hard. This is for you all, with much love.

Introduction

In the competitive and highly specialized world of commercial jewelry, technical information is as valued a commodity as precious metals and stones—and is as closely guarded, too. Within this community, there is a widely held (mis)belief that divulging trade secrets is on a par with the illicit trafficking of documents relating to national security. The sadly mistaken notion that mere possession of technical information somehow confers an advantage has bred an atmosphere of silence and secrecy. Each fellow practitioner is viewed suspiciously as a competitor, which stifles discussion and sharing of mutual professional concerns and aesthetic issues. The attitude literally slows the wheels of progress.

Each individual is left to reinvent the wheel, so to speak. We all use the same tools and techniques; it is what we do with them that establishes our individuality. Sharing information is a good thing. When you know how to do something, you often just do it automatically, without much thought. When you have to explain to someone else what, how, and why you do what you do, it forces you to think about your work, and the more you think about your work, the better it gets. It is in the spirit of sharing that I offer this material on stonesetting, my way.

I decided to write this book for two main reasons. The first involves an issue of social responsibility; I am one link in a social order, a metalsmithing tradition, that stretches back to the dawn of human civilization, and which will, I hope, stretch even further into the future. As workers in precious metal, we are—every one of us—stewards of our profession, privileged with the gift of information handed down to us (traditionally, mostly by word of mouth), perhaps adding a little something to it, and then passing it on. With privilege comes responsibility, and this gift of knowledge is actually less a gift than a loan. Though it's ours to use for the brief time allotted to us, it is incumbent on each of us to pass what we know along to others. I take this responsibility seriously.

I was fortunate to have had excellent teachers and instruction as a student. Now I teach, and try to pass along the lore and wisdom that was entrusted to me. However, there is a severe limitation on the number of people I can reach directly, in person. Dimming eyesight, graying hair and a gradually increasing assortment of minor aches and pains leads me to suspect that I won't be able to teach one on one forever. So here I sit, hunting and pecking, a one-fingered keyboard wonder. It is my hope that this book will reach a larger audience, and for longer than I can.

My second reason for writing this book is simple: perceived need. I have long noted, with some degree of surprise and chagrin, that there seems to be a dearth of written information that deals specifically, in any depth, with creative stonesetting. By creative stonesettings, I mean unique, original settings designed and fabricated from scratch. There are many jewelry books that describe simple settings like the basic bezel, but they seldom explore the range of possibilities. Most leave the topic of stonesetting at that plain thin band of metal, and for too many people that's where the lesson ends. There are also a number of technical manuals that describe step-by-step techniques for mounting stones in commercial settings. These are well suited for trade jewelers, but they are of limited use to most studio craftspeople.

When commercially manufactured settings are well-made and properly used, they do what settings are supposed to do: hold stones. Because they are churned out by the thousands, they have a built-in anonymity that stems from their mass-produced 'look-alike-ness.' More often than not, when we use them in original, handcrafted work, they look like tacked-on afterthoughts—functional, perhaps, but bland and featureless. They lack any correlation to the design of the piece on which they are mounted. Your commercial settings look just like everyone else's, and this lessens the visual impact of your work.

Anyone with competent soldering and fabrication skills can make the settings described in this book. Having the ability to create unique settings that are integral to a design greatly expands options and possibilities. You won't be restricted to the standard range of sizes and shapes commercially available. You can create settings for stones of any shape or size. And, there are other ancillary benefits, as well. As I say to my students: "More different is often more better." Creative, innovative settings invite second looks. They add interest and freshness to your work. Also, in the process of learning how to assemble the settings described in these pages, I guarantee that your manual, technical, and design skills will improve. When you can solder the ten solder joints of a basic four-prong basket setting—all with hard solder and all within a space no larger than a pea—all of your other soldering jobs will be a breeze.

Although the focus of this book is on stonesetting, it necessarily involves some practical information about gemstones. I do not plan to delve into gemology, mineralogy, or lapidary beyond a brief discussion of pertinent issues. Though these three areas of study are related to stonesetting, they require more attention than I can give them here. Fortunately, each area is well covered in its own literature. I encourage you to acquaint yourself with the various gemstones and their properties. You'll find that a basic knowledge of gem materials will come in handy in both the marketplace and the studio.

Now it's time to get started. Let's set stones!

Chapter One
Getting Ready

As mentioned earlier, a full description of lapidary or mineralogy is beyond the scope of this book, but it is important for jewelers to have a practical understanding of characteristics pertinent to stonesetting. It will be useful to establish a common vocabulary of terms that will be used throughout the book. Let's start with some basic nomenclature and practical considerations specific to stonesetting. For example, stones that do not depend on the introduction of light are customarily set in solid bezels, while those that benefit from light are usually set in more open structures like prong settings. However, this "white wine with poultry, red wine with meat" approach has more to do with convention than practicality or necessity. Since virtually all light that enters any stone does so from the top, any cut of stone can be set in any kind of setting that will hold it securely and attractively. That's useful to know. It is also important to know the parts of a stone, and some characteristics that may help you in the design of an appropriate setting.

Alan Perry | Commitment Ring
18k gold, amethyst, tourmaline, boulder opal
photo: Robert Diamante

Gemstone Terminology

Cabochons

Cabochons are polished gemstones with smooth, rounded tops (the crown, or dome) and flat bases. Some cabochons may be flat on both top and bottom surfaces (called buff-top) and some may have two rounded surfaces (called double, or double-domed cabochons). The outer perimeter of the cabochon, where crown and base meet, is called the girdle. Most cabochons are opaque (impenetrable to light), or translucent (allowing some light to pass through). Transparent stones are rarely cut as cabochons and are more likely to be cut as faceted stones to take advantage of the illumination and reflection that results from penetration of, and interaction with, light.

Parts of a faceted stone.

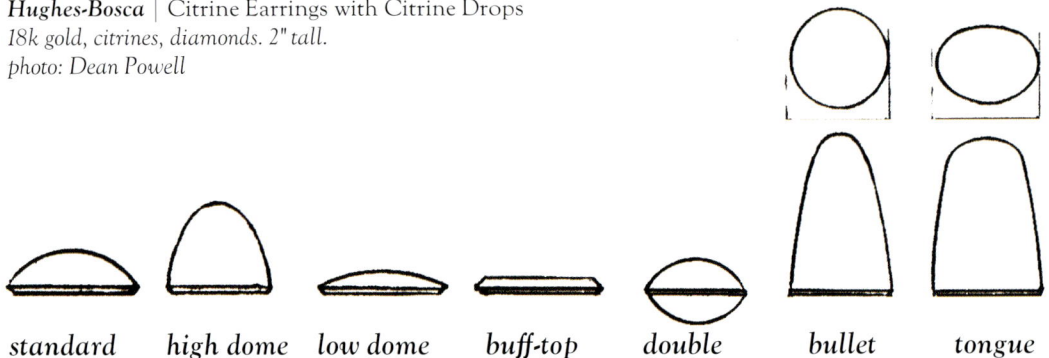

Hughes-Bosca | Citrine Earrings with Citrine Drops
18k gold, citrines, diamonds. 2" tall.
photo: Dean Powell

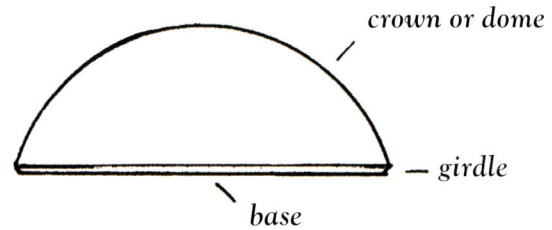

standard   high dome   low dome   buff-top   double   bullet   tongue

Cabochons are available in a variety of profiles.

Faceted

Faceted stones have reflective planes arranged in specific configurations to enhance the brilliance of a gemstone. The flat facet at the top of the stone, parallel to the plane of the girdle, is called the table. The faceted tip at the base of the pavilion is called the culet. Far and away the gems most often cut as faceted stones are transparent, but occasionally translucent and opaque stones are faceted.

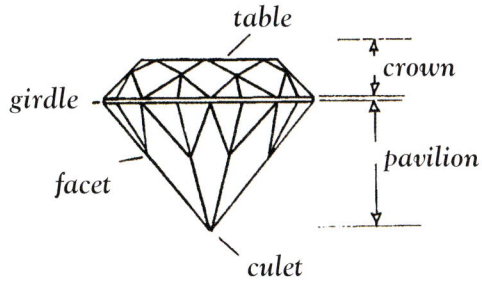

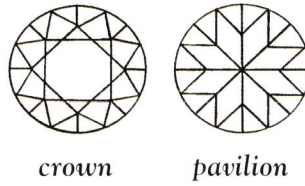

The proper names for parts of a faceted gem.

Stuart Cathey | LV Ring
18k gold, quartz
photo: Robert Diamante

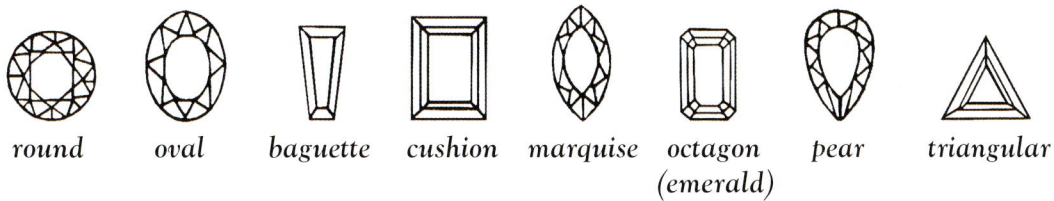

round   oval   baguette   cushion   marquise   octagon (emerald)   pear   triangular

Standard shapes of faceted stones.

Any given gem can be described in terms of its physical properties. Over the millennia, specific terminology and standards have been developed for these descriptions. Hardness refers to a gemstone's resistance to abrasion. The comparative hardness of gem materials is measured on a scale that rates materials from 1 to 10, on which diamonds (10) are hardest and talc (1) is softest. The scale bears the name of its inventor, the 19th century geologist, Frederick Mohs. Most familiar gems have a hardness of 6 or greater, allowing them to take, and maintain, a polished surface. However, some softer organic materials like amber, coral, jet, and pearls are used as gemstones because of their unique color, luster, or rarity, or because they can be carved into ornamental gems. Examples of these gem materials include shell cameos and carved ivory.

MOHS SCALE of Hardness

	mineral	common gem materials
10	diamond	diamond
9	corundum	ruby, sapphire
8	topaz	emerald, aquamarine topaz, spinel
7	quartz	amethyst, citrine, tourmaline
6	orthoclase	jade, opal, moonstone, turquoise
5	apatite	malachite
4	fluorite	jet
3	calcite	pearl, coral
2	gypsum	amber, ivory
1	talc	

Luster describes the visual quality of polished surfaces. The harder the stone, the higher the polish it will accept. The polish of soft gem materials are described as waxy, or greasy. Harder gems are described as vitreous (i.e., glass-like), and the hardest gems are called adamantine (diamond-like).

Cut refers to three separate issues:
• style (e.g., cabochon, faceted)
• silhouette shape (e.g., round, oval, pear, marquise, etc.)
• the quality of the workmanship

Is the stone lopsided? Is the girdle uneven? Too thick? Too thin? Are the facets distributed unevenly? Is the surface poorly polished?). The third consideration is obviously open to subjective analysis, and it has a lot to do with a stone's value, both market and aesthetic. Relevant to our concerns here, the quality of workmanship can also create problems when it comes time to set a gemstone. Uneven, asymmetrical, and otherwise poorly cut stones are more difficult to set than precisely geometric stones. An experienced setter knows to examine a gem carefully for cutting quality before beginning any job.

Color describes the hue of a stone—whether it is red or green or blue—but there is more to it than that. Color also includes these factors:
• depth or intensity (e.g., pale blue, dark red, deep purple, etc.)
• quality and distribution (e.g., uniform, zoned, cloudy, etc.)
• tone or shade (e.g., grass green, blood-red, etc.)

There is a tremendous range of variation in color, and subtle differences can greatly affect the value of a stone. A grass-green beryl of reasonable clarity is a very valuable emerald; a pale green or bluish-green beryl of comparable quality is a significantly less expensive aquamarine. To further confuse the unwary, many stones are routinely enhanced by being dyed, heat-treated, irradiated, or altered with lasers to improve color. Yet another kind of "creative no-menclature" can be misleading. A Cape ruby is actually a garnet and a Herkimer diamond is a clear rock quartz crystal. Color has no bearing on the setting of a stone, but plays a major role in the market-place. My advice: never buy a stone based on sales hype. Buy what appeals to you, even if other people would find it too pale or uneven. Sometimes, like people, stones are all the more beautiful and attractive for their idiosyncrasies. That said, I do advise that you pay attention to overall quality and stability, because these will matter later when you set the stone.

Clarity refers to the degree of transparency, the presence or absence of internal flaws, and purity of color. Like color, clarity is largely an aesthetic issue, important in the marketplace, but of little or no relevance to the stonesetter.

Flaws are imperfections that can be divided into two categories: cosmetic and structur-al. Both affect the value of a stone, but only one category is of critical importance when stetting the stone. Cosmetic flaws affect appearance, but not the physical integrity of a gem. Structural flaws weaken a stone, and pose a threat when setting. Structural flaws can be natural, and include cracks, fractures, feathers, and inclusions. Flaws can also be man-made and these include knife-edged girdles, thin tips on pointed stones, and similar cutting errors. Though not technically flaws, invisible structural weaknesses are associated with certain gem materials. These include cleavage planes, predisposition for chipping or splitting, and similar problems that have plagued stone setters for many generations. Examine each stone thoroughly to locate flaws and then make an educated call as to whether or not the stone is safe to set. If you have reservations, make them clear to the client before taking on the job.

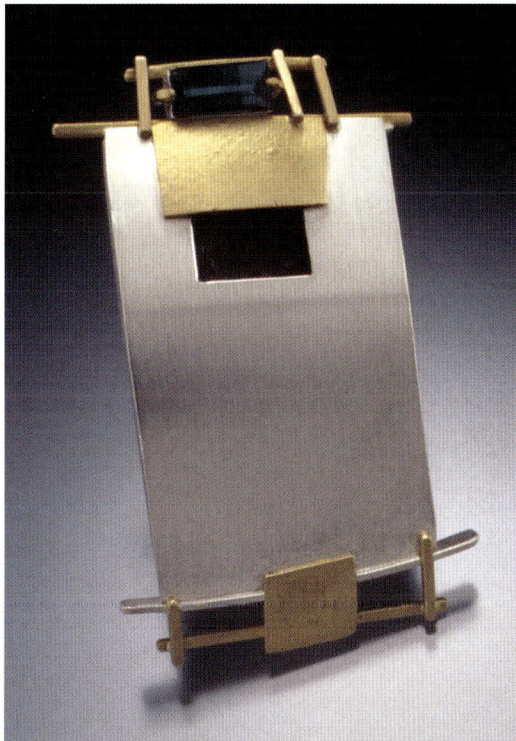

Bruce Anderson | Brooch
18k gold, sterling, tourmaline. 2½" tall
photo: Ralph Gabriner

Durability and **Stability** are characteristics that define a gem's ability to withstand stress (like the force on a stone when it is being set). This is different from hardness. The presence of flaws or inclusions and inherent characteristic tendencies play a role here. Opals are reasonably hard, but they are quite fragile because of the mil-lions of internal cracks and crevices. By contrast, jade has equal hardness but it is very tough because of its fibrous structure. Emeralds, though quite hard, are as brittle as they are beautiful. Some stones are dyed, heat-treated or irradiated to change or clarify their color, and if subjected to heat again, they may shift in color. Other gems are unaffected by high temperatures and can be soldered or cast in place. A little homework comes in handy here. Conduct a bit of research on each variety of stone as you buy it. Over time, you will compile a working knowledge of stone lore. You'll learn what to look for as well as what to look out for.

Design Considerations

When you set out to design and fabricate a setting, there are functional and aesthetic factors to consider. The primary function of a good setting is to securely hold and to protect a stone in the environment for which it is designed. For example, a setting for a pendant is not subjected to the same rigorous wear as a setting on a ring, so the pendant might be designed with a more delicate structure. On the other hand, burying a stone in a massive setting, though secure, would overwhelm the stone. The second design imperative is to display the stone to advantage, enhancing its beauty. The third element is the design integration of the setting and the piece on which it will be set.

These three considerations go hand in hand and should be addressed simultaneously. It is never, "First, I'll make the piece of jewelry. Next, I'll design a beautiful setting. Then, I'll figure out how to make it secure. And finally, I'll figure out how to put the two together." Always strive to design a secure, attractive setting that will integrate with, and be an essential element of, the overall design of the piece. The visual appearance of a setting will be determined by its safety, security, display, and location. I personally find it useful to make a mental checklist of the things I need to consider within each of the three categories.

Functional/Physical Considerations
- What is the specific environment of the setting—ring, pin, pendant, etc.?
- Is the setting appropriate for this environment and will it stand normal wear?
- Does the stone require special safety or setting consideration? Is it brittle or fragile?
- Does the stone have flaws, inclusions, or fractures?
- Is the stone hard and durable enough for the intended application?
- Does the cut of the stone necessitate special design consideration? Is it deep, or is the girdle liable to chip because it is too sharp?
- Will the setting snag? Poke? Be uncomfortable to wear?
- Will the physical design of the setting, or its final location, cause problems when it is time to set the stone?

Aesthetic Considerations
- What type of setting will it be? Prong? Bezel? Graver set?
- What will it look like?
- Can the setting be decorated or stylized? Can I add appliqués or embellishments? Can I cut away selected areas to visually lighten the setting?
- Will the design of the setting enhance the stone and display it to advantage?
- Is the setting interesting? Unique?

Overall Design Integration
- Will the setting fit in with the design of the rest of the piece, or will it look like a tacked on afterthought?
- Is the choice of stone, or its color, pattern, shape, or size significant to the design of the overall piece, or is this stone an arbitrary addition? Will a different stone, size, cut, color be better?

Chapter 2
Tools, Supplies, and Equipment

If you have reached the point where you are ready to consider adding stonesettings to your jewelry pieces, you probably have already accumulated many of the tools and supplies needed for fabrication and setting. The incorporation of stones is as old as the history of jewelry itself, and until the advent of machine technology, all settings were completely constructed and set with only a few simple hand tools. In many places around the world this is still the case, and it remains a viable option for us, too. However, the widespread availability of specialized tools and accessories (i.e., stonesetting burs, flexible shafts, and optical magnifiers) makes our work faster and easier. I am not suggesting that you run out and purchase everything on the following list of items, though the suppliers would certainly love it, and I know that most of us are avid tool collectors. Instead, I suggest that you add items to your collection as needed. When you know you need a specific tool or accessory, buy it.

One additional bit of advice: many of these tools are available in varying qualities and prices. Always shop carefully, and look for the best quality and best value. Get your money's worth. Especially in the case of the essential triumvirate of every jeweler's tool kit: saw, file, and pliers, these should be the very best you can afford. They will render superior service, outlast cheaper look-alikes many times over, and they will just plain feel good in your hand. And, hey, don't you really deserve the best?

The items on the following list reflect my personal preferences and recommendations. Some of these items require modification or special preparation before they're ready to use. In most cases, I will explain how to make these alterations, in detail, in the chapters where their usage is discussed. I have also separated these items into two categories: Essential and Optional.

Essential Tools
Bezel Pusher

This tool is simply a flat-ended metal rod mounted in a wooden handle. It is used to compress a bezel against a stone. Because the same tool is used to push prong tips over the girdle of a faceted stone, it is synonymously called a prong pusher. For the sake of clarity, I will simply stick with "bezel pusher." Though this tool can be used as purchased, I find that a simple modification increases its efficiency. This modification is described in Chapter 3, Bezels.

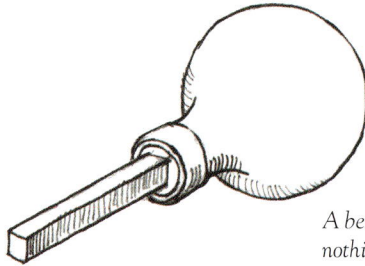

A bezel pusher is nothing more than a short metal rod in a bulbous handle.

Burnisher

Burnishers are used most often for rubbing out marks left on bezels from setting (i.e., pusher marks, filing and sanding scratches, etc.), and, to a lesser degree, for burnishing a rim of metal over the girdles of flush-mounted stones. Standard commercial burnishers (straight or curved) are used for the former, and homemade burnishers are used for the latter. The procedure for making these special homemade burnishers is described in Chapter 6, Flush Mounts.

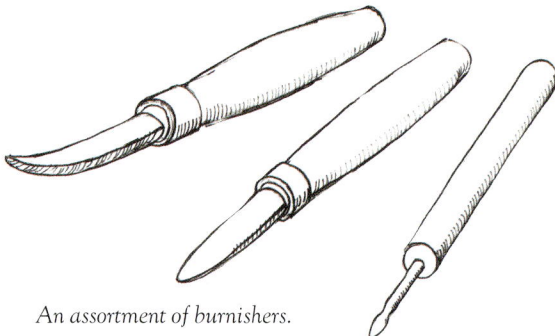

An assortment of burnishers.

Hughes-Bosca | Rings
18k gold, agate, fire agate, emerald, mandarin garnet, tsavorite garnet, mexican opal, yellow sapphires, tourmalated quartz. photo: Dean Powell

Burs

Burs for stonesetting come in many silhouette shapes (bearing, Hart, ball, etc.) and qualities (i.e., carbon steel, vanadium steel, high speed steel). Though generally offered in (rather expensive) sets of graduated sizes, burs of virtually any size and style can be purchased individually. This allows you to buy only the burs you need, assembling an assortment gradually. Different types of burs and their specific usage are discussed throughout the book. Before you rush out and buy a set of burs, make sure you know exactly what you need. Read first, buy later. One other consideration: burs are of use only when you have some means of rotating them to realize their cutting potential. Though you can secure a bur in a pin vise and cut a seat by hand, it is faster and easier to accomplish this operation with a flexible shaft machine.

Burs come in a dazzling range of styles and grades. Here are a few of the most commone.

Files

Along with pliers and the ubiquitous jewelers saw, files are among the most basic and essential tools in any jewelers kit. Files for jewelry use generally come in about a dozen different styles (flat, square, triangular, half-round, etc.), in three different size ranges. Files also come in a range of cuts, or coarsenesses (#0, #2, #4 and #6 are the most common cuts). Jewelry-quality files are often described as Swiss pattern or Swiss cut, which simply means that the teeth are created by the intersection of two rows of cuts that run lengthwise down the working face of the file. This produces a finer, smoother surface than the common hardware store variety of file that is often referred to as American bastard cut, or, simply, bastard cut.

Larger files, usually ranging from 6" (15 cm) to 12" (30.5 cm) in length (the numeric length designation refers to the length of the working portion of the file, not its overall length) are called hand files. All hand files require the addition of a handle to prevent injury to the hand from the tapered, blunt-pointed tang. These larger files are designed for rapid removal of material, and are used for leveling, truing, and preliminary clean-up of broad surfaces.

Intermediate-size files, known as needle files, mostly range from 4½" (11.5 cm) to 6½" (16.5 cm) in length, and are usually sold in

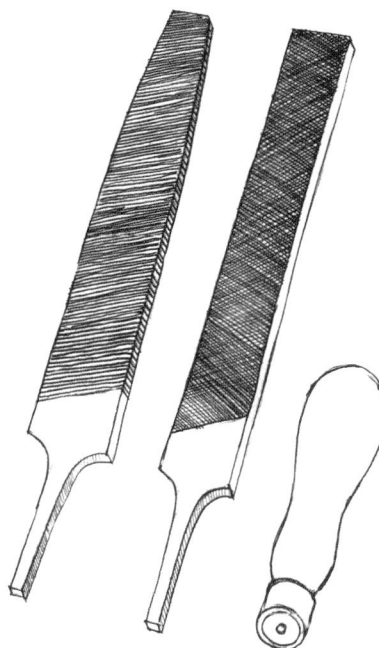

Two hand files: American Bastard cut on the left, and Swiss-cut on the right.

an assortment of 10 or 12 standard styles (also available individually). Jewelers use these files extensively; their various cross sections allow access to small, restricted spaces. They are particularly useful for refining and detailing. Needle files have cylindrical, partially knurled tangs with rounded ends, which eliminate the need for separate handles.

The smallest files were originally designed for watchmakers (escapement files), or tool and die makers (machinist files). These tiny files have working surfaces ranging from about 1½" (4 cm) to about 2½" (6 cm) in length. Escapement files usually have long, square handles with an overall length of about 5½" (14 cm), and machinist files are shorter, typically 3½" (9 cm) with cylindrical, knurled handles. These miniature files are ideal for getting into tiny recesses, and for shaping, detailing and refining prong tips

I find two specific files, one, a hand file and the other, a needle file, particularly

Susan Jo Klein | Strange Fruit: Ginko in Winter (Brooch) *photo: Peter Groesbeck*
Morrison Ranch jasper, sterling, 18k gold. 22¼" wide.

useful for stonesetting. A 6" (15 cm) or 8" (20 cm) flat hand file (with handle), #0 or #2 cut, is extremely useful for quick, efficient leveling and truing, and a smaller, finer, barrette needle file, #4 or #6 cut, is handy for trimming prongs and fine detailing. I refine both of the barrette file edges on fine abrasive paper to smooth and polish away any roughness prior to use to prevent possible damage to stones. Remember, it pays to buy the best quality files you can afford.

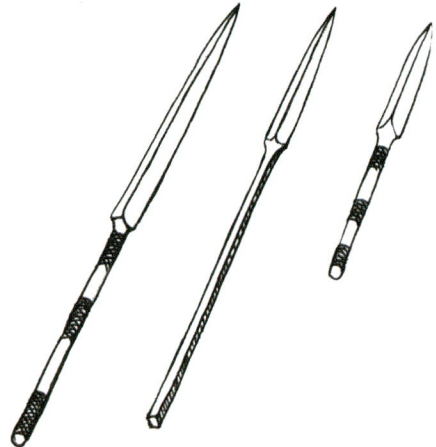

Needle files are available in three sizes: Standard (4½"–6½"), Escapement (around 5½"), and Machinists (3½").

Common cross sections of needle files.

Gravers

Gravers, and their handles, come in a wide range of shapes and styles, but only a few are really relevant to stonesetting. These particular gravers, their preparation, and their proper usage are discussed in detail in Chapter 5, Graver Settings.

Jewelers Sawframe

One of the three most important tools in your collection, your sawframe(s) should be the very best quality you can afford. I own a number of sawframes of different styles and throat depths. The traditional sawframe is wooden-handled, has a two-piece steel adjustable-length frame, and utilizes three thumbscrews; two to tighten the blade between knurled jaws at both ends of the frame, and one for adjusting and locking the frame at the appropriate length. Newer, ultralight or lightweight sawframes are not adjustable in length, relying instead on standard length blades and the springiness of the frame to properly tension the blade. Instead of moveable jaws to clamp the blade at each end, these newer frames use setscrews to tighten the blade inside receptacle holes located at opposite ends of the frame.

Throat depth refers to the distance between the mounted sawblade and the inner face of the rear of the saw frame. A deeper throat depth allows you to cut farther into larger pieces of metal, but, because of the tendency of the back end of the frame to wander from side to side, it makes it more difficult to cut straight. Shallower throat depth permits finer control and truer, more precise cuts. Since the cuts required for fabricating or setting are, obviously, quite small, a shallow throat depth is preferable. My favorite sawframe, a traditional-style beauty whose handle has worn comfortably smooth in my hand over many years of use, has a 2" (51 mm) throat depth that I find ideal. It just keeps getting better and better.

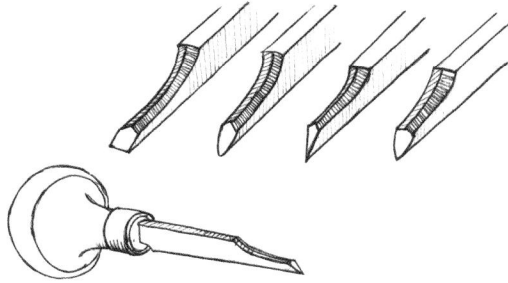

The most common styles of gravers are, left-to-right, flat, round, knife, and anglette.

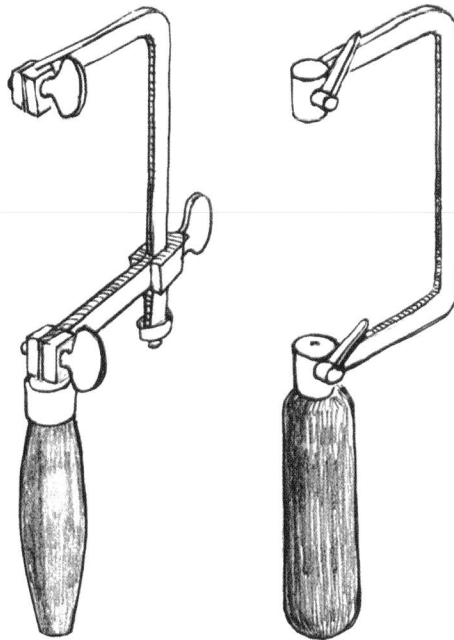

Sawframes are available in a range of sizes, measured from the blade to the back. The standard adjustable frame is shown at the left, with a "quick release" lightweight frame at the right.

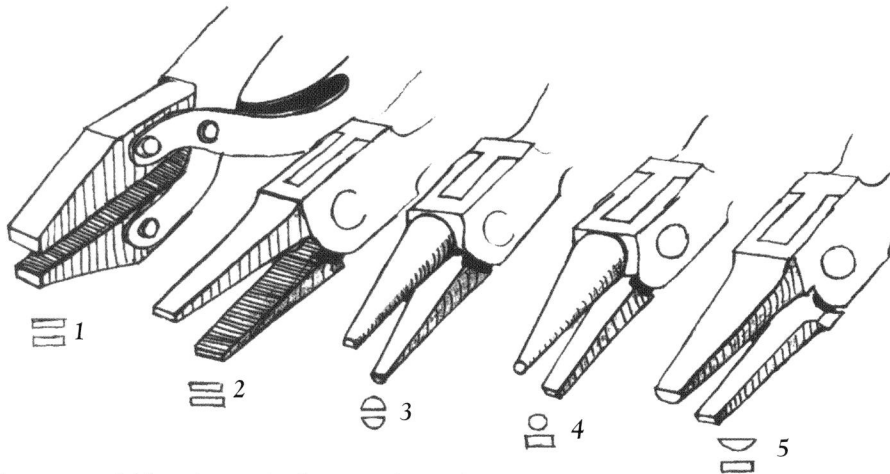

Pliers are available in dozens of styles, many designed for very specific uses. These are the most common, most versatile shapes. 1. Parallel Jaw, 2. Flat, 3. Chain-nose, 4. Round/Flat, 5. Half-Round/Flat

Pliers

Like files, pliers come in many styles, sizes, and qualities. All jewelry-grade pliers have smooth, untoothed jaws, preferably polished, and the best quality are assembled with a box joint construction. Cheaper pliers often employ a weaker lap joint construction. Some pliers have springs to facilitate opening and closing, and some are fitted with plastic handle covers for comfort. Always buy the very best quality pliers you can afford. You can skimp on some tools, but buying cheap pliers is false economy.

In addition to my standard pliers (i.e., flat-nose, chain-nose, etc.), there are three specific pairs of pliers that I find absolutely indispensable for stonesetting: parallel-jaw pliers, round/flat-jaw forming pliers, and half-round/flat-jaw forming pliers. Parallel-jaw pliers are very useful for holding small parts securely, particularly flat or uniformly thick items, while filing or refining. The two forming pliers are essential for shaping and forming curved parts, and also for adjusting the length of bezels. I describe in detail the proper usage of these pliers in Chapter 3, Bezel Settings.

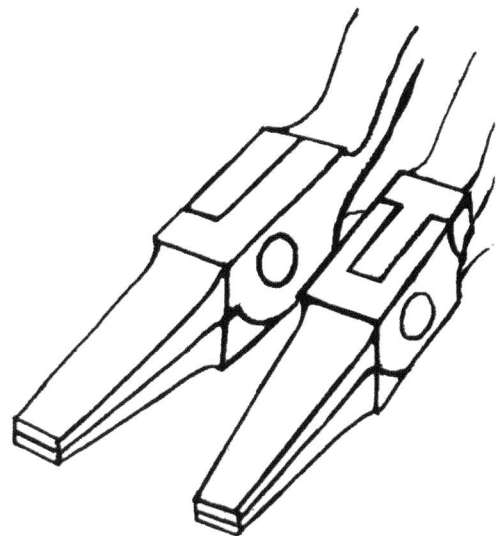

Pliers are constructed with lap joints (left), or the more rigid, more dependable box joint (right).

Ring Clamp

Ring clamps, as the name implies, are simple, double-ended devices for holding small items, like rings, while working. Ring clamps are most commonly fashioned of wood, but some are made of plastic or aluminum. Generally, ring clamps are rounded at one end to follow the contour of a ring, and flat at the other. The inner faces are usually lined with leather, rubber, or plastic to provide a sturdy grip and to prevent marring. Items are usually secured in position at one end of wooden ring clamps by driving a wedge between the halves at the other end. Some plastic and metal clamp styles use a wing nut or thumbscrew to tighten the jaws instead of a wedge.

I prefer the wooden clamps because they don't flex (I have had small items snap out of the far more flexible plastic clamps and go sailing across my studio), and I find them more comfortable and easier to handle than metal ring clamps (the wing nut on most metal ring clamps is awkwardly located on the side of the clamp). Also, I modify my stonesetting ring clamp by filing ¼" (6 mm) deep notches around the outer perimeter of the clamp, about an inch in from each end, that fit into a correspondingly shaped notch in my bench pin. This makes it easier for me to anchor and steady the ring clamp when I am filing or setting. Ring clamps and bench pins are so inexpensive and useful that I always keep extras on hand, modifying them to fit my needs.

Scriber

A fine-pointed, straight-tapered scriber is essential. Make sure it does not have an angular, beveled point. They are widely available from any jewelry supplier, or you can make your own. A sewing needle with its eye end driven into a short length of dowel makes a respectable scriber. My scribers are fashioned from old dental tools. I simply snapped off the worn-out

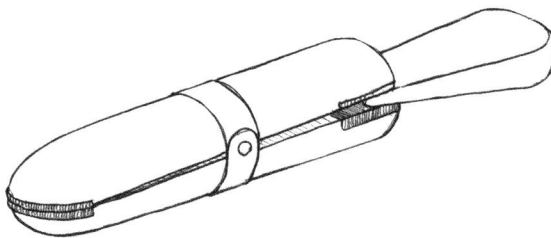

Ring clamps are used to hold onto small pieces when cutting, filing, setting, and finishing. In addition to making the work easier, using them will avoid unhealthy stresses to your hand and arm muscles.

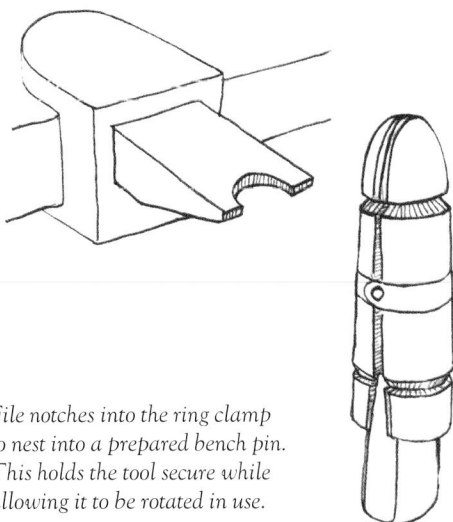

File notches into the ring clamp to nest into a prepared bench pin. This holds the tool secure while allowing it to be rotated in use.

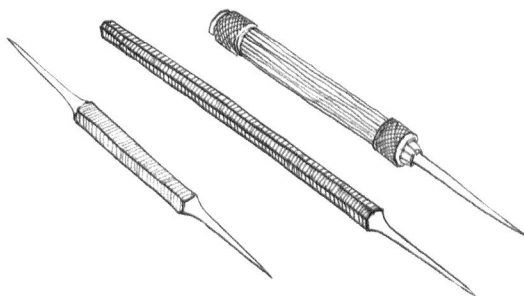

Assorted scribers.

working end, and file a straight-tapered point. This same fine-tipped tool also serves as a miniature burnisher, allowing me to get into the tiniest of spaces to rub out file marks, brighten hard-to-polish areas, and to tighten stitch prongs against small stones, described in Chapter 5, Graver Settings.

Spring Dividers

At first glance, spring dividers resemble a small compass. Upon closer inspection, however, you'll note that instead of one leg ending with a graphite point, both legs of the spring dividers terminate with sharp metal points. Spring dividers are used extensively for stonesetting (and for many other metalworking activities, as well). They are used for taking, and transferring accurate measurements, for describing arcs and circles, and for many other layouts requiring great precision (which is frequently, in the case of stonesetting). The numeric designation (2", 3", etc.) that describes the size of a pair of spring dividers refers to the distance to which the legs will open, which in turn defines the maximum radius of a circle that it will describe. For example, a 3" (76 mm) spring dividers will describe a 6" circle. A silversmith might use a 12" (30.5 cm) spring dividers to describe a 24" (61 cm) circle on a sheet of metal, while, conversely, a stonesetter might use 1½" (38 mm) to 3" (76 mm) spring dividers when laying out the dimensions for a stonesetting. Size really does matter. If your dividers are too large and ungainly, they will be awkward and clumsy, and will not satisfy your needs. An occasional rub on a sharpening stone helps to maintain sharp points.

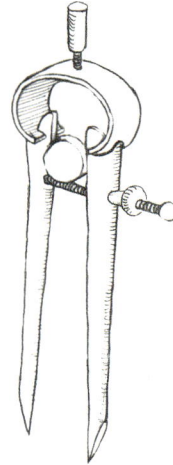

A spring dividers is an essential tool for finding and holding small dimensions.

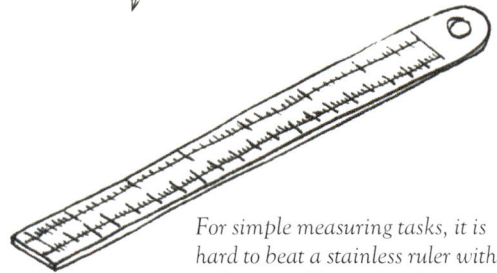

For simple measuring tasks, it is hard to beat a stainless ruler with inch and millimeter markings.

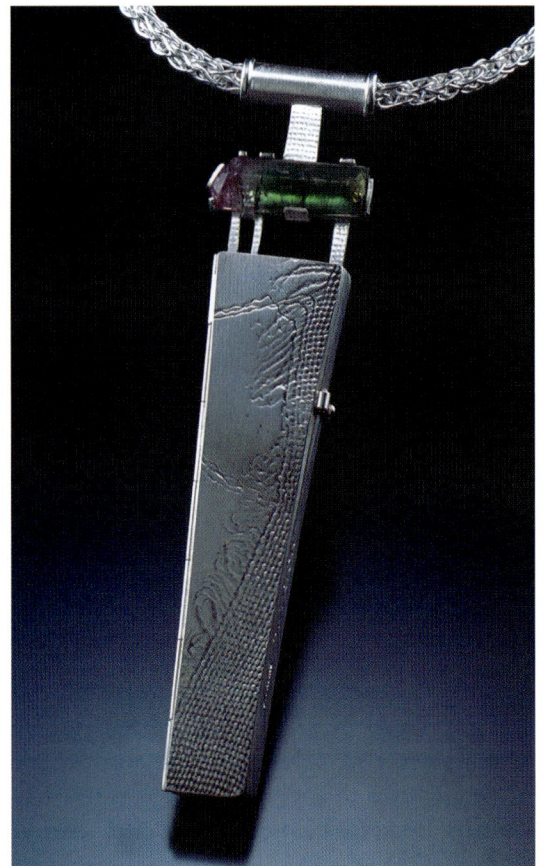

Mary Anna Petrick | Pendant
*Sterling, bi-colored tourmaline.
4½" tall.
photo: Larry Sanders*

Stone Gauge

Measuring cabochons is pretty simple because most cabochons are flat-backed and can be measured with a simple 6" stainless steel ruler that is marked off in millimeters. In fact, because bezels are fitted to the stone, and because they are relatively easy to adjust, you really don't even have to measure the stone. Unfortunately, however, such is not the case with faceted stones that will be set in prongs or, even more importantly, into bur-cut seats in solid metal such as graver settings and channel settings.

When cutting seats for faceted stones with burs, it is critical that you select a bur exactly the same size as your stone. A fraction of a millimeter means the difference between a seat that will fit the stone properly, and one that won't. With prongs, you may be able to adjust the prongs in or out a bit to improve the fit, but solid metal is not so accommodating. Either your stone fits, or it doesn't. Because of the complex, multi-angular form of a faceted stone (and the matching bur, too), it is impossible to measure it precisely with a ruler. You will need a more accurate way of doing this.

There are three basic types of measuring devices for measuring faceted stones with the degree of accuracy you will need. The least expensive, but also least precise, is called a sliding gauge. Usually made of brass, it measures in 1.0 millimeter increments. For intermediate fractional millimeter readings, you simply measure the stone and then, while maintaining the spacing between the two jaws, do a trial and error fit to select a bur of the same size. Not too sophisticated, but it works if you are careful.

The other two measuring devices, a spring gauge and a vernier caliper, cost a little more, but both measure in tenths of a millimeter, making them more accurate and dependable than a sliding gauge. The degree gauge has two spring-tensioned legs joined with a single rivet, that allows the legs to pivot opened and closed. At one end, the legs terminate in pincer-like jaws. At the far end, a millimeter scale is affixed to one leg

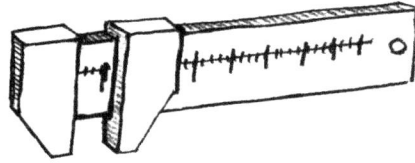

A sliding gauge, also called a sliding caliper, is a handy and economical choice.

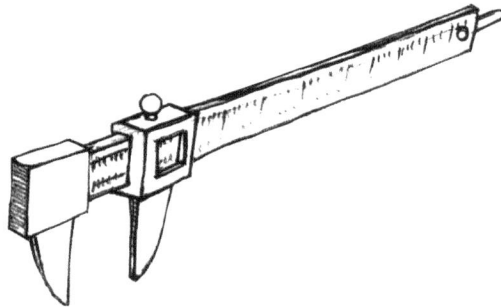

A vernier caliper provides much greater accuracy, especially when measuring small gems. In addition to the mechanical version shown, you will find models that display the measurement on a gauge or a digital read-out.

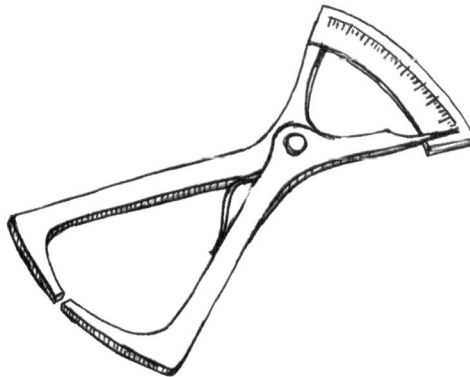

The time-honored spring gauge transfers an opening at one end into numerical readings on the other end.

and the other leg ends in a pointer. When you position the jaws on a stone's girdle, the pointer indicates the precise measurement of its diameter.

The vernier caliper is a larger, more accurate and somewhat fancier cousin of the sliding gauge—kind of like a sliding gauge all grown up and with a college degree. The vernier caliper has a movable jaw with a window for easy measurement reading, and a spring-loaded, or thumbscrew, locking mechanism that enables you to hold a setting. The jaws measure outside dimension on one side and inside dimension on the other, and a retractable flat metal rod attached to the sliding jaw allows you to measure the depth of concave forms. Fancier, more costly models (these have PhDs) have instant readout dials or digital displays, and have resolutions as fine as one hundredth of a millimeter.

Tweezers

Probably one of the most basic, most essential, and most neglected of all essential tool categories, tweezers are the workhorse of the soldering station. Over the years, I have observed countless individuals struggling with otherwise simple soldering operations simply for lack of a decent pair of tweezers in workable condition. Rendered useless from misuse, neglect, poor design, or decrepit condition, these simple, indispensable tools, instead of facilitating our activities, become instruments of anguish and frustration. I have seen eyebrow tweezers, tweezers whose tips don't meet, tweezers bent and mangled, tweezers encrusted with solder and flux, even tweezers with tips solidly soldered together nestled incongruously in otherwise respectable tool kits.

There are two pairs of tweezers that I think are critical to any jewelers collection: a pair of insulated grip cross-locking stainless steel soldering tweezers with tapered, slightly blunted points, and a pair of plain, sharp-pointed stainless steel tweezers. The

cross-locking tweezers are designed to hold small items securely while soldering, and they can safely withstand the heat of a direct flame while their insulated grips protect your fingers from conducted heat. Their stainless steel alloy composition doesn't become annealed during repeated heatings, so they maintain their shape better, and they won't rust like cheaper, inferior, chrome-plated look-alikes. A simple modification to the tips of these tweezers, described in Chapter 4, Prong Settings, turns them into a specialized soldering jig, ideal for holding the parts of a prong setting in the proper alignment for solder assembly.

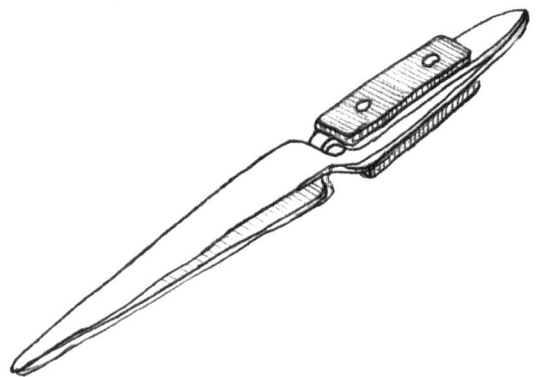

Insulated cross-lock, or "self-locking" tweezers are useful to hold parts while soldering. I also use them to hold onto small elements so they don't get lost on my bench.

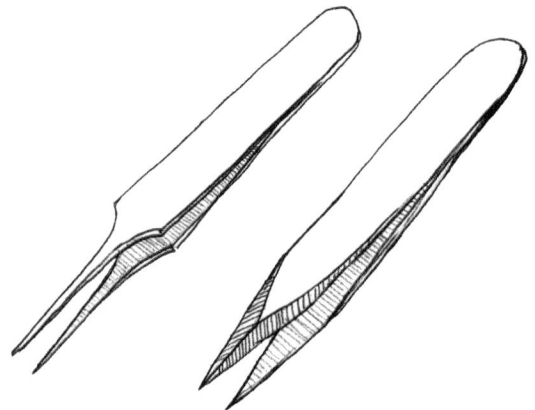

A nice pair of fine-pointed tweezers is like a good paring knife in the kitchen—once you get used to them, you will never want to do without. If the tips become worn, file a symmetrical and delicate point.

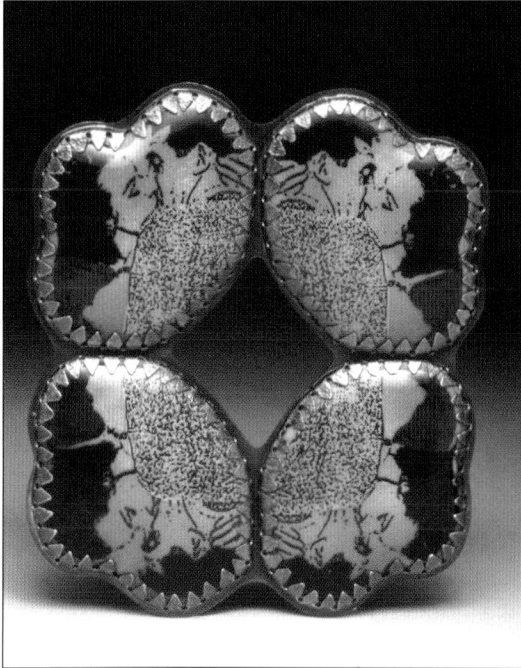

Kathleen Browne | Quartet Brooch
Fine silver, sterling, vitreous enamel.
4" by 3½"
photo: Kathleen Browne

The fine-pointed tweezers are used for picking up and placing chips of solder and other small items, and should never be subjected to direct heat. The rule is, when flame comes down, tweezers go up. Like cross-locking tweezers, they are rustproof and easy to maintain.

Neither of these tweezers is expensive, which may explain the widespread negligence in their maintenance. If they cost more, we'd probably take better care of them. An occasional adjustment with a pair of pliers to correct any misalignment, or a few strokes with a sanding stick to keep the ends clean and well-shaped are about all the standard maintenance they require. With a little care, they will provide many years of dependable service.

Optional Tools
Bezel Mandrels

My students take great delight in watching dear old (surely senile) Dad wander around the studio in search of the perfect mandrel around which to bend some specific curve. It may be a water pipe, a gas cylinder, the handle of a hammer, anything with the right cross section. I constantly tell them, "All the world's a mandrel. You just have to see it." It is absolutely true. There are mandrels everywhere, some specifically designed for that purpose, and others that, though not really meant to be mandrels,

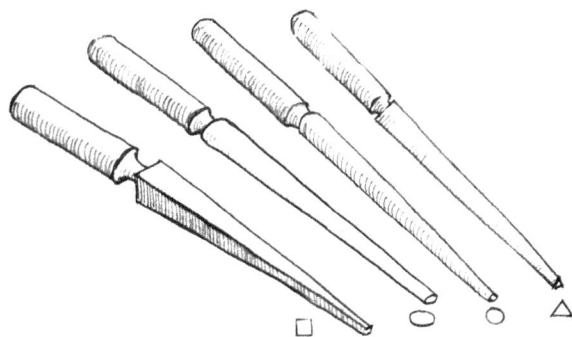

Commercial bezel mandrels come in many shapes; the most common are square, oval, round, and triangular.

just happen to be the right size and shape, and, serendipitously, just happen to be right there in front of us, in the right place, at the right time. Bezel mandrels are no exception.

There are commercial bezel mandrels in many cross sections, but round and square mandrels are the only ones that will always produce settings that will fit those shapes accurately and reliably. Triangular, rectangular, oval, and pear-shaped stones vary so widely in relative proportions (length to width, or comparative length of a stones sides) that no single mandrel can accommodate them all, and hence, these mandrels are of limited use.

Over the years, I have assembled a sizable collection of mandrels that include such diverse items (in addition to the real bezel mandrels) as plumb bob weights, automotive drift punches, center punches of varying size, and drill bits (a standard drill index has sixty sizes). Any port in a storm. If it fits, it is a mandrel. Keep your eyes open, and soon, you too, will start seeing mandrels everywhere. Note: although they are called bezel mandrels, they are equally useful when fabricating prong settings.

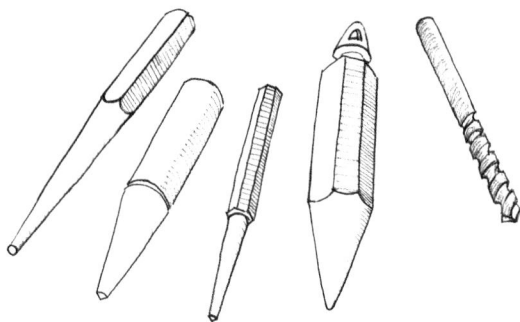

Useful mandrels appear in many places, including hardware stores, junk shops, and flea markets.

Beading Tools

Beading tools come as a set of about a dozen short cylindrical rods and a mushroom-shaped handle into which they all fit interchangeably. The working ends of the rods are conically tapered, terminating in smooth concave depressions of varying sizes. The cup-shaped end of the beading tool is used to roll and burnish graver-raised burrs or stitches into tiny polished beads. These tools, and their proper usage, are described in detail in Chapter 5, Graver Settings.

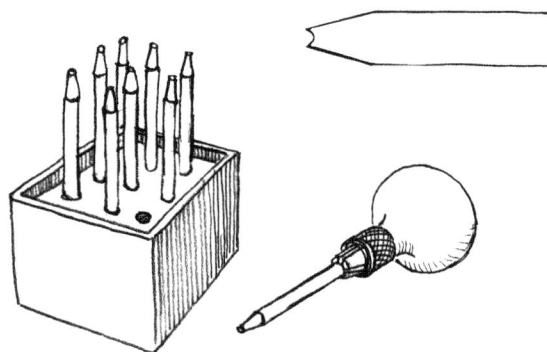

Not all settings require a set of beading tools, but in some situations they are just what is needed.

Flush Cutters

Flush cutters, also called flush-cutting nippers, are extremely useful for many stonesetting-related operations like trimming prongs and cutting wire sections or bezel strips to length. The precision-ground jaws of these nippers are thin and relatively fragile, and are only designed for cutting thin-gauge, soft metals (gold, silver, copper, etc.). Heavier, less expensive bevel-edged utility cutters are used for cutting harder materials like binding wire or base metals like nickel and brass.

As the name suggests, these nippers produce a perfectly flat cut, but on only one side of the cut. The other side of the cut will always be beveled. When used properly on both sides of a seam, these nippers produce a perfectly true, close-fitting joint that requires no further preparation for soldering.

Flush cutters are available with three different jaw configurations: diagonal, offset (or oblique), or end. The pointed tips of diagonal flush nippers allow access

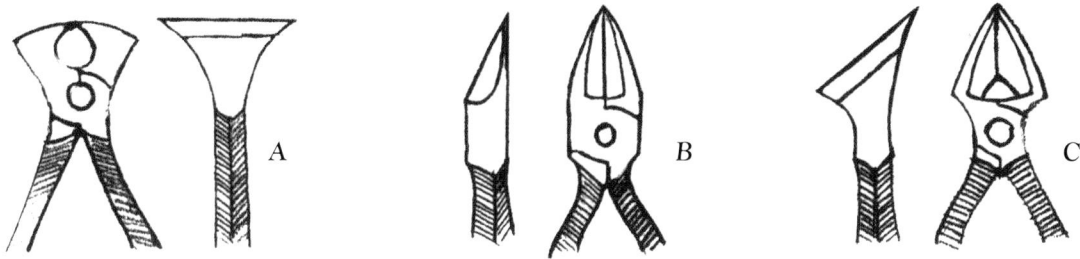

Diagonal cutters are offered in these three formats: A. End Cutters, B. Diagonal Cutters, and C. Oblique Cutters.

to very tight spaces, but are weakest at their delicate tips and strongest closer to the hinged joint. End cutters have jaws perpendicular to the lengthwise axis, are substantially stronger, and cut equally well along the entire length of their blades. However, their broad, blunt-ended profile restricts access in close quarters. Offset nippers fall in between, combining the best traits of the other two styles, and are my favorite for stonesetting.

Be careful when shopping for flush cutters. Good quality nippers that produce true flat cuts are often, but not always, expensive. Don't let price alone be your determinant, however. You can purchase inexpensive flush cutters designed for electronics from Radio Shack for less than ten dollars, that cut true and accurately, but are not made from the same high quality steel as their more expensive counterparts, and won't last as long. On the flip side, there are expensive, yet inferior quality cutters. Whenever possible, if you have the opportunity to physically inspect the tool before making your decision, take it for a test drive. Try it out and examine the quality of the cut it produces. Look carefully at the way the whole tool is finished. If the overall quality of the tool is lacking, chances are the cutting jaws are too.

When shopping for nippers, don't be fooled by misleading descriptive terminology. Nippers are often described as semi-flush, flush, full-flush, or ultra-flush, Flush is flush. Like pregnancy and honesty, its all

or nothing. If the nippers don't produce a perfectly flat cut, they are not truly flush. My advice: Stick with reliable tool suppliers and well-established name brands. Lindstrom, one of the best known and best quality brands, is my personal favorite.

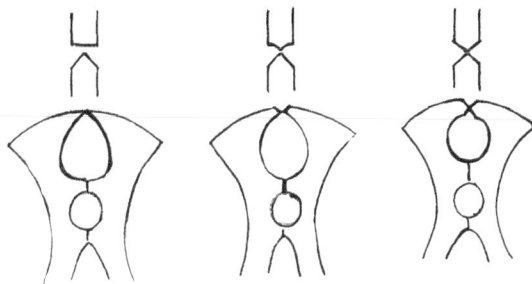

Full-flush, Semi-flush, and Beveled Cutters. In practice, the quality of the tool is more important than these minor distinctions.

Millegrain Tools

Millegrain tools are not actually used for the fabrication or setting of stones. They are, instead, used to produce a decorative beaded border after the stone is set. Like beading tools, millegrain tools come in sets of various sizes that fit interchangeably into a single handle. Each tool consists of a tiny, flat roller with concave depressions around the outer perimeter, affixed to the end of a rod. When rolled along a sharp edge, it produces an ornamental beaded trim.

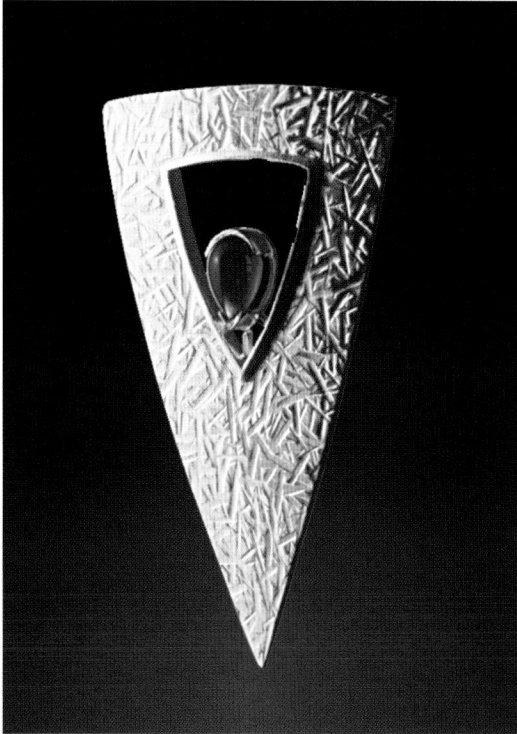

John Cogswell
Brooch
Sterling, blue
chalcedony
3 tall"
photo: John Cogswell

Magnifying Devices
Opti-visor, Mag-Eyes, and Loupes

When I was younger, my eyesight was very acute and I required no magnifiers of any sort, even for the finest and most delicate of operations. Students trembled at my approach, familiar with my legendary visual acuity and my unerring ability to spot even the most skillfully camouflaged flaws. Alas, the passage of years has exacted their toll, and now, without some sort of optical assistance, everything within a 10" range of my nose is fuzzy around the edges. Presbyopia, which comes to many of us, as my dictionary points out rather indelicately, in old age, has robbed my eyes of the ability to focus properly at close range. My long range vision is as good as ever (fortunately, I do not need corrective lenses), but since fabricating stonesettings and the like at arms length is awkward and unwieldy at best, I am forced to rely on optical enhancers for closer work.

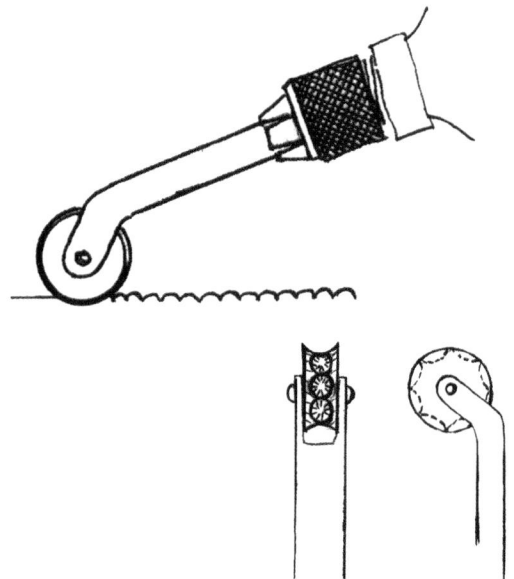

Millegrain tools are used to add decorative detail and sparkle around delicate settings.

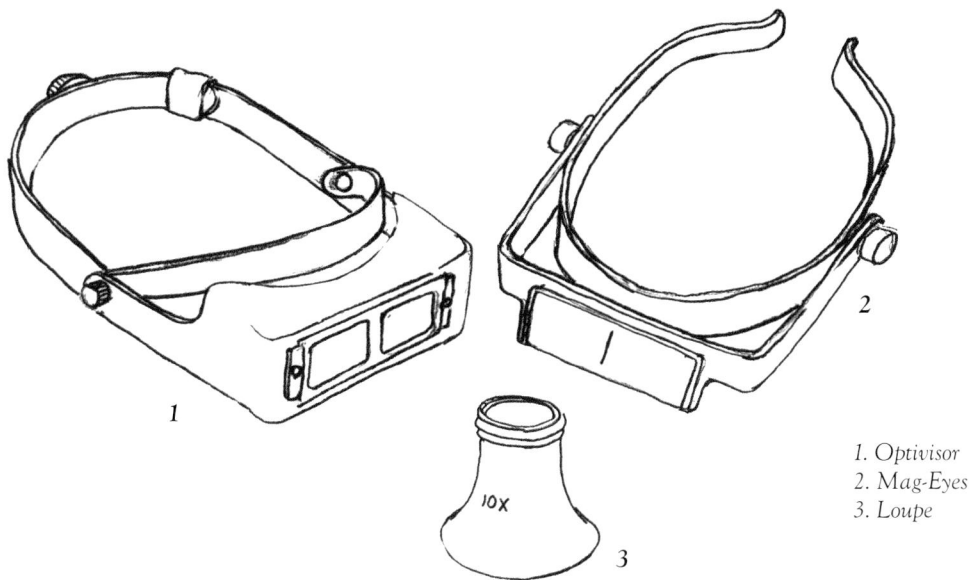

1. Optivisor
2. Mag-Eyes
3. Loupe

There are all manner of magnifiers available to those of us who need them. I have gradually accumulated a rather impressive collection, ranging from low-tech, non-prescription, 1X magnification drugstore variety reading glasses to more impressive, and substantially more expensive, binocular loupes boasting a 10X magnification. In my search for the ultimate visual enhancer, I have discovered several immutable, universal truths: (1) none of these wretched devices ever does what I need, (2) all are hot, uncomfortable, and clumsy, and (3) numbers 1 and 2 are moot, since I have absolutely no choice but to wear them. My search continues.

If you, too, find yourself in need of occasional, non-prescription magnification, here are several personal observations and suggestions that I hope will prove helpful. Inexpensive monocular jewelers loupes are handy for high-magnification inspection, as in searching for flaws in a stone, but their extremely short range and limited focal field render them useless for general bench work. Binocular magnifiers, which are substantially more expensive, are a bit unwieldy and have a limited field of

view as well. Lightweight Optivisors and MagEyes, both moderately expensive, have interchangeable lenses of different magnifications and working distances and are handy for close-up detail work such as stonesetting. Believe it or not, I find that the ubiquitous drugstore reading glasses are sufficient for all but the smallest work, and are often the simplest, most comfortable, and least expensive alternative for general bench work (but remember, I don't need corrective lenses). I try to find the shatterproof variety made of polycarbonate or acrylic lenses, wear them only when I really need them, and use the least amount of magnification necessary.

One final note to my students: I still see every little flaw...

Supplies

Abrasive Paper

I prefer wet or dry abrasive sheets (long-lasting silicon carbide, emery or aluminum oxide abrasive grit resin-bonded to a sturdy waterproof paper backing), which are a bit more expensive than less durable, hardware store variety sandpaper (quartz abrasive glued to non-waterproof paper). I generally use only two grits when fabricating settings: #320 (medium coarse) and #600 (fine). 3M and Norton are my favorite brands.

I find it very useful to make sanding sticks by scoring and folding abrasive sheets around flat wooden strips 12" in length, 1" wide, and ¼" thick. I place an abrasive sheet grit-side down on a flat surface and align the wooden strip with one long edge of the sheet. With a scriber, I lightly score the sheet along the inner edge. When I flip the stick 90°, this produces a crisp fold. I repeat this scoring and wrapping until I reach the far end of the sheet. I like to secure this paper wrapping at one end of the stick with a fabric hair elastic, though you can also use masking tape, a rubber band, or a thumbtack. I find that tacks last longer than rubber bands, which tend to dry out and break quickly. All four surfaces of this stick are useable, and as one surface becomes excessively worn, I simple peel off that layer, exposing the fresh one below. Using a sanding stick is far more effective, and less wasteful, than simply folding a piece of abrasive paper.

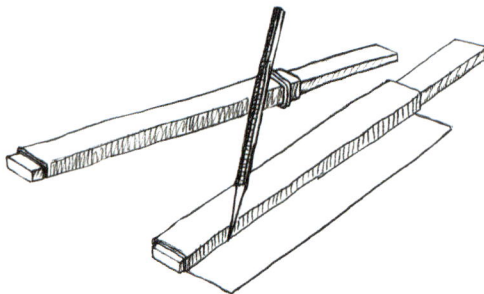

To gain control and leverage, wrap abrasive papers around conveniently sized sticks.

Beeswax or Sticky Wax

A small piece of beeswax or sticky wax (a soft microcrystalline wax used in casting for joining or repairing model parts) is useful for picking up and positioning small stones during the setting process.

Use beeswax in a lump, shaped into a cone, or pressed onto the tip of a small rod like a discarded bur.

Epoxy

Epoxy is the preferred adhesive for stone-setting purposes, mostly for securing pearls and beads. Jewelry grade epoxy comes as a two-part set: resin and catalyst. Equal parts of each are mixed together to create the epoxy. A good epoxy, when properly cured, should be water-clear, and won't discolor with age. The best epoxies usually have an initial set time of about 10 minutes, but achieve maximum strength after a final cure time of 12 to 24 hours. After application, the epoxied item should be set aside and left to cure, undisturbed, for the entire time suggested by the manufacturer to produce a strong, durable, and waterproof bond. EPOXY 330 is my favorite brand. I have used it for many years with dependably consistent results. It can be purchased from any jewelry supplier, and at many good hobby and craft supply stores.

Epoxies should not be confused with quick-set adhesives (cyanoacrylates like

Sue Ann Dorman | Necklace 3
Ametrine, sterling
photo: Steven Alfano

Daphne Krinos | Collection of Rings
Sterling, 18k, various beryls, topaz, tourmalines, quartz.

photo: *Joel Degen*

Crazy Glue or Super Glue). Though the quick-set adhesives conveniently set in seconds, they lack the durability and strength of true epoxies. Their bond degrades rapidly, and they are brittle, having little or no shear strength. Cyanoacrylates were developed during the Korean War to temporarily close wounds until soldiers could be transferred to field hospitals for proper treatment. Because they bond body tissue so quickly and securely, exercise great care if you use these products, never allowing them to come into contact with your skin or eyes.

Temporary Adhesives
When you are working with small items, holding them can be difficult. The task is made far simpler and safer when you have some means of temporarily securing these items to a handle of some sort. Sometimes, simply clamping them into the wooden jaws of a ring clamp works, but often, and

this is especially true in stonesetting, you may be working with fragile wire basket settings or thin-walled bezels which would be crushed by this method. At times like this, some sort of temporary, moldable, removable adhesive provides a safer alternative. A few of the most popular solutions are flake shellac, chasers cement, Jett-Sett, Aquaplast, Plastiform, Setters Grip.

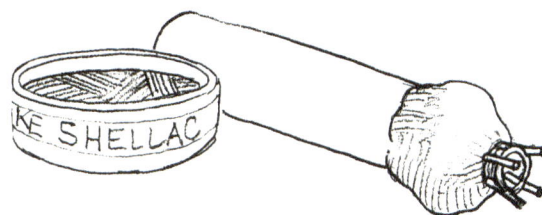

Shellac is a temporary holding material that has been used for generations. Warm flake shellac just enough to melt the pieces and build up several layers on the end of a comfortable handle. To use, warm the shellac, press the work into place, and allow it to harden. To release, warm the shellac again, or give the handle a sharp tap, which often snaps the piece loose. Tiny bits of shellac that stick to the work can be dissolved in alcohol.

Applying one of these malleable, thermoplastic materials to the end of a suitable handle, such as a short section of wooden dowel, produces the equivalent of what stonecutters know as a dopstick (to which a stone is temporarily affixed in preparation for cutting). The cement is warmed to soften, the workpiece is partially imbedded, then the cement is allowed to cool, leaving areas to be worked exposed. Later, after the work is completed, the cement is rewarmed, and the item is removed. These temporary adhesives are discussed more fully in Chapter 3, Bezel Settings.

Flex Shaft Accessories

A quick leaf through any jewelry supply catalog will reveal all manner of miniature felt wheels, buffs, rubberized abrasives, emery points, pumice wheels, burs, drill bits and other flexible shaft-related accessories. Armed with these, you can bur, drill, grind, sand, and polish just about anything. Most of these items are very inexpensive and once you assess those particular operations for which you will use them, you'll gradually build a customized assortment that will suit your own specific needs. Note: as with any piece of power equipment, eye protection is a must.

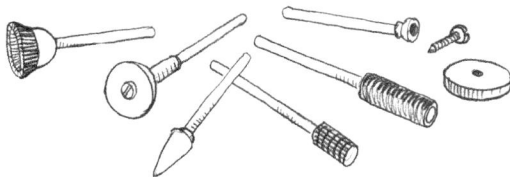

There are hundreds of tools made for the flexible shaft, with more arriving every year. Experiment to see which ones are right for you.

Sharpening Stones

There are two basic sharpening stones that you will need for establishing and maintaining the pointed tips of your gravers. An oilstone (often called an India oilstone, or a bench stone) is a rectangular, double-sided, aluminum oxide composite block, with coarse grit on one side and fine grit on the other. Its name refers to the traditional practice of applying a light oil to the surface prior to each use in order to prevent glazing of the surface with the steel particles being abraded away.

The other stone is not abrasive, but is a hard, fine-grained, flint-like stone used for honing and refining an already sharpened graver. This stone is called a Hard Arkansas stone, its name referring to the location from which it is quarried. With a hardness greater than that of steel, it burnishes and smoothes a graver's cutting tip, which then produces a bright, reflective cut. I discuss the proper use of both of these stones and the sharpening and honing of gravers in Chapter 5, Graver Settings.

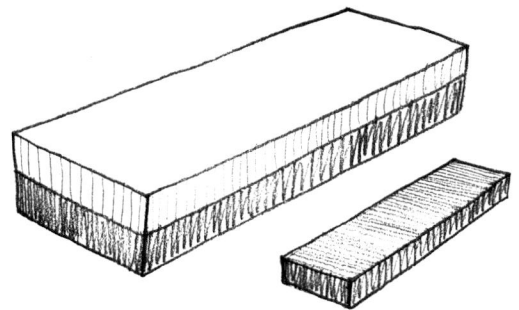

An India Stone (a.k.a. Combination Stone) left, is the best all-around choice of whetstone. For a really high polish, invest in the smaller Arkansas Stone.

Harold O'Conner | Brooch
18k gold, sterling, spectrolite. 3" wide
photo: Harold O'Connor

Steel Bench Block

A small, 2" x 2" hardened steel bench block is very handy for flattening, straightening, light forging of small wires, quality stamping, or any other small-scale operation requiring a perfectly smooth, flat surface. These inexpensive blocks can be purchased from any jewelry supplier.

Wide-nibbed Permanent Markers

I use wide-nibbed permanent markers to darken metal surfaces at locations where I plan to scribe. The subsequent white line on a darkened ground is clear and easy to follow. No need to remove the ink prior to soldering, as it burns away without residue. If you don't plan to heat the surface, or just wish to take it off, denatured alcohol washes it away, or a light rub with a nylon scouring pad will do the trick.

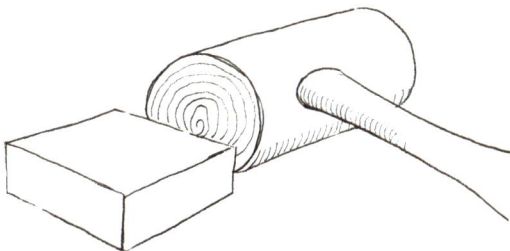

The simple bench block is one of those tools you will wonder how you got along without.

Equipment

Flexible Shaft Machine

Though this is a relatively costly piece of equipment, its versatility and the range of activities for which it can be used (sanding, drilling, burring, polishing, etc.) make it a most desirable tool for any number of jewelry studio operations. For general light work, a $1/10$ hp motor is sufficient. For extended, heavy-duty use, choose a model with a stronger motor ($1/8$ to $1/3$ hp). Gear reduction models produce lower speeds with higher torque, which is handy for drilling, grinding, and burring, though similar results are possible with standard models with a good foot-controlled rheostat and a little practice.

Electronic, solid-state foot-controlled rheostats are virtually maintenance and trouble free, but often offer only three or four speeds. Carbon resistance rheostats are more fragile (don't drop them!), but offer infinite speed control. I prefer these infinite range controls in my studio, but take a solid-state model when I travel for workshops.

A range of interchangeable handpieces (i.e., reciprocating hammer handpieces, quick-change handpieces, heavy-duty handpieces, slim profile models, etc.) further expands the machine's range of applications. Most current models come with sealed ball bearing motors that need no lubrication and only require minor maintenance in the form of an occasional greasing of the flexible cable inside the sheath. Foredom (my favorite) and Pfingst are the two best-known domestic brands, though many suppliers offer their own proprietary brands as well.

Beware of cheap, inferior-quality knock-offs. They may, at first glance, look like their brand-name counterparts, but are often of poor-quality, and potentially hazardous construction. I was once asked to field test one such comparable quality machine that was touted to be of equal quality at half the price of its competitors. At a workshop, on the occasion of its very first use, I, and a studio full of astonished participants, watched, slack-jawed, as it popped, sizzled, then burst into a pyrotechnic display of sparks and smoke. Fortu-nately, no fire or injury ensued, and it was, I must admit, entertaining in an alarming sort of way.

The preceding list reflects my personal recommendations and preferences, distilled and refined over the years by practical, hands-on experience and objective studio observation. However, as the old saying goes, "Ask one expert, and you're okay. Ask two, and you're in trouble." The same goes for stonesetters: Ask ten of them for their favorite tools and techniques and you'll get ten different lists. They will all, most likely, achieve the same results—just differently. As with any other activity you undertake, you will simply have to determine what works best for you. Experiment. Observe. Assess. Eventually, you'll assemble your own favorite collection. Then, you, too, can be an expert.

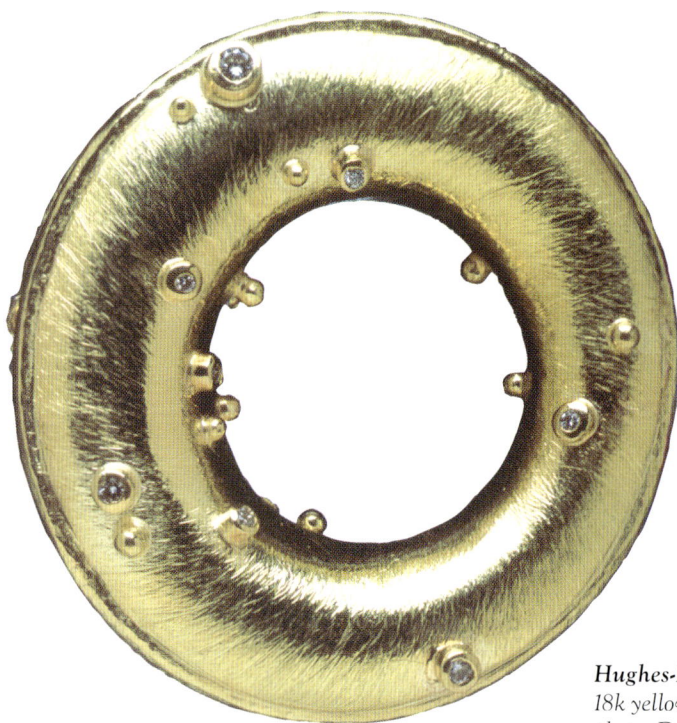

Hughes-Bosca | Sea Urchin Bead
18k yellow gold, diamonds
photo: Dean Powell

Chapter 3
Bezels

For many contemporary jewelers and metalsmiths, stonesetting begins and ends with the basic bezel setting. Bezels constitute, by far, the largest family of stonesettings. No other setting is more adaptable to the many shapes, sizes, and cuts of stones, and none offers a greater range of custom design possibilities. Regardless of shape, design modification, or degree of complexity, all bezels begin exactly the same way. Though the term bezel may bring to mind a plain, nondescript band of metal that encircles a stone, there are, in fact, many variations, some bearing little resemblance to the basic bezel at all.

Bezel Materials

Many metalsmiths first learn to make a bezel using one of two commercially available alternatives: bezel wire, a thin strip (usually fine silver) available in several standard widths, gauges, and cross sections; or, gallery wire, a decoratively pierced and patterned strip. Both can be purchased from jewelry suppliers and refiners. Because commercial bezel wire is thin and soft, it is easy to shape, and later on, easy to push over the girdle of a stone. However, this material has many limitations. It comes in a narrow range of thicknesses and widths, and because it is so thin, it can easily be melted during soldering or over-thinned during final finishing. Even if it survives the perils of fabrication, bezels fashioned from this very thin wire may look flimsy and fragile and can wear quickly or loosen gradually from the rigors of normal daily use.

Gallery wire, too, has its limitations. Because of its lacy character, it is more fragile than bezel wire, and it must be formed carefully to avoid breaking. The decorative scroll-work patterns make it difficult, to integrate a bezel made from this material into a contemporary design. Commercial gallery wire is rarely used by professional jewelry designers.

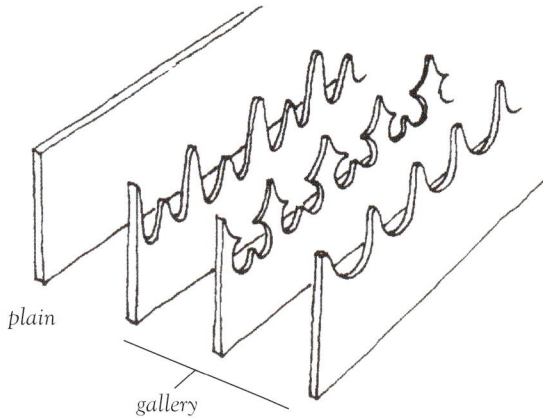

plain

gallery

Rather than relying on these commercially prepared bezel materials, I prefer to cut a strip from a sheet of metal. The height, length, and thickness can then be matched to the specific requirements of each individual stone and situation. Further, because sheet metal is available in a wide range of gauges and materials (like copper, brass, nickel silver, etc.), and can be easily milled to desired specifications, it eliminates the restrictions imposed by the meager selection of commercial bezel materials.

A good bezel—in fact, every stone setting—should meet several criteria. It must hold the stone securely; it should display the stone to advantage without overwhelming it; and it should integrate well with the design of the piece. Consider carefully the physical environment in which the bezel will exist, the aesthetic effect you are after, and the specifics regarding the stone it will hold. What kind of wear will the setting be subjected to? Rings and bracelets are exposed to a lot more wear than earrings or pendants, for example. Is the stone soft or fragile? Does it have structural flaws? Can it safely bear the pressure of setting required for the gauge or material being considered? If not, perhaps a softer material (fine silver or high karat gold), or a thinner gauge may be safer. Might a thinner bezel, even though it may be perfectly secure, look too flimsy? Only after all of these considerations have been carefully weighed should the specific gauge and material be determined. Generally, most bezels range from 26 gauge (0.4 mm / light-walled) to 18 gauge (1.0 mm / heavy-walled). In some designs, even thicker gauges are used. In my experience, 24 gauge (0.5 mm) makes a handsome bezel, requiring little muscle to set, and allowing ample material for cleanup and wear.

Eleanor Moty | Agate II Brooch
Sterling, 18k & 22k gold, carved agate (Dieter Lorenz), garnets. 2½" x 1½" x ⅜"

Making a Basic Bezel
(for a round or oval cabochon)

When fashioning a bezel, certain measurements are critical. If the strip is too short, it won't fit around the stone. If it is too tall, it will hide too much of the stone, and may wrinkle when set. If it is too low, there may not be sufficient material to hold the stone properly. Within reasonable limits, however, just how thick or thin a bezel may be is a matter of preference, but the decision should be based on a number of aesthetic and functional considerations.

Measuring and Cutting the Bezel Strip

The height of the finished bezel should be approximately a third to a quarter of the height of the stone, depending on the wall thickness. Make the strip slightly wider than actually needed—the bezel can always be filed shorter, but it can't be filed taller. Thicker bezels can be slightly shorter than thinner bezels, with greater mass making up for lesser height, but even they should never be less than one-fourth the height of the stone. A very short bezel presents little material to push onto the stone and may require a lot of force to do so.

The bezel strip must be long enough to completely encircle the stone; a measurement that can be determined by several methods. You can wrap a strip of paper around the stone, and mark it where the ends overlap. Add a little extra to accommodate the thickness of the metal, and cut at this point. Another method requires a simple computation and knowledge of basic geometry. For round stones, multiply the diameter of the stone by 3.5, which is an approximation of the formula $C = \pi D$ (pi times the diameter). I use a slightly inflated figure instead of true pi (3.14) to allow a little extra length. (Example: a 10 mm stone would require a strip about 35 mm long: 10 x 3.5 = 35 mm).

For oval stones, add the length and width of the stone (the X and Y axes) and divide the total by two; then multiply that number by 3.5. (Example for an 8 x 10 stone: 8+10 = 18 ÷ 2 = 9 x 3.5 = 31.5. This stone will require a strip 31.5 mm long. These computations yield minimum, close approximations. The exact length will depend on the thickness of the strip. The thicker the strip, the longer it must be. When employing either of these methods to determine strip length, it is always wise to allow a little extra. Better the strip be too long than too short.

Easier and faster than either of those two methods, simply estimate the length

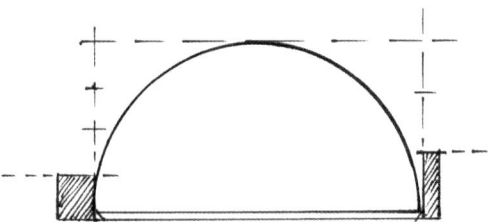

Use one quarter of the stone's height for heavy bezels.

Use one third of the total height for heavy bezels.

For round stones, multipy the diameter times 3.5 (a rounded version of π.

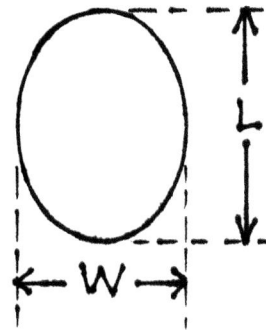

For ovals, add the length and width, then divide in half to get an average. Mutiply this times 3.5 (a rounded version of π.

required and then cut a strip longer than that estimate. I usually cut a strip the entire 6" width of a standard sterling sheet. This is easy to handle and will often yield several bezels with little or no waste.

Determine the height for the bezel, then use a pair of 2" or 3" dividers, draw a line parallel to the edge of the sheet. Let one leg of the dividers run along the edge of the sheet while the other leg scratches a line where the strip will be cut. Darkening the area parallel to the edge with a marker makes the scribed line stand out clearly and easier to follow while cutting.

I usually cut sheet metal of 20 gauge or less with plate shears. These heavy-duty scissors make a clean cut, and for that reason I prefer them to aviation snips, which create a serrated edge that requires additional cleanup.

To prevent distortion to the edge of the sheet from which the strip is being cut, keep the left blade of the shears pressed firmly against the underside of the sheet while the right jaw pivots down, cutting off the strip along the scribed line. Use bench shears or a jewelers saw when the sheet is too thick to be cut with plate shears.

A strip of metal cut with plate shears will curl and develop a lateral curve (it's better to have the strip distort than the larger sheet from which it was cut). This is easily corrected. Carefully unroll the curled strip (watch out for possible sharp burs) and use a rawhide mallet to flatten and straighten it. I work on a flat, hard wooden

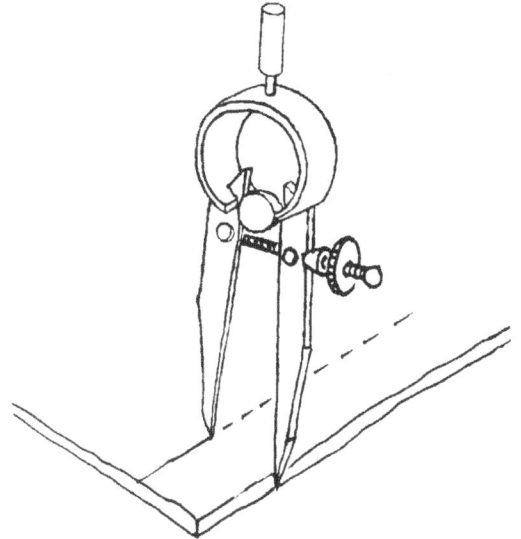

Use a dividers to mark a line parallel to the edge.

surface like the top of the workbench. Malleting on a steel block quickly hardens the strip and makes it more difficult to shape.

Shaping and Fitting the Bezel Strip

The shaping of the strip is best done with forming pliers. Half-round/flat forming pliers have one gently rounded jaw and one flat jaw and are used for shaping gentle curves. Round/flat forming pliers have one conical, tightly radiused jaw and one flat jaw. They are used to make tight curves, and will be useful only for very small bezels. The curved jaw of the pliers is always kept to the inside, concave side of the metal strip, which puts the flat jaw on the outer, or convex side. Reversing this

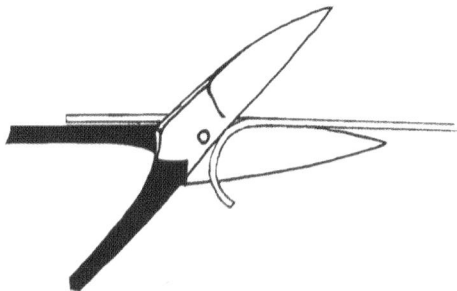

Holding the shears tight against the underside of the sheet will minimize distortion.

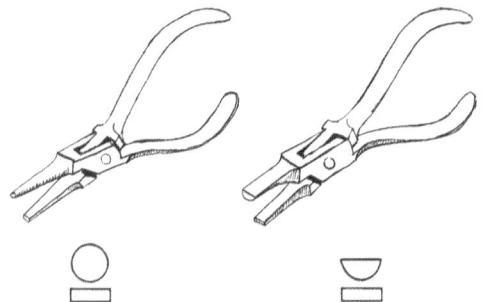

The pliers on the left is OK for small work, but the half-round/flat pliers are needed for larger curves.

YES   NO

Always position the rounded jaw on the inside of the curve.

positioning of the pliers will cause kinks and a sadly misshapen, scarred strip.

Determine where the seam will eventually lie, and begin to form the strip from that point, fitting it as closely to the shape of the stone as possible. The location of the seam is not an arbitrary matter. Two considerations must be taken into account: (1) will the location of the seam affect the final appearance, and, (2) might its location play a role in the setting of the stone later on? If the seam is well-fitted and properly soldered, it should be virtually invisible after clean-up, so the cosmetic issue is of less concern in the case of a round or oval bezel (though it will be of greater concern in the case of certain other types of bezels that will be addressed later on). It is, however, a matter of practical and aesthetic concern.

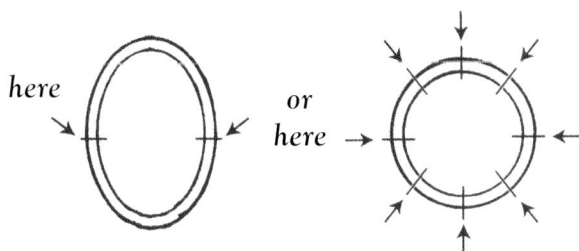

here   or   here

On oval stones, locate the solder on the long curves.

Solder contains copper and zinc, and this makes it less malleable than silver. For this reason, locate the seam where it will require the least amount of compression. On an oval bezel, the seam should lie in the middle of a long, less sharply curved side rather than at an end where the curve is tighter. On round bezels, where the curve is uniform, the location of the seam doesn't matter.

While shaping, it is very important that the sides of the bezel strip be kept absolutely vertical. The goal is a bezel in which the stone fits securely without gaps between the inner wall and the stone's girdle, and into which the stone can be fitted snugly, without excessive pressure. Getting a perfect fit consistently, without the need for further adjustment, is a skill that comes with practice.

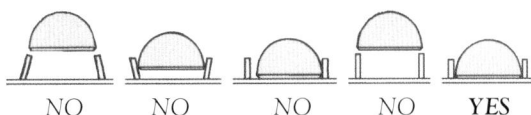

NO   NO   NO   NO   **YES**

The bezel walls must be vertical and accurately matched to the size of the stone. Fudging here will only lead to problems later.

Aim for a good fit, but bear this in mind: It's less work to make a bezel that is too small a little larger than it is to shrink a bezel that is too large. A slightly under-size bezel requires only a little stretching to fit (the emphasis is on the "slightly" undersize). If it is significantly smaller than needed, excessive stretching may thin it too much. In this is the case, it is usually best to simply start over. To correct an oversize bezel, however, you must remove a small section of the bezel by cutting on either side of the seam, then re-solder the joint. Determining just how much to remove requires some guesswork and experience.

When the bezel is the correct size and shape, the stone should fit equally well from either direction. That is, there is no top or bottom to a proper bezel. If the strip is worked with the pliers from only one side, it will develop a slightly tapered profile. This can cause major problems later because the stone can enter the bezel from only one side. If the smaller side of the taper fits the stone, and the bezel is soldered in place with the larger side down, the stone will fit loosely once dropped down inside the bezel. Even though the upper edge of the bezel may be pressed tightly against the stone, the girdle of the stone will be loose within the setting because of the taper. This situation will be revealed by a characteristic rattle that can be heard when the piece is held close to the ear and gently tapped with a forefinger near the bezel. Though perhaps barely perceptible at first, this slight movement within the bezel can eventually allow the stone to work itself loose. Conversely, if only the larger side of a tapered bezel fits the stone and this larger side gets soldered down, the stone won't fit in at all. Attempts to open up the restricted upper edge of the bezel at this stage may result in damage to the bezel or to the area around it.

If the bezel is too large at its base, only the top edge will be touching the stone. Eventually the stone will rattle and the bezel may open.

These unnerving and unnecessary scenarios can be prevented by simply remembering to keep the bezel walls vertical. Work back and forth with the forming pliers from one edge of the strip to the other while fitting the strip to the stone. It is also important to understand that pliers are tools around which metal is formed. Gripping and bending the bezel strip with pliers can produce undesirable marks, and make it difficult to achieve graceful curves. Instead, the strip should be held gently with the appropriate forming pliers, and then pushed and pulled around the jaws with the fingers until the required curves are produced.

The bending and shaping process will begin to work-harden the strip somewhat as it stretches and compresses to accommodate the curves. As it begins to reach its final profile, the bezel can often be pressed

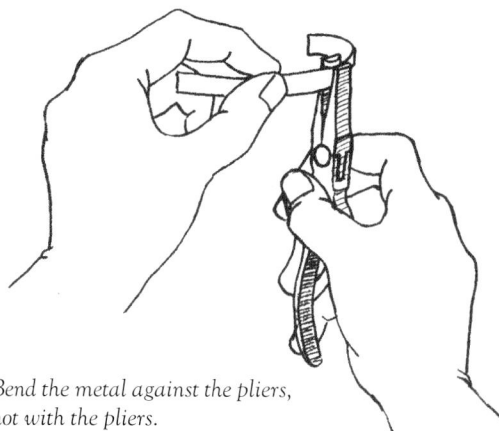

Bend the metal against the pliers, not with the pliers.

into place around the stone to check the fit. The extra length of the strip provides a handle that allows the stone to be picked up, silhouetted against a light, and checked for areas needing further adjustment. When the fit is precise the strip can be marked and cut.

Excess material can be cut off with flush-cutting nippers or with a jewelers saw fitted with a fine saw blade (e.g. #3/0 or #4/0). If plate shears are used here, they will cause unnecessary distortion to the ends, requiring straightening and readjustment with pliers to bring them back into alignment. In preparation for soldering, true up the ends with a flat needle file. If the ends of the bezel are first flexed past each other several times, spring tension will hold them tightly together. Don't worry if the bezel becomes slightly misshapen during this operation—this can be easily corrected after soldering.

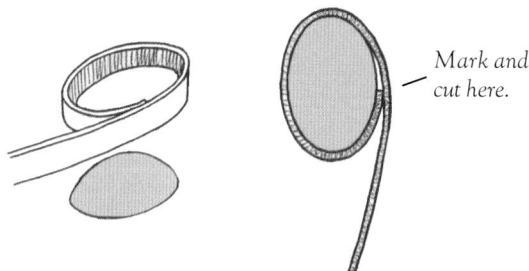

Mark and cut here.

Bend the bezel strip so it goes around the stone and continues along the same curvature, then cut.

If filing does not make a perfectly smooth seam, use a fine sawblade to trim away the irregular edges that are causing the problem. Hold the bezel on a bench pin with firm but gentle downward pressure from the fingertips. Don't squeeze the bezel from the sides while sawing. The spring tension should be sufficient to keep the seam closed. Cut straight down through the center of the joint. The sawblade will pass through the seam with a parallel-sided cut, removing metal from both sides and eliminating gaps or irregularities. As the sawblade exits the cut, the ends should snap together, forming a perfect seam ready for soldering.

Use a small blade to saw the bezel strip. This will trim away a tiny amount of metal and create a perfect seam.

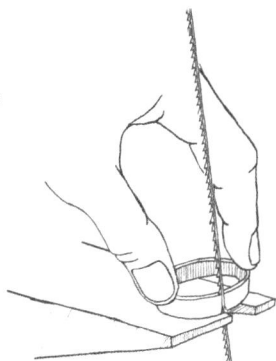

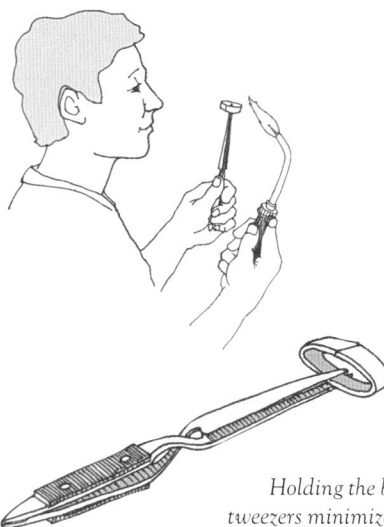

Soldering the Seam

The soldering process has two stages: the first will melt the flux and stick the solder in place. The second step takes the work to a higher temperature, which causes the solder to flow. When I'm working on precise soldering operations like this, I grip the work in cross-lock tweezers, (for bezels, at a point opposite the seam), they hold the work in the air above the soldering bench. I bring the work up in front of my face— far enough away for safety, of course, but near enough to permit close observation. When bezels or other small metal objects are placed directly on a soldering block there is a risk of melting because the torch flame reflects off the block, intensifying the heat of the flame. In delicate work, this can happen so fast that the damage often occurs before the danger is realized. Even

Holding the bezel in tweezers minimizes the heat-sink caused by a soldering block. It also allows me to bring the work close to my face.

when the flame is withdrawn, heat continues to be transmitted from that refractory surface, either through reflection or convection, or both. When possible, supporting small items on an iron mesh soldering frame placed on the refractory surface helps somewhat. Holding the object with tweezers in the air is even better. I find I can monitor the process better and control the heating more precisely. With a flick of the wrist the flame can be removed and the temperature of the piece immediately lowered into a safe range.

This is probably the appropriate moment to discuss an important related issue—manual dexterity. Whenever I am involved with a multi-step solder assembly, I am faced with the minor dilemma of figuring out how to juggle all the tools, implement, and parts simultaneously. There are a variety of third-hand jigs, props, and wire structures that I might use to position parts for soldering, which in theory will free up my hands to do other things. Unfortunately, these are cumbersome, time-consuming to set up, and generally turn out to be more of a hindrance than a help. Turning the torch on and off between heatings is also a waste of time and interrupts the process.

Kristin Diener | Eye Pendant (detail)   *photo: Margot Geist*
Sterling, fine silver, eye agate, beach glass, buttons, shells, pottery
10" x 8" x 1"

Instead, I take advantage of the two best jigs at my disposal—my hands. I have learned to hold multiple items between the fingers of each hand. I often hold the torch (lit) and the cross-lock tweezers holding the item to be soldered with the fingers of my left hand, while I flux and place solder chips with my right hand. Whenever I am doing something precise or delicate, I steady my hands by pressing my wrists together. With experience, I have learned to move these implements around as needed. With a little practice, you will find this to be a most useful skill. One word of caution however: Be careful with heated tools. Like when you are driving, keep an eye on everything, especially when your torch is lit.

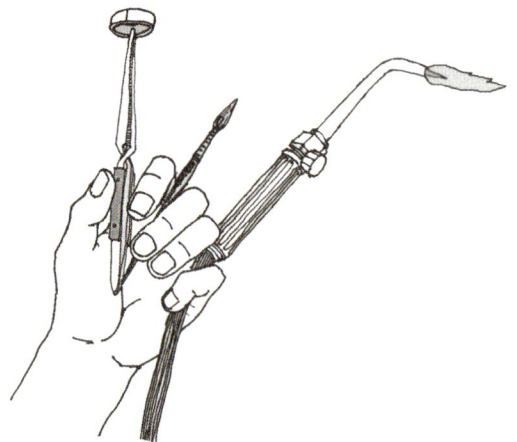

In one hand I hold the bezel clamped in tweezers, (seam-side up), and in my other hand I hold the torch with its flame pointed up. First, I carefully preheat the bezel using a soft reducing flame, directing the flame back and forth along the side opposite the seam until the flux becomes clear. Next, I place a fluxed piece of hard solder directly on the outer surface of the bezel—I put it here because it will be easier to remove any excess. Thinking carefully about how much solder to use and where to place it can reduce or eliminate tedious clean-up later on. The flux on the chip of solder will instantly melt and hold it in place.

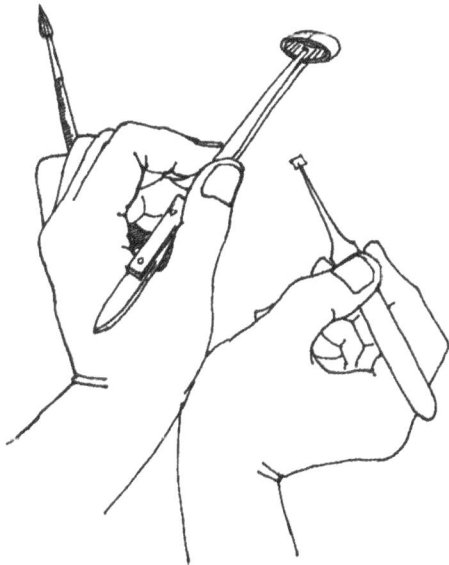

With a little practice, you will be able to manage several tools at once.

At no time should the flame be played directly on the seam. Focusing the flame directly on the seam will cause the bezel to relax, and the seam will open up. It may also cause excessive oxidation that can inhibit solder flow. Remember that it is the heat of the metal that melts the solder, not the flame.

Again, use a soft flame (a sharp, focused flame can easily overheat the strip). Move the flame back and forth along the strip evenly, gradually advancing the flame closer to the seam with each pass. This will cause the strip to expand toward the seam, keeping the ends tightly closed. When the metal reaches the appropriate temperature, conducted heat will melt the solder, causing it to flow into the seam. Withdraw the flame as soon as the solder melts. Allow a few moments for the soldered bezel to drop below red heat, and then quench it in water. Quenching at or above red heat can fracture the metal.

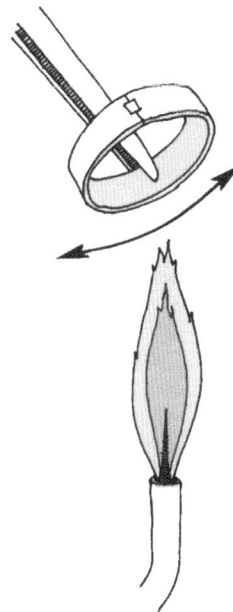

I like to move the bezel over the flame, which is stationary and pointed straight up. It takes a little getting used to, but this method offers the best view of the soldering process.

If the seam is not completely and properly soldered, analyze why it is not and correct the problem. If there was insufficient solder to completely fill the seam, simply re-flux, add another small piece of solder (use hard solder—do not be tempted to use a lower melting grade of solder), reheat and reflow. If the seam opened up during heating, the flame was misdirected. Solder that flowed to one side of the seam, but not into it, indicates that one side of the seam was hotter than the other. Re-flux, add a tiny bit of new solder, and reheat evenly. Only after the solder joint is successful should the bezel be pickled.

After pickling, the shape and fit of the bezel can be adjusted as needed. First, if any solder flowed through the seam onto the inner surface, it should be removed using either a needle file, a scraper, or a flex shaft bur. If the bezel is properly fitted, excess solder inside the bezel will prevent the stone from fitting properly. The removal of this solder is the only clean-up that should be conducted at this point. Take care not to thin the bezel; remove only solder, just to the surface of the bezel wall. Do not remove any solder on the outer surface of the seam area. It will serve to temporarily reinforce the seam should reshaping or size adjustment be required. In the event that later adjustment is necessary, any marks on the exterior surface that may result are best removed, along with any exterior solder, in one single operation. It is an unnecessary waste of time and material to repeatedly clean the same area. Refine an area only when, after careful consideration, you have determined that it will be too difficult, or impossible, to clean up later on. Any refinement that can be easily done later on is better left until, well,… later on.

Adjusting the Fit

Once any solder inside the bezel has been removed, make whatever minor adjustments to the shape and fit of the bezel are necessary. The heat of soldering leaves the bezel annealed, so any minor reshaping is accomplished by gentle manipulation with the forming pliers. Even when properly shaped, however, the bezel may not fit the stone. As mentioned earlier, if the bezel does not fit at this point, it is far easier to correct if it is a bit too small, rather than a little bit too large.

To stretch a round bezel, slide the bezel on a tapered round mandrel and tap it further along the taper with a rawhide mallet. Reverse the bezel on the mandrel occasionally to avoid making a tapered profile. In situations where a little more stretching may be required, the bezel can be lightly planished with a small rivet hammer or planishing hammer. Because both the bezel and mandrel are round, the adjustment doesn't alter the shape. However, for most other shapes of bezels, stretching up a bezel on a mandrel is usually, at best, impractical, and, at worst, poses a risk to the integrity of the bezel.

Stones come in many shapes and so do bezel mandrels. A selection of round mandrels is very useful, and these mandrels have numerous applications in other metalsmithing activities besides stonesetting. Round mandrels come in a variety of tapers, from short and conical, to long and narrow, and come from many sources. Heavy-duty machinists center punches; the pointed, conical end of a carpenters plumb bob; automotive drift punches, or even the tapered jaw of a pair of round-nose pliers are useful supplements to bezel mandrels sold by jewelry suppliers.

Mandrels for standard shapes (round, oval, square, rectangular, triangular, pear, etc.) are commonly available, and relatively inexpensive. Except in the case of squares, there is tremendous diversity and variation within each of these categories. There are long, narrow ovals and short, squat ones. Triangular only means three sided, not necessarily equilateral. The length of each of the three sides of a triangular stone may vary widely. This is also the case with rectangles and other "standard" shapes like pears and octagons—proportions within any given shape may vary widely, but a steel mandrel can only fit one specific profile exactly. Specialty bezel mandrels like ovals seldom match a given stone, and have such limited application elsewhere that I find them of little value. There is an old saying that any tool that performs only one function is probably not a tool worth owning. Fortunately, there are cheaper and more suitable alternatives at hand.

The same forming pliers that were used to initially shape the bezel can be used after soldering to adjust it. By walking the pliers around the bezel, it can be stretched along a single axis until it fits the stone properly. Directional stretching can be used to enlarge a bezel of any shape in a controlled manner, with minimal thinning or marring, and little of the distortion that might result from stretching up on an ill-fitting mandrel. Any shallow concave marks left on the inner wall of the bezel by the rounded jaw of the pliers will be hidden when the stone is set, and any slight, flat faceting on the outer surface is easily sanded away.

Directional stretching is accomplished by gripping the bezel strip deep in the jaws of the forming pliers, close to the hinge-point, with the jaws perpendicular to the bezel—curved jaw on the inside, flat jaw on the outside. Firmly squeeze the pliers hard enough to slightly thin the metal. Move the pliers a tiny step along the bezel, and repeat. Continue walking around the bezel this way, moving sequentially along the strip. As the metal is pinched by the pliers it will stretch at a right angle to the jaws. Round/flat forming pliers stretch a bezel quickly; half-round/flat pliers stretch more slowly.

The jaws of most pliers form an angle when open. When a piece of flat metal is gripped in the jaws, the greatest pressure is exerted closest to the hinge, with little or no pinching action exerted at the tips, furthest from the hinge. If the stretching action is confined to one edge, the bezel will curve in an arc, making it lopsided and giving it a tapered profile. To prevent this, any time the bezel is gripped and pinched at any point along one edge, it must be

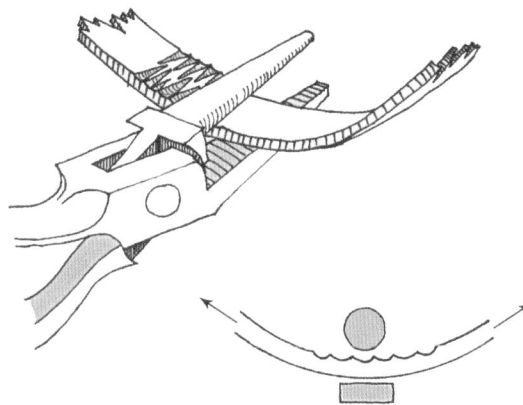

One way to stretch a bezel is to use round/flat pliers to make tiny pinches thath will push the metal outward from the point of contact.

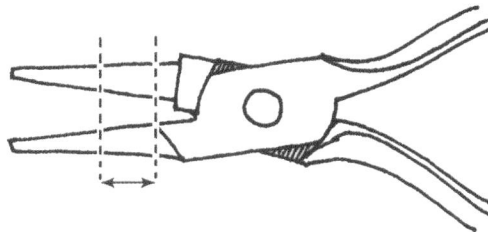

The fact that the jaws of the pliers open at an angle means that they get their first and greatest grip close to the joint. For this reason, it is necessary to work from both sides of the bezel.

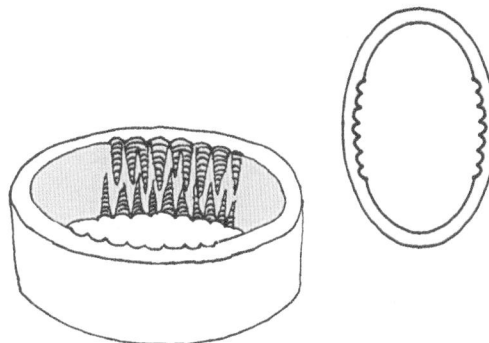

The notches on the inside and corresponding flat facets on the outside of the bezel will be easily removed in the normal course of setting. To maintain symmetry, always work equally on opposite sides.

pinched exactly the same amount along the opposite edge. Whenever it is necessary to maintain the symmetry of a bezel, the stretching action should also be applied evenly, not only to opposite edges of the strip, but to opposite sides of the bezel as well.

Only slight adjustments should be required, and because the annealed bezel will stretch quickly, use a light touch, advancing cautiously. I count the number of pinches applied to an edge, then repeat the entire sequence on the opposite side of the bezel. I check the fit frequently as work continues and stop as soon as the stone fits neatly into place. The bezel should be annealed again and its shape adjusted if necessary. If it is not annealed at this point, tension in the work-hardened bezel may cause it to warp as stresses are relieved during subsequent heating. If the bezel changes shape while being soldered down, it will no longer permit insertion of the stone. If the bezel is thin-walled, this annealing is best done after the exterior of the bezel is cleaned up; the work-hardening temporarily strengthens the bezel, making it less subject to distortion caused by handling during clean-up.

Leveling and Adjusting the Bezel Height

Once fitted to the stone, the bezel edges are trued, and the height is adjusted. In preparation for the final height adjustment, file one side of the bezel perfectly flat, perpendicular to the axis of the bezel wall. Use a hand file to remove any burs, then follow this with sandpaper. Tape a sheet of medium grit wet/dry abrasive paper onto a flat, waterproof surface (e.g., a piece of

Donald Friedlich | Translucence Series Brooch
18k gold, glass.

sheet acrylic), and wet-sand the piece in a circular motion. Wet-sanding keeps the paper from becoming clogged with metal residue, extending its usable life span. Change the position of your fingers as they pressing down on the bezel to create an edge that is flat, finished, and true.

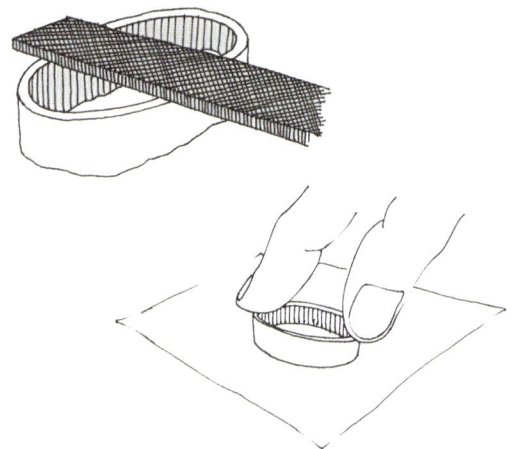

Use a file to remove high spots, then switch to a piece of abrasive paper taped to a board to make one edge flat and straight.

Once leveled on one side, a line parallel to the trued edge can be marked off with a pair of small spring dividers set to the desired height of the bezel. To make this line easier to see, darken the bezel with a marker. The ink will burn away during the next soldering operation, or you can wipe it off with denatured alcohol. File the edge to the scribed line, then repeat the de-burring and sanding as before. Temporarily place the stone in the modified bezel and check that the fit and the height are correct.

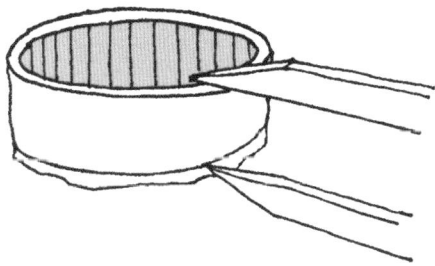

Use a dividers to transfer the straight edge of the finished rim to the opposite side.

Up to this point, the exterior wall of the bezel has been left virtually untouched. In most cases, this is the time to clean up the outside of the bezel, before it is soldered down. Take the piece to a fine sandpaper finish, but do not polish unless the design of the work will make it impossible to polish the bezel after it is in place.

If the bezel is heavy-walled and too thick to push over safely and easily, you may want to thin the upper, outer edge of the bezel by filing it to a beveled profile. This will reduce the thickness of the portion of the bezel that will be pushed over the stone. The beveled taper should start approximately a third the height of the bezel from the upper edge, and should reduce the thickness of the bezel wall at the top to no less than a third of its original thickness. In no event should this tapered edge be filed to a knife-edge that might, at best, spoil its appearance, and at worst, ex-

cessively weaken it. Be careful when filing this beveled angle to preserve the definition and clarity of the form. The bezel is now ready to be soldered down in its final position.

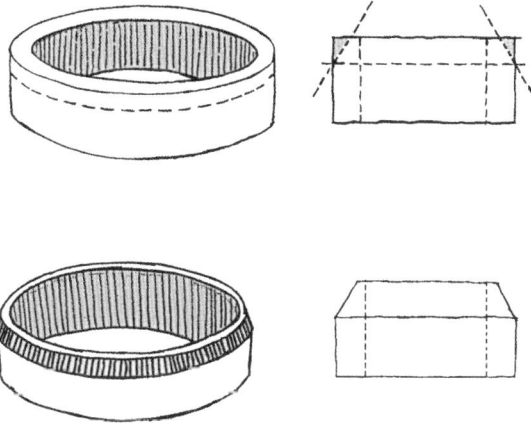

When a bezel is thick, it is often helpful to taper the upper edge. This makes it easier to press the metal over, and contributes to a graceful appearance.

Soldering Down the Bezel

Assuming that the background surface to which the bezel is about to be soldered is clean, flat, and free of blemishes, the bezel is ready for permanent attachment. Generally, bezels and other stonesettings are attached in the final stages of construction. This protects them from damage during the construction and early finishing of the work. For strength, better color match, and to ensure a margin of safety during subsequent heating, I use hard solder to make the bezel and construct the piece, but use easy solder to attach bezels onto jewelry pieces. Not only does the lower melting point lessen the likelihood of opening existing seams, but parts that were originally attached with easy solder create less risk if the piece must be dismantled for repair in the future.

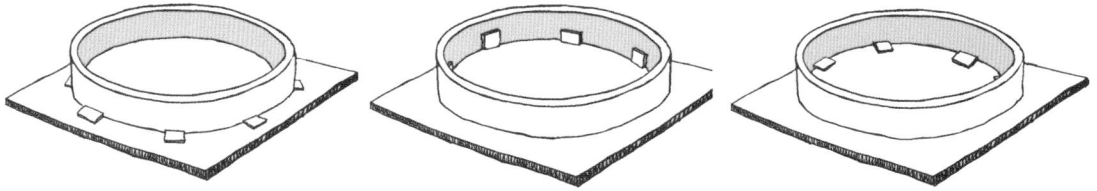

Here are the three most common options for solder placement when attaching a bezel to a base. Each method has its advantages and disadvantages.

Once again, concerns specific to this solder operation should be weighed carefully. The three major considerations are where place the solder, how to orient the solder, and how much solder to use.

In the case of a simple bezel on a flat background, placement of solder, inside or outside, is primarily a concern of cosmetics and elbow grease. Capillary action will draw the solder into, and along, the seam equally well from either side. But, the residue from solder placed outside the bezel is generally harder to remove without damaging surrounding areas. Solder flowed from within, if done carefully, often requires no further attention at all.

If solder flows onto the inner wall of a tight-fitting bezel it may be impossible to insert the stone. To prevent this from happening, lay the solder pieces flat on the base surface, adjacent to the bezel. If heated properly they will flow neatly into the seam, rather than up the inner wall. In this case, proper heating means focusing heat on the base. Remember that the fundamental principle of proper soldering is that the heat of the metal melts the solder, not the flame. Never direct the flame at the bezel. Solder is drawn to heat, so if the bezel itself is the hotter element, that's where the solder will go. To keep the solder on the base, see that it is slightly hotter than the bezel.

With regards to how much solder is needed, the obvious response is "just enough." Too much will be unsightly, and will create a thick fillet of excess solder that may prevent the stone from fitting all the way down into the bezel. Use as little solder as you can—additional solder can always be added later if it's needed.

Once soldered into position and pickled clean, it is time to deal with the area inside the bezel. It adds unnecessary weight, but normally serves no useful purpose. Many's the sorry soul who, eager to see how a stone would look in the setting, prematurely popped it into a tight, closed-back bezel, only to find it impossible to get out without damage to stone, setting, or both. Or, consider the case of a transparent stone in such a closed-back setting, under which moisture, dirt, and debris can accumulate, or where tarnishing may occur. In yet another scenario, even though bezels may appear to be tightly sealed around a stone, they are not watertight, and immersion (e.g., when being cleaned and rinsed) can result in water becoming trapped under the stone, and possibly oozing out later.

Most of the time, only a small rim of metal is needed to support the stone. Cutting out the back of a bezel has several advantages:
• allows the back side of the stone to be seen (it is sometimes as attractive as the front)
• facilitates removal of the stone, either during the trial fitting and setting stage, or later, should a repair be needed
• precludes entrapment of water or grimy matter
• simplifies washing, rinsing and drying
• allows light to pass through transparent or translucent stones

I don't recommend drilling a hole in the middle of the floor. From a practical standpoint, even though it may allow a stone to be pushed out from behind, it does not prevent the gradual build-up of grime or moisture, does not eliminate the potential for visible tarnish or discoloration behind clear stones, and does not allow drainage or drying of accumulated moisture. From an aesthetic point of view, a single bullet hole in the back of a bezel is seldom visually pleasing.

If, as a matter of carefully considered choice, drilled holes are used, there should be at least two (one to let air in, and the other to let moisture out), strategically placed on opposite sides of the bezel, as close to the inside wall of the bezel as possible. Multiple holes, placed in a decorative pattern, would be even better. In most cases, the best and simplest solution involves the total removal of extra backing material. Simply saw out all the backing sheet except for the rim around the inside perimeter, then neatly file and burnish the exposed edge.

There are several notable exceptions to the total removal of the metal backing inside the bezel. These exceptions usually occur in applications requiring direct attachment of parts to the reverse side of the setting. For example, when bezel settings are used as earrings, and the posts or screwbacks are going to be applied to the backs of the settings, leave a bridge of metal for the attachment. Another common exception involves camouflage. The reverse side of certain stones, usually cabochons, may be unattractive. The back side of a stone may not have been polished, or may exhibit undesirable flaws or blemishes. A well designed, carefully pierced pattern is sometimes preferable to a solid, closed back, or, worse yet, a single bullet hole.

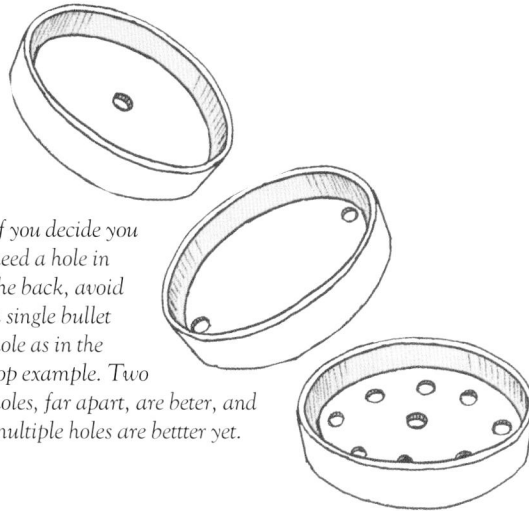

If you decide you need a hole in the back, avoid a single bullet hole as in the top example. Two holes, far apart, are beter, and multiple holes are bettter yet.

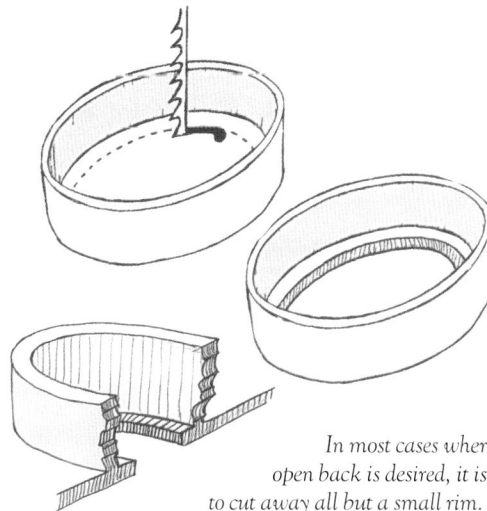

In most cases where an open back is desired, it is best to cut away all but a small rim. This is more practical and more elegant than a single hole.

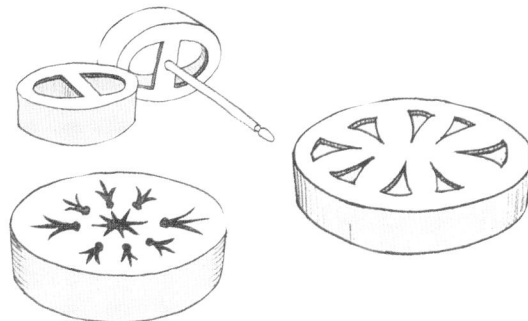

The practical value of having openings behind a stone are matched by the opportunity to use these openings for decorative embellishment. A few minutes with a sawframe can change bullet holes to pattern.

Securing the Work for Setting

The actual setting of the stone begins only after all solder construction, clean-up, patination, and preliminary polishing has been completed. The pressure required to set a bezel usually makes it difficult to hold the item with the fingers alone, so the first step is to securely anchor the piece into which the stone is being set. Because of the tremendous variety of shapes, surfaces and structures to which bezels are attached, there is no single solution that will be appropriate for all settings.

Some forms, like rings, for example, are relatively simple to hold. They can be gripped in a ring clamp or supported on a ring mandrel during the setting process. Some other forms lend themselves to being supported on a sand bag. Delicate or fragile items may prove too difficult to hold by conventional means or may require additional support or temporary reinforcement during setting to prevent bending, denting, or distortion. Traditionally, these items are temporarily secured to a short piece of stout dowel (a section of broom handle works well) or to a small block of wood with an adhesive such as chasers cement or orange flake shellac.

Chasers cement comes in either block or stick form. It is heated with a small, soft flame (e.g., with a small torch or over an alcohol lamp) and melted onto the end of the dowel, which is rotated in the fingers, or over one entire surface of the wood block. The shellac usually comes in flake form, and is melted in a small tin can, heated from below with a soft flame. Take care not to overheat—it could ignite. Pour the shellac onto the block or, in the case of the dowel, gathered onto its end in a rolling motion. Shellac is more brittle than chasers cement. I add a small amount of dry plaster of Paris powder (slightly less in volume than the amount of shellac being melted) to the shellac to render it more workable.

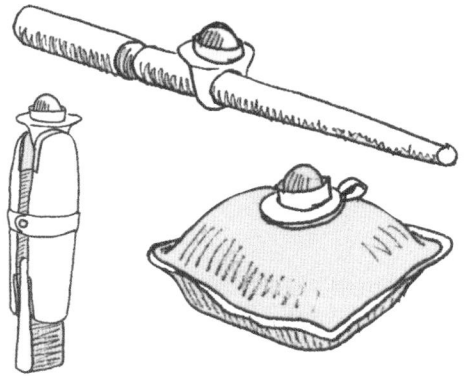

Three popular ways to hold rings while setting a stone.

Here is a set-up for making a shellac stick.

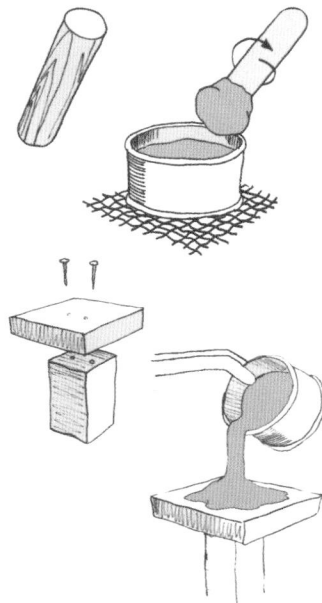

For small objects, coat the end of a dowel with shellac or chaser's cement. For larger objects such as pins and pendants, attach a piece of board onto a handle with screws, then build up a layer of adhesive thick enough to support the work

Apply either adhesive to the dowel or block in sufficient quantity to allow the work to be firmly secured. To imbed the item in the cement or shellac, hold it with crosslock tweezers and gently warm it with a small, soft flame. It should only be heated enough to allow it to melt down into the cement. Be careful not to overheat these adhesives. When molten, they adhere readily to the skin and can cause nasty burns. It's a good idea to keep a small container of water nearby. The cement can be shaped and kneaded around the work while still warm, if necessary.

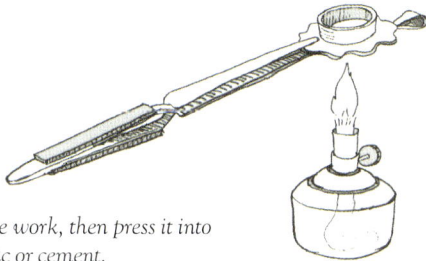

Warm the work, then press it into the shellac or cement.

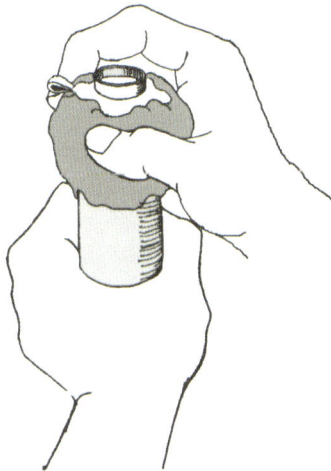

Mold the soft cement or shellac with dampened hands as it cools.

Any material that oozes up inside the bezel is most easily removed while still warm; use small wooden scrapers or toothpicks. If left until later, after the adhesive has cooled and hardened, the removal of this unwanted material is considerably more difficult, usually requiring the use of burs or other sharp steel tools that risk

Patty Bolz | Brooch
22k gold, chrysoprase, diamond.
photo: Robert Diamante

damage to the item. Once securely imbedded, the piece can be dipped into cold water, or left to air cool to harden the adhesive.

In use, hold the prepared dowel in your hand, much like a ring clamp, braced against the benchpin during the setting process. Clamp the wooden block in the jaws of a small vise, freeing both hands. This is most often used when closing heavy-walled bezels with a chasing hammer and setting punch.

After the setting process is complete, remove the work from the stick or block by carefully chipping away the adhesive cement around its perimeter with a pointed scribe or graver, taking care that you don't scratch the surface. This is generally safer than heating the piece and cement with a flame—while this would soften the adhesive, it might also damage sensitive stones. To remove bits of cement or shellac that stick to the piece, soak the work in denatured alcohol for 15 to 20 minutes, then brush or wipe off the dissolved adhesive.

If the gem material you are setting may be damaged by alcohol (e.g., dyed stones, amber, pearls, etc.), there is a safer, water soluble alternative. Recently, a number of thermoplastic/ceramic materials have become available through jewelry suppliers, marketed under names like Jett-Sett, Plasti-form, Aquaplast, and Setters Grip. These materials arrive in the form of small beads or pellets which, when heated in water, can be compressed and molded into any shape. When cooled in air (or, more quickly, in cold water), they harden, becoming tough and resilient, but not brittle. You can use them in much the same manner as chasers' cement or shellac to hold items for setting. The best part is that these materials do not stick to metal or stones, so they are easily removed by rewarming the plastic in hot water. They leave no residue. These thermoplastics are also reusable. In addition to their use in holding settings, they can also be modeled into all sorts of ergonomic tool handles, small mallet heads, and forming tools.

Setting Tools

Contrary to popular lore, a burnisher is not the best tool for closing a bezel. The rounded, convex surfaces of a burnisher can easily slip on the rounded, convex surface of a bezel, and its pointed tip can wreak havoc on the surrounding surface. A burnisher is designed for smoothing, rubbing and polishing, and is better reserved for those activities. Other tools, such as bezel rockers, may work well on thin bezels, but are also prone to slip under the pressures involved in setting heavier bezels. Reciprocating hammer handpieces (fitted to a flexible shaft), designed specifically for stonesetting, work best on thinner bezels, but are relatively fragile, expensive and maintenance-intensive.

In my opinion, the safest and most efficient tool for closing light- or medium-walled bezels is a bezel pusher, a steel or brass rod with a flat end that is secured in a mushroom-shaped handle. I find

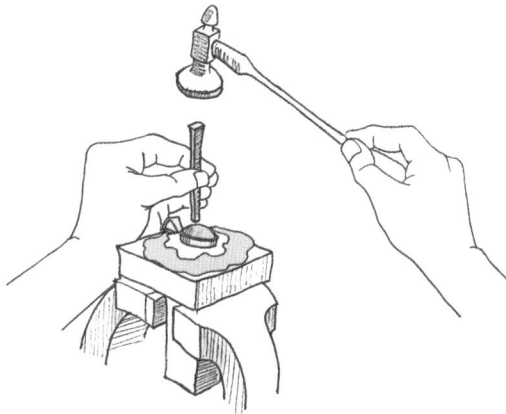

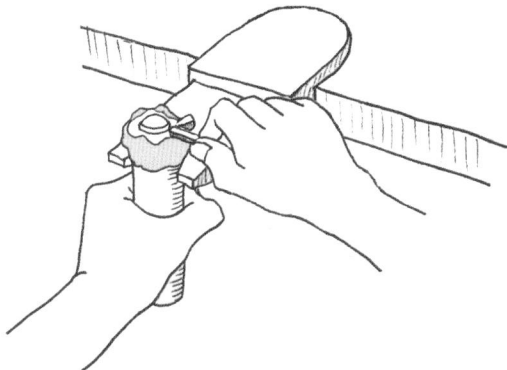

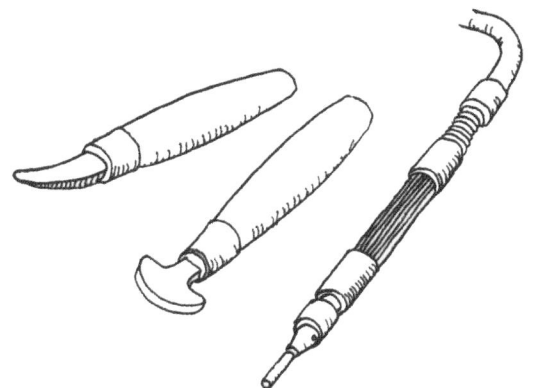

When the work is properly gripped, you can focus your attention on moving the metal over the stone.

These three tools — burnisher, bezel rocker, and reciprocating handpiece — are often used to set stones, but in my opinion, the simple bezel pusher offers more control.

that when this tool is properly prepared and used, it is safer and less likely to skate across the surface than a burnisher or a bezel rocker.

Bezel pushers can be purchased from jewelry suppliers or made in the studio. These simple tools consist of a short length of square or rectangular rod fixed into a mushroom-shaped graver handle. The size should be whatever is comfortable in your hand—most pushers use rods about ⅛" thick (3 mm). The length, including handle, is typically around 3" (80 mm).

Steel or brass can be used to make a bezel pusher. Because these tools don't have to be hardened, you can use something as simple as a heavy nail (16 pennyweight, or #16-D common). Drill a slightly undersize hold in a wooden handle and drive the nail in. File the tip to whatever shape is needed for the job at hand. Because bezel pushers are so easy to make, most stonesetters build up a collection of specially shaped pushers designed to fit into tight spaces, or that address other specific setting situations.

For general setting purposes, I use a pusher with a rectangular shape. When held against the bezel with its wider dimension in a vertical position, this tool localizes the area of point of contact, which focuses the applied force. When the bezel is mostly pressed against the stone, I rotate the pusher ninety-degrees, so the wider axis is horizontal (parallel to the edge of the bezel). In this position, I rock the tool in a sideways back-and-forth motion as I advance around the perimeter. This smoothes out irregularities, and tightens the bezel against the stone.

Thicker bezels, too heavy to be set with the pusher, are best closed with a setting punch and small chasing hammer. This punch is usually about 3½" long, and, in order to withstand the stress of the hammering, should be made from square tool steel at least 3⁄16" on a side. Its working face should be forged and/or filed to a rectangular shape having the same dimensions as the pusher described above. Because it is hammered, it requires hardening and

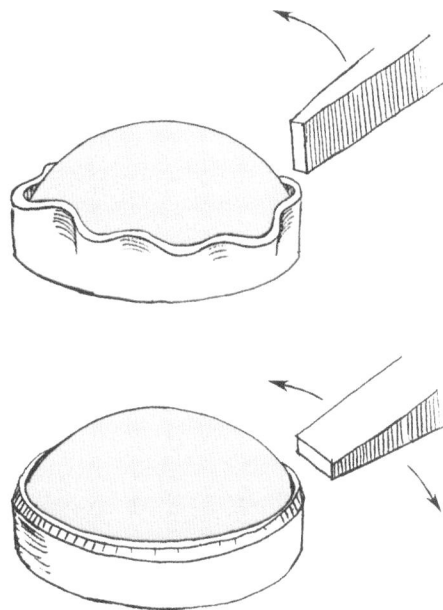

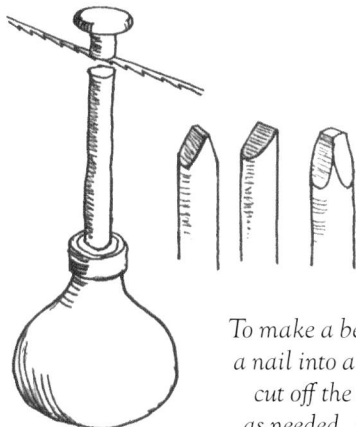

To make a bezel pusher, drive a nail into a wooden handle, cut off the head, then shape as needed. A few commonly used tips are shown here.

A bezel pusher with a rectangular face allows greater control than the more familiar square rod.

tempering after being shaped (hardening and tempering are discussed in Chapter 5, Graver Settings). To properly condition the working end of the stone pusher (or the setting punch), first slap its face lightly and repeatedly with an old flat hand file (medium or fine cut). Alternatively, sand the face of the punch with coarse abrasive paper. In both cases, the goal is to create a face that is flat and has a non-slip surface. Only a slight, subtle texture is necessary—or desirable. If the face is too coarsely textured, it will produce an unnecessarily roughened surface on the bezel, requiring additional cleanup.

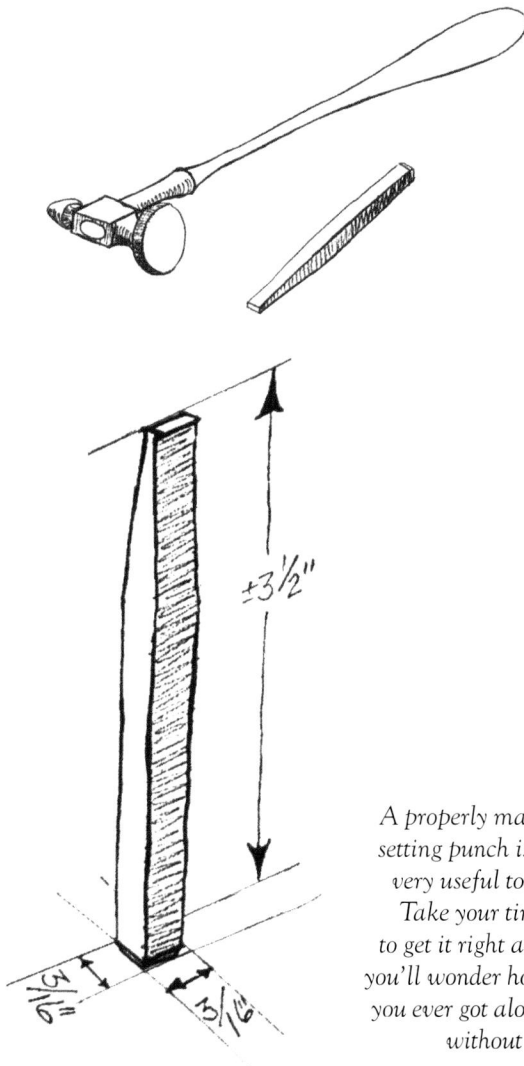

±3½"

3/16"

3/16"

A properly made setting punch is a very useful tool. Take your time to get it right and you'll wonder how you ever got along without it.

Setting the Stone

Securing a stone in a bezel exploits the characteristic plasticity of precious metal. During the setting process, the metal is actually compressed in on itself toward the surface of the stone, effectively reducing the circumferential measure of the upper edge of the bezel. The combination of compression and consequent work-hardening yields a setting of great strength and durability.

The first step in compressing the bezel is to create a number of evenly spaced crimps around the stone. Locate the first crimp directly on the bezel seam. Soldering will have completely annealed the bezel, and the seam is now in its softest and most compressible state. If the seam is crimped and compressed at a later stage, when the bezel is considerably more work-hardened, more effort will be required to push, and the bezel may crack.

Position the second crimp directly opposite the first, and repeat the process. Continue in this way, making the crimps in pairs, opposite one another, in a north/south, east/west compass-point fashion. This alternating sequence produces a scalloped border, each successive set of crimps producing progressively smaller scallops as the bezel is compressed. The first four crimps should lock the stone securely in position. Consecutive sets of crimps, centered between the preceding ones, gradually tighten the bezel against the stone. Working evenly back and forth around the perimeter of the stone ensures that it remains centered and flat inside the bezel. Once all of the scallops have been compressed flat against the stone, go around the bezel again, using the pusher to smooth out and eliminate any small gaps or irregularities. Hold the pusher with the wider axis parallel to the upper edge of the bezel, rocking the pusher slightly from side to side while circling the stone.

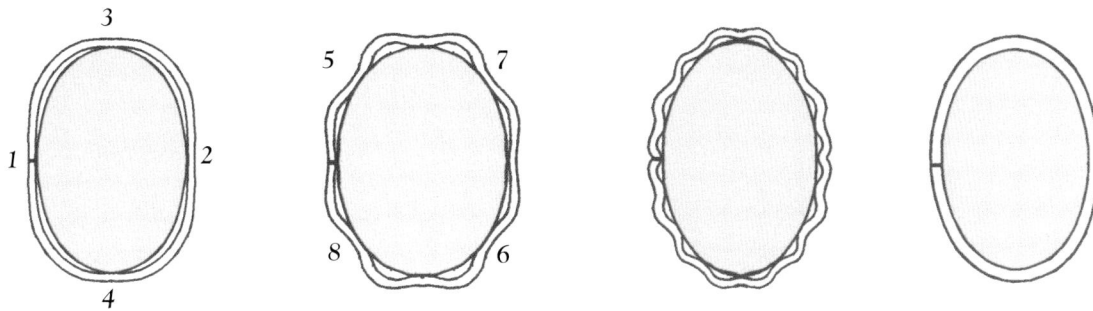

To make a smooth tight bezel, it is important to compress the metal evenly all the way around. Start with four crimps at the cardinal points, then locate four more crimps evenly spaced between the first series. Continue from here pressing in the bulges, always hopping back and forth across the stone, until the bezel is smooth.

Using the Bezel Pusher

Thin- to medium-walled bezels are usually best set with the bezel pusher. Exactly how thick a bezel can be set by hand depends on the strength of the individual. If the effort required seems too great, you should switch to using a hammer and a setting punch. Hold the pusher so the flat face is firmly against the bezel with its wider axis in the vertical position. Arc the handle of the pusher upward and forward in a continuous motion, forcing the bezel tightly against the stone at that point. When pushing the bezel over, always make sure that the face of the pusher remains in full contact with, and perpendicular to, the wall of the bezel. This will insure full contact of bezel to stone. Avoid pushing in such a way that only the upper edge of the bezel is pushed over. This will simply curl the bezels edge, even though the top edge may make contact with the stone, it will leave a gap between the wall of the bezel and the stone.

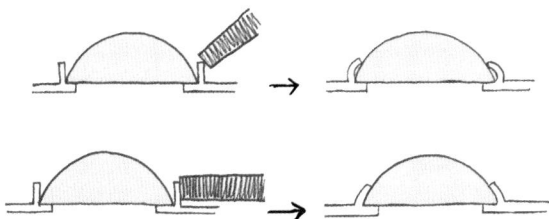

In the upper drawing, the tool approaches at a steep angle and leaves a gap at the base of the stone. In the lower example, the entire height of the bezel is in contact with the stone, giving a stronger result.

Using a Setting Punch and Hammer

When a bezel is too thick to press down by hand, or in cases when pushing by hand doesn't get the job done, the solution is to use a setting punch and a hammer. When used properly, even a small hammer can deliver a concentrated bit of energy that will close a heavy bezel. Of course this same blow can damage the stone or the jewelry piece, so great care is needed.

As mentioned earlier, in preparation for setting, the upper edge of a thick bezel should be beveled to a tapered profile, the slanted face produced sloping down approximately thirty-degrees from horizontal to a point about a third of the way down the bezel wall from the upper edge. This reduction of the wall thickness lessens the force needed to push it against the stone, and facilitates the compression of the metal.

I usually secure items that I'm going to hammer-set on a shellac (or cement) block that is clamped in a vise. This frees my hands to hold the punch and the hammer. For rings, I usually slide them snugly onto a steel mandrel, then place the smaller end of the mandrel into a hole drilled into the front of the workbench. During the setting process, I brace the larger end of the mandrel against my chest. Remember to reverse the ring on the mandrel repeatedly during the setting sequence.

A thick bezel is compressed against the

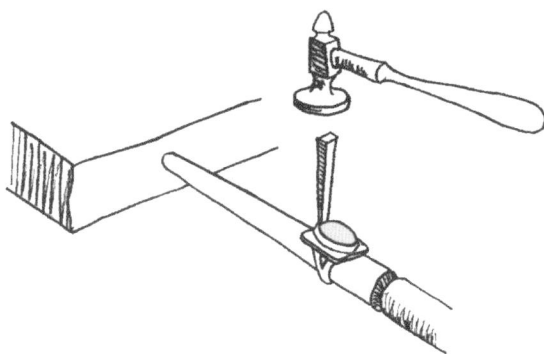

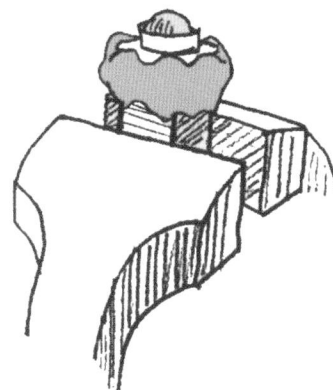

Rings are usually pretty easy to secure for setting. Slide onto a mandrel that is then supported against a hole in the front of the worksbench, or afix with cement or shellac into a block that is then gripped in a vise.

stone in two separate stages. During the initial phase, set the lightly textured face of the punch flat against the beveled edge of the bezel, then tap the opposite end of the tool with light, rapid blows. In exactly the same sequence as described earlier, crimp the bezel in a series of opposing points (north, south, east, west on a compass face) to lock the stone in position. At each crimp, the bezel should be tapped into full contact with the stone. As described above, follow the first four crimps with another four, these located between the first, and again moving across the bezel each time. The result of these eight crimps is a roughly scalloped pattern around the bezel. Using the same hammering motion, tap each of these bulges flat down against the stone.

In the second hammering sequence, hold the punch vertically on the upper edge of the bezel and tap it continuously as the punch is advanced slowly around the stone. Position the inner edge of the tool lightly against the surface of the stone. It is important to hold the punch absolutely upright—this way the force of each blow is directed straight down onto the bezel, compressing it. If the punch leans outward, the force of the hammering will be directed at the stone; if the punch is tilted to one side or the other, the edges will leave a series of

jagged cuts and depressions on the upper edge of the bezel. Continue this vertical hammering until the beveled edge is completely flattened and forms a right angle to the side of the bezel. When done properly, this second hammering phase will produce a thickened, flat upper edge that makes the bezel appear to be fabricated from a substantially heavier gauge of metal than it actually is.

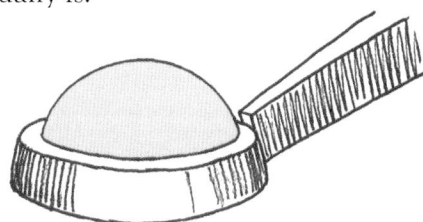

With the tool held at a low angle and the rectangular face oriented vertically, tap at the same alternating locations described earlier.

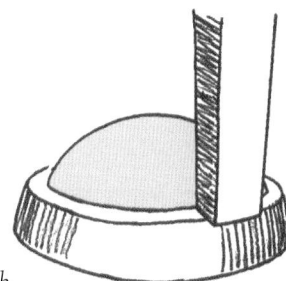

On a second pass, hold the tool vertically with the face along the top edge of the bezel. Planish with many light repeated strokes to smooth and compact the top edge of the bezel.

Filing

The crimping and compression of the bezel may have left unsightly marks and generated some distortion at its upper edge. The original crisp profile of its planes may have become rounded during the setting operation. Now that all of the heavy-duty tooling of the bezel is finished, any marks from the pusher or punch are removed and the planes and edges of the bezel are refined in preparation for final finishing.

Using a fine-cut barrette needle file (e.g., #4 cut), the edges of which have been sanded bright and free of any roughness that might damage the stone, carefully remove any tool marks and re-establish the crisp, defining planes on the exterior surfaces of the bezel. Normally, no filing of the upper edge of a bezel set with a stone pusher, where it lies against the stone, is necessary unless it is excessively uneven and wavy (referred to as a roller coaster edge). The hammered edge of a bezel set with a setting punch, however, will usually require some refinement with the barrette file.

Take care, during this file refinement, not to mar the background area surrounding the bezel. To help prevent unwanted scratches or file marks, the background surface can be protected with masking tape or with a piece of heavy paper (e.g., a piece of manila file folder) with an opening cut out to the size and shape of the bezel, and closely fitted over it. A fine, knife-edged pumice wheel, mounted on a mandrel in a flex-shaft, may be used after the barrette file to further refine the filed surfaces, so long as the stone is suitably hard, and the wheel is carefully controlled. Because of the high speed at which it is used, and, consequently, the speed with which it can create irreparable damage, it should be used with great care, and then, only after much practice. Never use a sanding stick around a stone—the abrasive grit will damage the surface of all but the hardest stones.

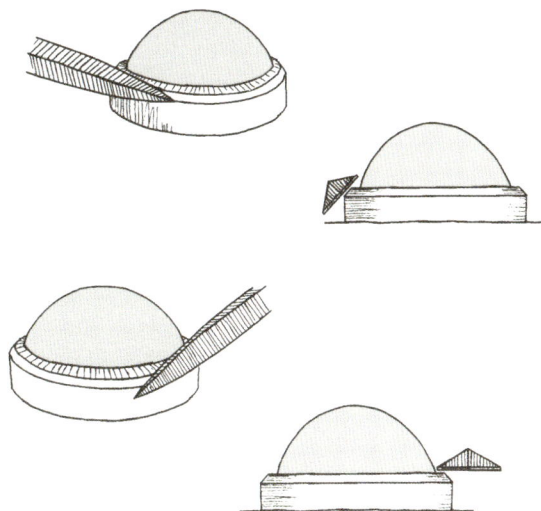

Refine and recover the crisp edges of a bezel with a barrette needle file that has had its rough edges removed. The first step on a thick bezel is to establish a uniform angle (top). Once this is filed, use a light touch to clean up the edge next to the stone.

Da Gama Designs | Necklace
18k gold, Brazilian tourmaline, diamond, platinum
photo: Robert Diamante

Burnishing

After filing, use a burnisher in short, carefully controlled, back-and-forth strokes to rub out any file marks on the exterior surfaces of the bezel, maintaining the clarity and definition of any changes in plane. Lubricating the burnisher (with soapy water, oil, or, traditionally, saliva) helps it slide smoothly and easily. Once properly burnished, a bezel should require only light buffing to complete the finish.

Especially for thin and medium bezels, burnishing is the best way to smooth, tighten, and polish.

Bright Cutting and Polishing

The flat upper edge of a bezel, when viewed from above, constitutes a significant visual element—a shiny, decorative border that encircles and frames the stone. Though perhaps a relatively small detail, this edge can greatly enhance the overall appearance of the setting, and should be handled carefully. The edges produced by the two setting methods discussed earlier differ in subtle yet significant ways, and each is finished off in a different manner.

The broad, flat edge produced by a setting punch on a heavy-walled bezel, extending out from the surface of the stone at an obtuse angle, permits easy access, and normally presents no special finishing problems. It is first filed with the barrette file, and then polished with rouge, first with a small felt wheel (either mounted in a flex shaft, or mounted on a polishing arbor) and later, with a muslin buff.

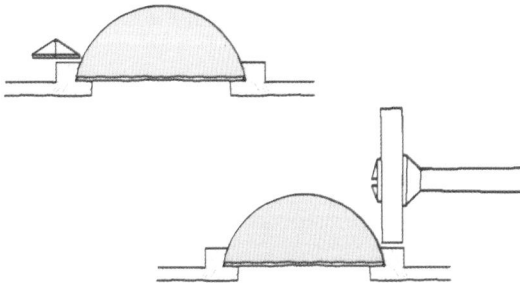

After setting a thick bezel with a hammer and punch, refine the surface with a needle file, then use a hard felt buff on the flex shaft to polish.

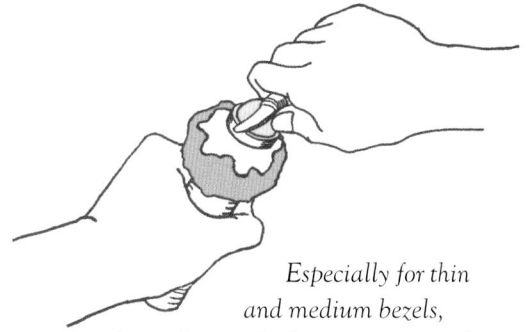

The narrower edge produced by hand setting with a stone pusher presents an inwardly sloping inclined plane, perpendicular to the surface of the stone. The juncture of this inwardly banked edge and the slope of the stone creates a shallow, right-angled notch that might be lost if filed. The best means of dressing this edge is with a flat graver.

A properly honed and polished flat graver produces a highly reflective cut—hence the name bright cutting. The graver is used, in effect, like a miniature chisel, gradually shaving away imperfections, planing away uneven areas on the edge until a uniformly smooth, flat surface is produced. A #42 flat graver is a good all-purpose choice for stonesetting.

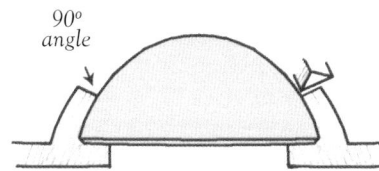

90° angle

Use a polished flat graver to slice away irregularities until the top edge of a bezel is mirror bright.

Hold the sharpened graver at a shallow angle with its cutting edge gently pressed flat against the upper edge of the bezel, perpendicular to the stone's surface. The side of the graver blade near the tip will slide along the stone as it skims along

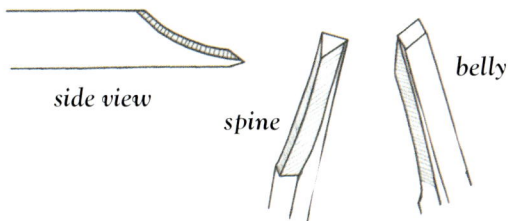

A properly shaped and honed flat graver will shine like a mirror and be as sharp as a razor.

the bezel to make a clean, bright cut. It is important to keep the tool in exactly this position because if you increase the angle, the corner of the graver might scratch the stone. Also the handle end should not be lifted during the cut, which will cause it to dig down into the bezel. To repeat: hold the graver at a constant, shallow angle and slide it forward along the edge of the bezel with steady, overlapping strokes.

No pressure is required. The graver's razor-sharp edge will do all of the work as it skims along the edge, shaving off any high spots and irregularities until, in a single, continuous final pass, a uniformly flat, reflective plane is achieved. Dip the tip of the graver into a small container filled with cotton saturated with oil of wintergreen to create a smoother cutting action. The tip of the tool must be mirror bright and extremely sharp—check it frequently during cutting and hone it on a hard Arkansas stone when necessary. (See Chapter 5 for information on preparing a graver.)

A perfectly flat, uniform cut all the way around the perimeter of a bezel requires a degree of skill that is acquired only after much practice. The final bright cut edge should require little or no buffing. If it is buffed, it should be done gently, with a fine muslin buff or a soft-bristle polishing brush, charged lightly with only rouge.

Because the graver is a burnishing as well as a polishing stroke, the bright cut edge is surprisingly durable. This final treatment of the bezel is an indicator of fine craftsmanship to a trained eye. When done

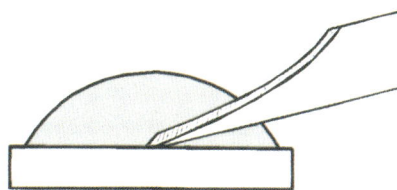

This is the proper angle for the graver to slide along the rim of the bezel.

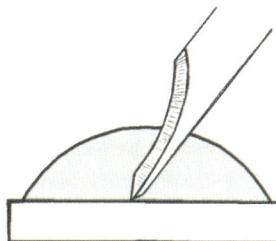

This drawing illustrates the wrong angle of approach. A graver held this way will dig into the metal, leaving marks and threatening the stone.

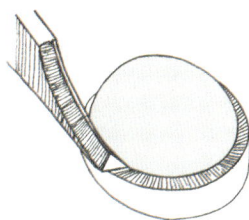

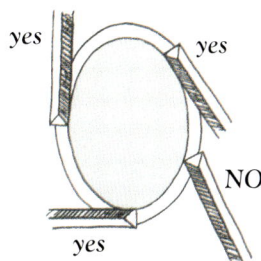

The goal of bright cutting is to achieve a smooth stroke that glides evenly around the entire bezel. When looking straight down onto the stone (lower drawing), the tool will appear to swing a wide arc as it travels. Be careful, though, that you don't swing too far and press the corner of the graver against the stone.

well and with skill, the time spent refining, burnishing and bright cutting a bezel represents time well spent. These operations can elevate an otherwise commonplace bezel to the Rolls Royce of bezels. Remember, little details make a big difference. It is what we do with our hands and our hearts, and how well we do it, that gives our work its true value.

Shoulder (or Bearing) Bezels

A basic bezel satisfies the fundamental requirements of a good handmade stone-setting: it is strong and secure, visually unobtrusive, simple to make, and easily adapted to cabochons and faceted stones of any shape. But basic bezels are not without limitations. The overall height is determined by the thickness of the stone, almost always restricting it to a low profile. It can only be soldered to a flat or nearly flat surface. Also, because of its low profile and relatively thin gauge, there is insufficient material to allow embellishment without compromising strength and security. Decorative appliqués cannot be soldered to its exterior surfaces because they would interfere with the proper closing of the bezel.

In addition to the functional disadvantages and limitations of the basic bezel, there exists another, more personal, design-related consideration. While a basic bezel may physically hold a stone in place, duct tape or epoxy might work too. The point is not only to secure the stone but to create a setting that integrates with the design of the piece. No single setting can be correct for every situation, and this applies to the basic bezel.

Fortunately, a modification to the simple bezel—the addition of an internal shelf or bearing—offers hundreds of possible variations. This upgraded bezel is commonly referred to as either a shoulder or bearing bezel.

A bearing is a shelf inside the bezel upon which the stone rests. The introduc-

Robert Grey Kaylor | Pendant
18k gold, lapiz lazuli, pearl, diamond
photo: Robert Grey Kaylor

tion of a bearing effectively eliminates most functional restraints and opens up many design possibilities. Because a flat shelf is provided, independent of the background surface, the bezel can be fitted to a surface of any contour. Its height now becomes a matter of maker discretion, and its exterior surface can be greatly modified. Metal can be selectively removed above or below the

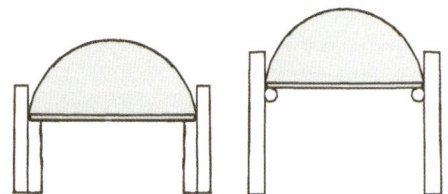

Two common ways to create a rim inside a bezel are to make an interior bezel from sheet or a supporting ring from round wire.

bearing as long as you leave enough metal to safely hold the stone and to support the bezel. Decorative trims like textured appliqués or ornamental borders of differently colored metals can be added to the outside of the bezel. Remember to keep these below the bearing where they won't make it difficult to close the bezel. Especially when portions of the bezel are removed by sawing or filing, the result can look more like a prong setting than a conventional bezel.

The traditional method of making a bearing bezel is to start with thick sheet (16 gauge or thicker) and make a bezel that is too small to admit the stone. Cut a bearing with gravers or burs while simultaneously creating a bezel that is sufficient to close over the stone. This time-honored method produces a great shoulder bezel, but requires skill with gravers and burs, and the ability to figure out the correct size of the starting bezel.

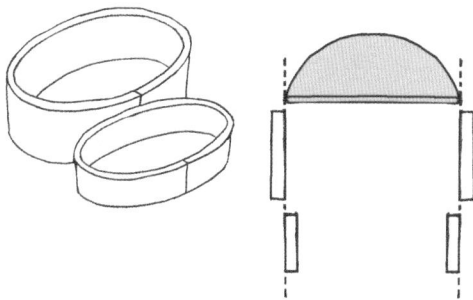

Two views of a shoulder bezel assembly.

For most metalsmiths it is far simpler to assemble a shoulder bezel from two parts: an inner shelf to support the stone and an outer bezel to hold it—basically a bezel within a bezel. The inner bezel, or bearing, must be sufficiently lower than the outer bezel to allow the stone to be properly set. The height of the wall of the outer bezel must exceed that of the inner bearing by a third to a quarter the height of the stone (i.e. the same amount needed to set a basic single-walled bezel).

A variation on this creates a bearing by soldering a ring of wire into a bezel. In certain instances, where a tall bezel would require too much material, or, in the case of earrings, where a solid bearing would add undesirable weight, the bearing can be made of wire rather than from a solid strip of metal. In either case, the bearing is eventually tightly fitted to the inside of the bezel and soldered in position.

Making a Shoulder (or Bearing) Bezel

Build a shoulder bezel like a single-walled bezel, with a few minor differences. Make the bezel (i.e., the outer unit) first, exactly fitted to the stone. The thickness of the bezel wall is a matter of personal choice, but the thickness of the bearing should be 24 gauge (0.5 mm). Thicker material is not necessary and only adds unnecessary weight. On the other hand, a thinner gauge may not provide enough support. The bearing should fit snugly inside the bezel.

Solder the seams on both strips with hard solder. If there is excess solder on the outside of the bearing, file it away so the inner tube will fit tightly inside the bezel. If there is solder on the outer bezel, don't bother to remove it until the two-layered assembly is complete.

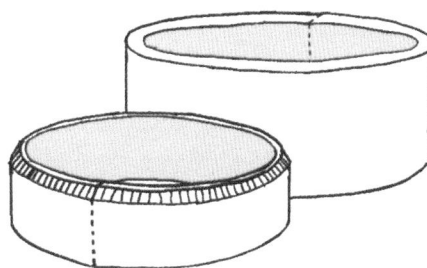

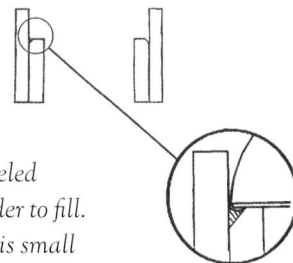

The outer edge of the interior ring (the shoulder) should be beveled to allow a space for solder to fill. As seen in the detail, this small angle will accommodate solder that will othersise prevent the stone from sitting flat.

The height of the outer bezel can be lowered later if necessary, so leave it a little taller than needed. Before sliding the two parts together, file the upper, outside edge of the bearing to make a small bevel. This beveled edge does two things. First, it helps as you slide the tight inner bearing into the bezel. Second, the tiny gap where the bearing meets the inner wall of the bezel prevents an undesirable fillet of solder that might disturb the fit.

Place the bearing, beveled side up, and center the bezel on top of it with the seams opposite each other. Using a small piece of hard wood (the flat side of the wedge from a ring clamp works well), firmly press the bezel down and over the bearing until the two are fitted together.

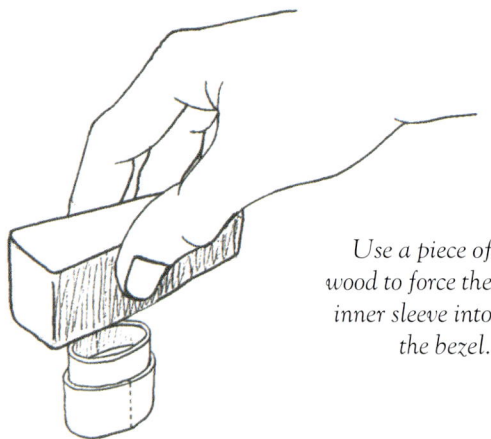

Use a piece of wood to force the inner sleeve into the bezel.

A wire bearing is fashioned and fitted in much the same way and can be made from either square or round wire. Round wire has certain advantages; because of its circular cross-section, it provides a ready-made solder-stopping gap where it lies against the inner wall of the bezel, and, if the setting is intended for a faceted stone, provides a ready-made seat to accommodate the stone pavilion.

To seat the wire bearing for solder assembly, place it on a flat surface and locate the bezel on it squarely. Again, use a small wooden block to press the bezel down over the wire. Use the stone itself to press the

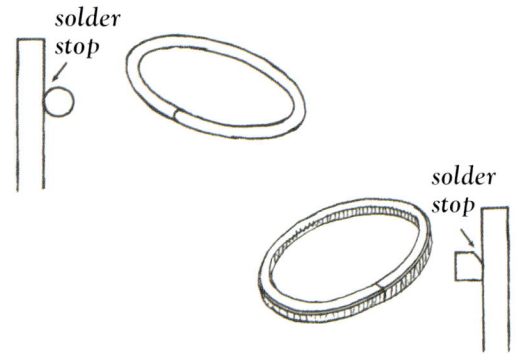

The cross section of a round wire naturally provides a solder stop. When using a square wire bearing it is necessary to file the edge.

wire bearing to the proper depth. If the stone is fragile, use a wooden or plastic tool instead—the plastic handle of a toothbrush, cut and filed to shape, makes a handy tool to press the wire into position. Check to make sure the bearing is level and parallel with the bezel's upper edge.

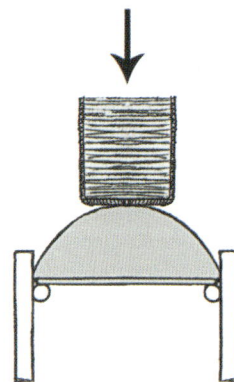

If the stone is tough enough, use it to press the wire shoulder into place. If there is a chance of breaking the stone, work the wire into position with whatever tool comes to hand.

To solder, grip the assembly, upside down, in crosslock tweezers. Flux the seams, inside and out, and preheat to the clear, glassy stage. Place small fluxed pieces of hard or medium solder on the seam between the two layers (or along the underside of a wire bearing), and heat from below with a soft flame. Waft the flame on and off the bezel, allowing the metal to reach the appropriate temperature, until the solder flows. Hard solder is preferable, but medium is perfectly acceptable and

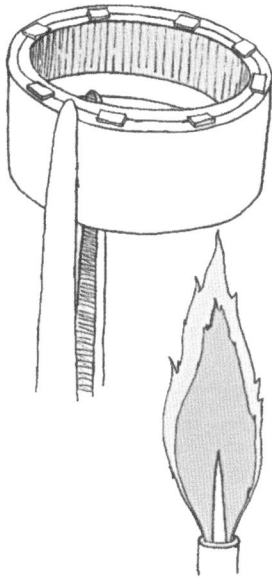

Soldering the bearing into a bezel.

may be safer, since it precludes remelting of existing seams. Also, since this will usually be the final soldering required for the actual construction of the bezel assembly, the next soldering sequence will likely be its attachment to the background, which is typically done with easy solder.

Be careful not to add too much solder, but use enough to completely fill the seam between the two layers. Unfilled gaps in a seam may trap pickling acid and cause problems later. After pickling, the completed shoulder bezel can be cleaned up and readied for attachment to the base structure.

Bezels for Angular Stones

The most familiar use of bezels is to set round or oval cabochons, but they can accommodate almost any shape or cut, geometric or otherwise. Most cut stones are geometric and described by their silhouettes: round, oval, rectangular, square, triangular, octagonal, pear, heart, and marquise. All of these are generally, though not always, symmetrical along at least one axis.

These geometric shapes can further be divided into three sub-categories: curvilinear cuts without any angular corners (e.g.,

round and oval); curvilinear cuts having one or more angular corners (e.g., pear and marquise); and straight-sided cuts having multiple angular corners (e.g., rectangular, square, triangular, and octagon). Bezels for non-angular stones (previously discussed) are the simplest to construct and the simplest to set. The latter two groups, both of which must accommodate angular corners, require special construction and setting consideration.

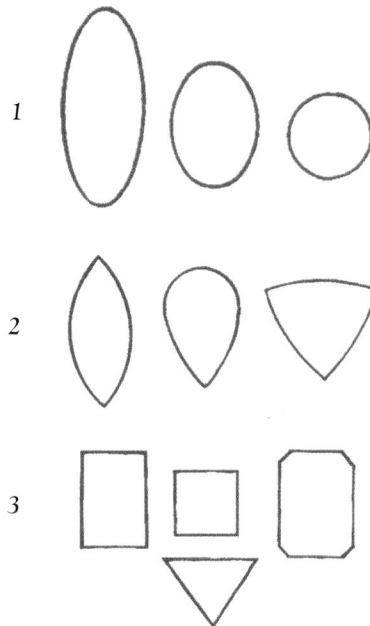

Cut stones generally fall into three categories:
  1. Curvilinear
  2. Curvilinear with corners
  3. Straight-side with corners

Constructing Shoulder Bezels for Rectangular and Square Stones

Great care must be used when dealing with corners, both while fitting the bezel and during the setting process. Sharp corners can be easily chipped when pressure is applied in an attempt to force a stone into a poorly fitting bezel. Also, because the adjustment of angular bezels is more difficult than round or oval bezels, precise measuring and accurate layout are critical as well.

On a properly constructed angular bezel, all solder seams should lie at the corners, for three good reasons. First, a joint in the middle of one side, between two adjacent corners, represents an additional, unnecessary seam; second, a seam between two corners may be visible and unsightly; and third, the setting of the corners of an angular bezel requires the removal of some material at those points, and it makes sense that the material being removed should come from a soldered seam.

Rectangular and square bezels have four right-angle corners. At first, it might seem logical to cut a strip long enough to go all the way around, mark it off into four sections, and bend it into its final form. This is possible but not recommended—its not quite as easy as it appears.

Woodworkers are familiar with a problem referred to as *dimensional buildup*.

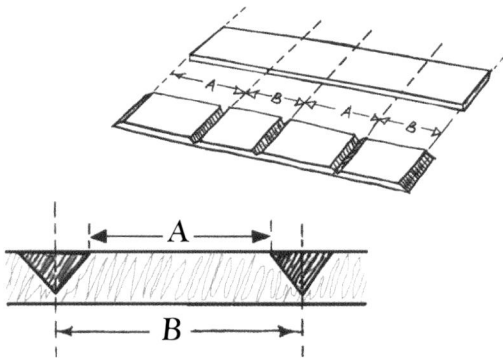

At first blush it seems like this is a logical way to construct a square or rectangular frame. There are several factors that make this difficult, including the fact that A (the inside dimension) becomes much smaller than B, the original marked length of each side.

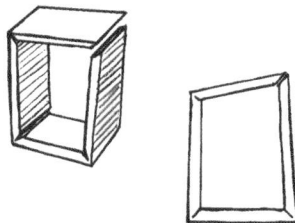

Even with careful measuring, this is an all-to-familiar result when building a frame from a single strip.

This phrase alludes to a cumulative error in measurement, usually reflecting a failure to take into account the small amount of material removed with a sawcut or mitered corner. The drawing shows how an inside dimension is reduced when a corner is filed and bent. The shortfall can be accommodated through careful calculations, but there are two much faster and easier methods.

Method 1

In the first method, the bezel and bearing are made separately and are later fitted together, one inside the other, as in the construction of round and oval shoulder bezels described earlier. Begin by cutting two strips of annealed metal, each at least 5 mm longer than the combined total length of two adjacent sides of the stone, and of the desired width (i.e., this width will actually be the height of the bezel). Be sure to allow for the height of the bearing that will be fitted inside later on. Adjust a pair of spring dividers to a dimension slightly longer than the stones shorter sides, measure in from one end of each strip and mark off this distance.

Use a square needle file to score a notch at this point across each strip, perpendicular to the lengthwise axis. File the

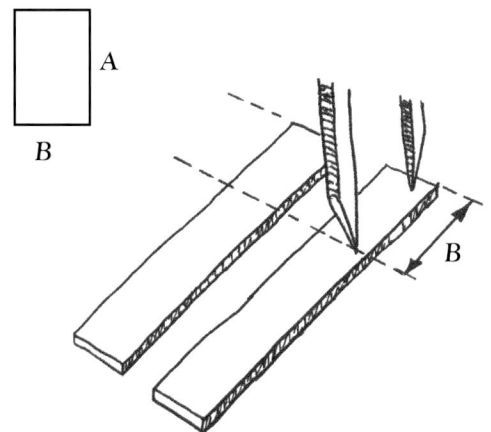

Start with two strips of metal, each equal to an end and a side (A + B) plus a little extra.

notch to a depth of about three-fourths the thickness of the strip. If the notch is not deep enough, the bend will be rounded instead of crisp.

Carefully bend each strip to a right angle at the scored notch. Handle the piece gently and avoid bending it back and forth

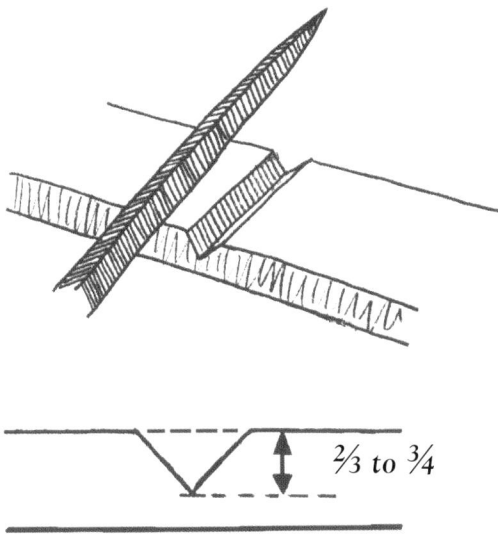

$$\frac{2}{3} \text{ to } \frac{3}{4}$$

Use a square needle file to create a sharp groove. The cut should be at least two-thirds of the thickness of the sheet. Anything less will yield a rounded corner, as shown below.

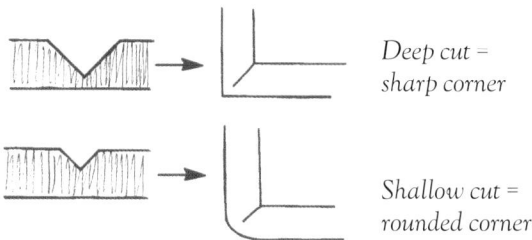

Deep cut = sharp corner

Shallow cut = rounded corner

(it might break). Check the accuracy of each angle with the square end of a small stainless steel ruler, or by placing the stone (which should be upside down, lying on its flat table) up against the inside perimeter of each bent strip. If adjustment is necessary, do so gently.

Before proceeding to the next stage, stabilize the two fragile L-shaped sections. Flux both scored joints, place tiny solder chips atop each, and carefully solder. Both angled sections can now be handled safely, without changing the angles.

Place the stone, table side down, on a flat surface. Position one of the L-shaped units against the stone, lining up a shorter end of the stone with the shorter leg of the strip. Carefully and accurately mark off the exact length of the edge on the inner face of the strip with a fine-pointed scribe. Repeat the same operation with the other angled unit. Trim the excess material from each to the scribed mark, making sure that the

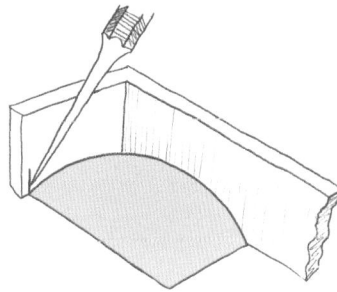

Set the L-shaped piece against the stone and mark the exact length of the shorter side. Do this on both pieces and cut away metal up to the mark.

ends remain perpendicular. Both of these trimmed, shorter legs should be exactly the same length now—exactly the same length as a short side of the stone. Check them against each other.

If the two L-shaped sections are now positioned around the stone in such a way that the shorter leg of each section lies

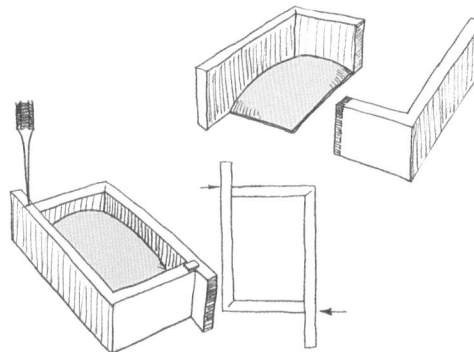

When the two "L" pieces are properly formed, mark the proper position and solder them together.

against a corresponding short side at opposite ends of the stone, the two sections can be slid along one another until they rest closely against the stone on all four sides. Again, use a fine-pointed scribe to mark the exact location where the short end of one L meets the longer side of the other. Remove the stone, realign both sections, flux, and solder. After pickling, rough trim the two projecting, overlong ends (no need to file flush or sand at this point) and check the fit. Adjust, if necessary, by selectively walking the bezel with forming pliers to directionally stretch as needed.

The bearing is now fashioned in exactly the same manner, the only difference being that it will be lower than the bezel and will be sized smaller to fit the interior of the bezel. Once constructed and adjusted, its upper, outer edge is beveled, and it is pres-

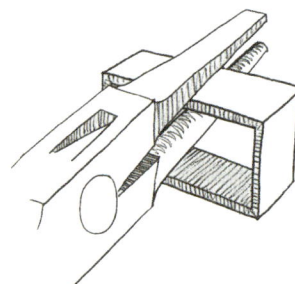

If the frame is a little small, squeeze gently with forming pliers as the tool slides along the short side.

sure fitted into the bezel. Stagger the seams (which lie at opposing corners) with those of the bezel for reinforcement and security. Solder the two together and pickle. Note that sometimes when the bearing is fitted into the bezel, the sides will bulge slightly from the tension fit, creating a space between the two walls. Simply clamp the two walls in the tips of the cross-lock tweezers. As the assembly is heated and approaches annealing temperature, the walls will relax and be pressed into contact by the tension of the tweezers tips. Once soldered, the exterior surfaces of the completed bezel can now be filed, sanded, and the height of the outer bezel adjusted if necessary.

Position the frames so the seams are in opposite corners, file a bevel on the inner sleeve to accommodate solder, and press the parts together. If the inner wall buckles, hold the piece in tweezers as you anneal.

Susan Jo Klein | Coral Reef Brooch
Red coral, black agate, beach stone, 18k gold, 3½" x 2"
photo: Peter Groesbeck

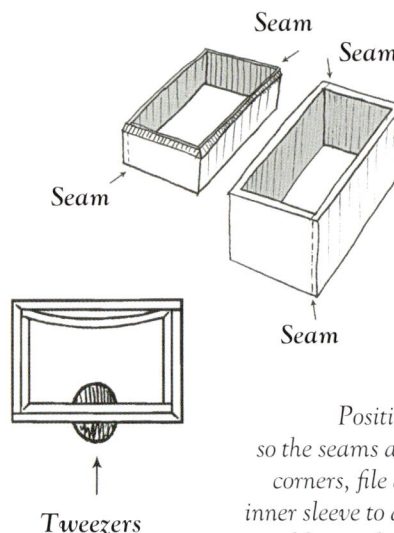

Method 2

In the second method, the bezel assembly again begins with two L-shaped units. However, the flat strips for both bezel and bearing are first soldered together as a single, double-layered unit that is later cut into two halves. Remember, this pre-soldered bearing/bezel strip must be comfortably longer than the total of the lengths of the four sides of the stone. It is imperative that when the strips are being soldered together they maintain accurate, parallel alignment. The width of each strip, and the distance between the upper edge of the bezel and the upper edge of the bearing of both strips, must be constant from end to end. If this distance varies even slightly, the upper edges of the bearing will not meet at the same level later, when the halves of the bezel are assembled. Solder the two strips together with hard solder, pickle, and cut into two equal sections.

From here the assembly is the same as described above. Both of these methods work equally well, but, depending on the specifics of a particular piece, one may prove faster or simpler. It should be noted that the second method is less forgiving with regards to adjustment, so it requires greater precision at every step. Refining the fit of the bezel with forming pliers is significantly more difficult in this latter method because of the uneven thicknesses of the bezels cross section.

Constructing Shoulder Bezels for Triangular Stones

Triangular shoulder bezels are usually most easily assembled by joining two separate units (Method 1, above). Obviously, because there are three sides, not four, two matching L-shaped pieces are not called for. Once again, there are several alternate layout and fabrication sequence possibilities.

In the first method, the bezel is constructed from a single strip, equal in length

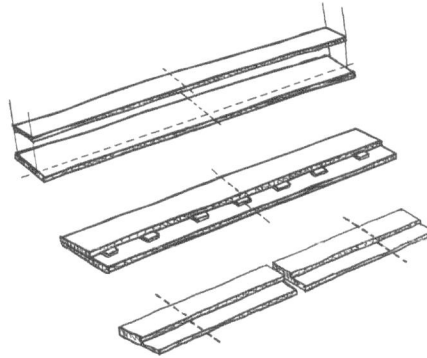

For efficiency and consistency, solder two long strips together, long enough to make the entire frame. When the soldering is complete and cleaned up, cut the strip into two equal pieces.

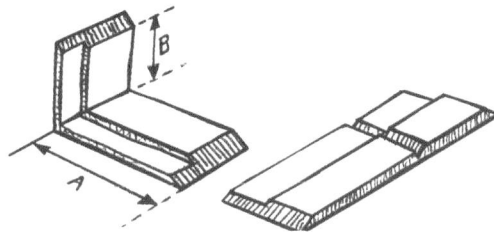

As before, cut a 90° notch with a square needle almost all the way through. Bend the corners with your fingers and solder the joint for strength.

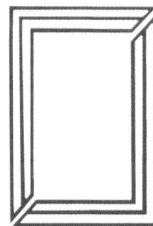

File a 45° angle on each end so the parts fit together into a symmetrical frame.

to the total of the three sides of the stone. The strip is marked off into three appropriate lengths. The ends are first beveled (the final mitering of the seam will be done by sawing), and the two interior corner locations are scored and bent. The scoring can be done with either a triangular or a square needle file. In most cases, neither will remove sufficient material to allow the strip to be bent into the required angles in one single operation, so begin by scoring with a file, bend, then use a saw to carefully cut into—but not through—each scored joint. Each saw cut will remove a tiny bit of metal from the inside of the corner. Repeat as many times as necessary to accomplish the correct angle. Solder all joints and pickle. Because no allowance is made for the thickness of the metal, the resulting bezel will be slightly undersized, but so long as it is of sufficient thickness—24 gauge (0.5 mm)—the individual sides can easily be adjusted longer with the forming pliers.

The other method involves assembly

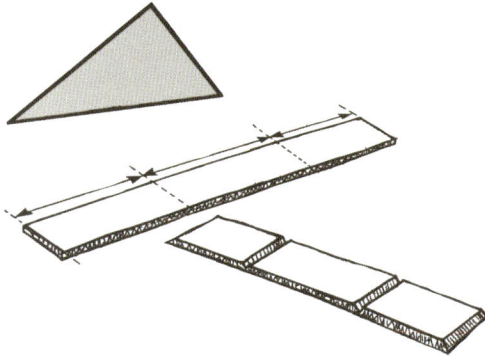

Measure each side of the stone and mark off sections a little longer. File and bend the bezel in your fingers.

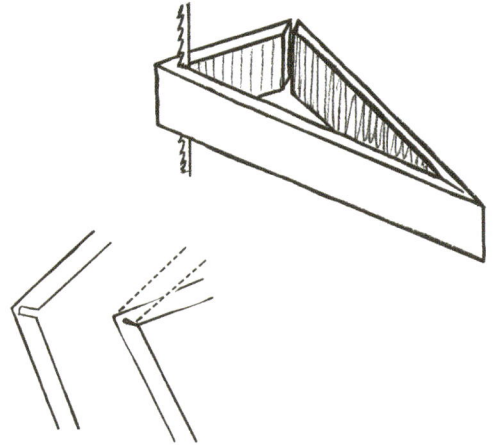

In an angled stone like this, it is often necessary to bend further than the grooves made with needle files allow. After making the initial bend, insert a sawblade and cut three-fourths of the way through the corner. Bend and resolder.

Michael Boyd | Ammonite Necklace
Green beryl, 18 & 22k gold, pearl, ammonite, mookaite, diamond.

photo: Steve Bigley

from two sections, one slightly longer than the sum of the lengths of two adjacent sides of the stone, and the second, slightly longer than the third side. The longer strip is scored (by a combination of filing and sawing), bent at its center point and soldered. The legs of this "V" are now filed back to match the exact length of the stone. The ends of these legs should also be filed at an angle, flush with, and in line with, the third side of the stone. The other strip is positioned against these beveled ends and soldered. A small right-angled bend will keep this strip upright during soldering.

If fitted properly, this method requires little or no additional adjustment. The bearing is constructed in exactly the same manner. Remember to stagger the end seams. Refining and clean-up, as usual, is done after the construction of the bezel is completed.

Sequence of Steps for Making a Geometric Bezel from Two Separate Pieces

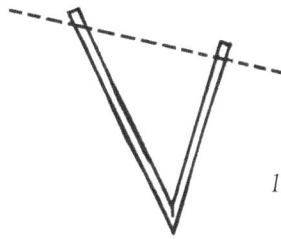

1. This is the idea.

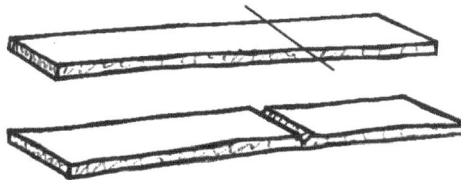

2. Start by filing a groove into the longer strip.

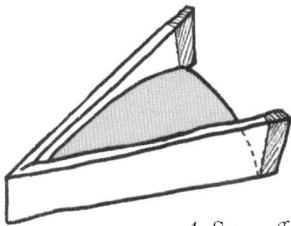

3. With the stone in place, mark the extra material at the top of the "V."

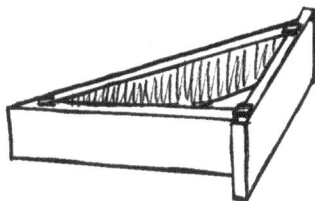

4. Saw off the extra and file the ends neat and square.

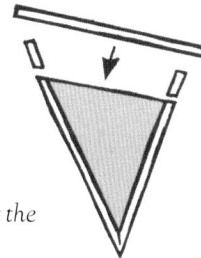

5. Solder a top piece across the top of the "V."

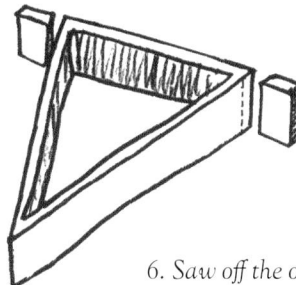

6. Saw off the overhanging metal and clean up all joints.

Bezels for Pear and Marquise Stones

Shoulder bezels for stones of these two shapes, which combine curvilinear profiles with one or more angular corners, are slightly more difficult to make than round and oval bezels. Here again, the bearing can be pre-soldered to the bezel strip, or fitted separately later.

To make a pear-shaped bezel, cut a strip longer than needed to completely encircle the stone. Begin shaping and fitting the strip along one side of the stone, starting at the pointed tip. When the strip is fitted all the way around the stone, mark and cut it where the ends cross. Saw through the joint to create a mitered seam and solder. Adjust the fit as necessary with forming pliers. Shape, fit, and solder a bearing in exactly the same manner (if the bearing was not already pre-soldered to the bezel). When fitted together, both solder joints of a pear-shaped bezel will be in alignment at the pointed tip, there being no reasonable way to stagger the seams.

To make a bezel for a marquise-shaped stone, first lay the stone upside down on a

Steps in making a bezel for a pear-shaped stone.

piece of paper. With a sharp pencil, trace the curvature of one side. Find a small, cylindrical object that is slightly more curved than this outline—medicine vial, small jar, etc.). Bend the strip around this with your fingers. The strip will spring back slightly,

which is why you start with a mandrel that is a little smaller than the desired curve.

Hold the stone, still upside down, against the inner wall of this curved strip so that one end extends slightly beyond the tip of the stone. Mark the inside of the strip where the stone ends. Score with a square or triangular needle file and bend, recutting into the joint with a sawblade if necessary until the bezel lies against the edges of the stone all the way around. Mark the point where the seam will lie and remove any excess. Saw through the joint to create a mitered seam and solder the joints at both ends. Adjust the fit, and then make a bearing in exactly the same manner. Fit and solder the two pieces together.

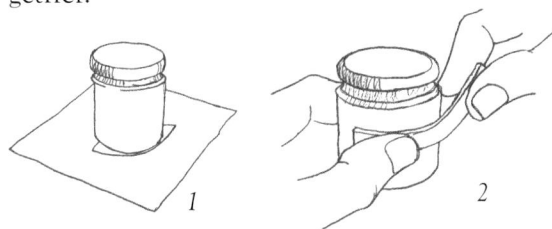

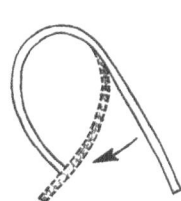

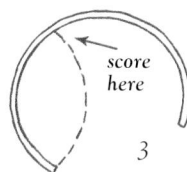

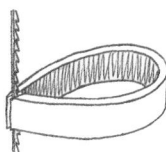

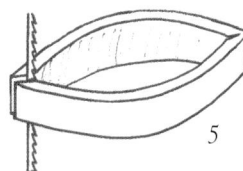

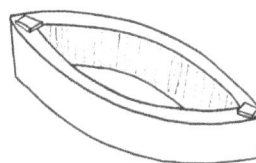

Marquise Bezel

1. *Find a temporary mandrel.*
2. *Wrap a strip around mandrel to achieve an even curve.*
3. *Score and bend.*
4. *Trim off extra.*
5. *True up the seam with a sawblade.*
6. *Solder.*

Constructing Bezels for Emerald-Cuts

Octagonal-shaped stones are usually, but not always, faceted, and are often referred to as emerald cut stones because that precious gem material is so often cut to this shape. Octagonal bezels are probably the most difficult to fashion because of the eight sides. Matching the lengths of each side and the angles of each corner of the bezel to the corresponding angles and corners of the stone requires precise measurement, layout, and workmanship.

Carefully examine the stone. Note that the sides are of three basic lengths: two long sides; two short ends; and four shorter corners. If the stone is accurately cut, the lengths of the individual sides within each group should be exactly the same. If this is the case, it will simplify the layout for the bezel (if this is not the case, each side and corner must be fitted individually, which is considerably more time-consuming). Comparing the measurements of each set of sides is best done with a small pair of fine-pointed spring dividers.

Begin the construction of the bezel by pre-soldering the bezel and bearing strips together. Make this double-layered strip comfortably longer than the total length of the stones eight sides. Make sure the bearing will be tall enough to contain the pavilion. Select a corner of the stone to begin and mark it with an indelible marker. As long as the stone does not have a porous surface, the ink can be removed later with denatured alcohol.

Looking straight down on the stone, note that there is a straight line that bisects the angle of each corner. These radial lines subdivide into two smaller angles of slightly more than 60°. Hold a small strip of metal, the same gauge as the bezel, against the edge of the stone where the fitting will begin. Allow the end of the metal strip to extend a little bit beyond the corner of the stone. Visualize the straight radial lines extending out beyond the girdle of the stone at both ends of that side of the stone, and, using a fine-tipped scribe, carefully mark

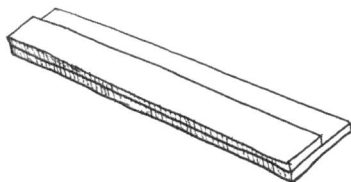

1. Start by soldering two strips together to make a bearing bezel.

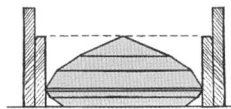

2. The width of the inner strip must be as tall or taller than the pavilion.

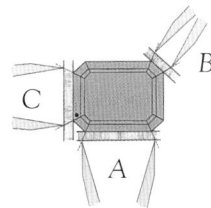

3. Use dividers to measure and hold the three lengths. Make an ink dot on the stone to identify a consistent point of reference.

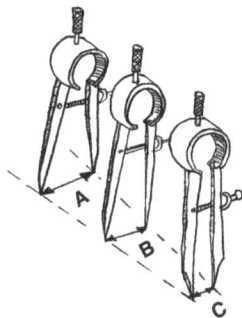

4. Confirm that the sides that should be the same length really are; i.e., that the stone is symmetircal.

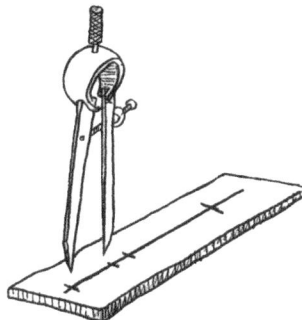

5. Mark off the appropriate sections with the dividers.

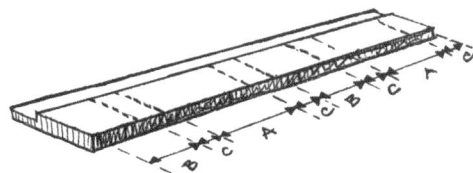

6. Mark off the divisions in preparation for scoring. Use a square to be sure the lines are perpendicular to the edge.

the points where these imaginary lines cross the outer edge of the strip.

The distance between these two points will be slightly greater than the actual length of the side of the stone. If you work from the actual length of the sides, the finished bezel will end up being too small. The slightly exaggerated measurements I'm describing here allow for the thickness of the bezel.

Adjust the tips of the spring dividers to this exact length, and transfer this measurement to a small, temporary measuring template. To make the template, select a small scrap of flat sheet, and scribe a straight line across its surface, somewhat longer than the longest side of the stone. Make a small mark with the point of a scribe at one end of this line. Place the tip of one leg of the divider in this indentation, and swing the other leg in a short arc crossing the scribed line, to record the length just measured.

Repeat this sequence of measuring and recording for each of the next two adjacent sides. Because these three consecutive sides include one short end, one corner, and, one long side, they provide the essential information with which to lay out the location of the scored joints along the bezel strip. Taking these measurements from the template is simpler than resetting the dividers' tips to the stone itself. If you have three pairs of dividers, set each one to a different length to expedite the process. Starting at one end of the prepared bezel strip, use the dividers to mark off the series of alternating lengths in proper order. These points show where the bezel wall will be scored.

Scoring for an octagonal bezel is done with a medium-fine sawblade (#2/0 or #3/0) rather than with angular needle files. Both a square and a triangular file will remove too much metal and result in a noticeable gap at the scored corners. Re-saw into each bend, as necessary, until the correct angle is achieved. As each successive corner is scored and bent, check it against the stone. When a corner is correct, solder the joint with hard solder to lock it in position.

When all of the interior joints have been scored, bent, and soldered, the two ends of the bezel strip (which form a small V-shaped notch where their inner edges meet) should be mitered with a saw cut and soldered. If the measuring, layout, and mitering are all done carefully, the bezel should fit the stone. If a side is too short, it can be stretched with forming pliers or the inner wall of the bezel can be carefully trimmed back with a flat graver. Any side a little too long must be recut at a corner seam and then resoldered.

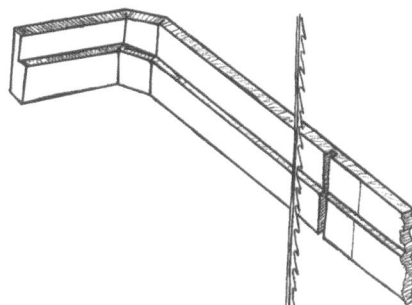

Use a sawblade to score the bends on an octagonal bezel.

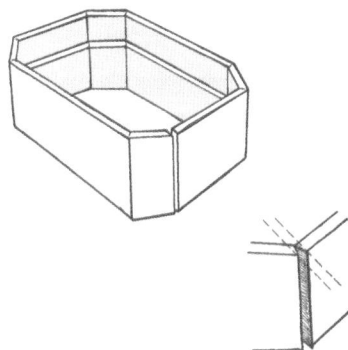

Bend the bezel around in your fingers, and clean up the joining corner with files and then a sawblade to make a perfectly clean joint. Use as little solder as possible here.

Setting Bezels with Angular Corners

Closing a bezel with one or more angular corners is done in much the same manner as for a regular bezel, with the exception of the treatment of the corners themselves. Scored and soldered corners are very strong and structural and it is neither possible nor desirable to try to compress the metal against the stone by pushing or hammering directly on these angular points. Attempting to do so would likely damage the bezel, the stone, or both. Instead, corners are "relieved" in one of two ways.

"Relieving" angular corners refers to the process of selectively removing a tiny amount of metal from the inside of the corner. This allows the bezel to be closed safely and securely against the stone with less pressure exerted on the fragile corners. One method involves cutting with a fine sawblade, and the other involves the filing away of part of the metal at each corner. Both methods work equally well, but, after setting, each yields a corner of slightly different visual aspect.

In the first method, position the stone in the setting and begin crimping and compressing the bezel in exactly the same manner as for any other non-cornered bezel, but leaving three or four millimeters on either side of each corner untouched for the time being. The corners will be set last, after the rest of the bezel has been closed against the stone. Work evenly, back and forth around the perimeter of the stone until the bezel has been compressed against the stone, locking it in place.

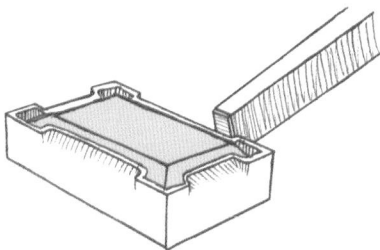

Use a bezel pusher to press the bezel over enough to lock the stone in place.

Using a very fine sawblade (6/0 or 8/0), carefully cut straight down through each corner all the way to the stone. A heavier sawblade will make too wide a cut, which will be difficult to close later. If the stone being set is faceted, the cut will extend all the way to the top edge of its girdle. In the case of a cabochon, the cut will end slightly above the girdle. Saw at an angle parallel to the stone's surface. As the cut approaches the stone, saw slowly and without pressure. If the stone is soft enough to be marred by the blade, cease sawing just before reaching its surface.

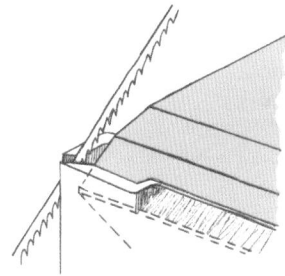

Saw directly into the cut, then press the two edges together. Repeat as many times as necessary to make a clean corner.

Press the bezel with a bezel pusher on both sides of the cut toward the stone until the top edges of the cut corner meet. Saw through this contact point, in the same path as the original cut, and push the edges together again. Repeat this alternate sawing and pushing as many times as necessary, until both sides of the cut at each corner lie directly against the stone. Use a burnisher to further close and tighten the seam, rubbing toward the corner from either side of the cut. Burnishing will make the cut invisible. Once the setting and refinement are completed, the bezel will appear as a band of uniform width paralleling the edge of the stone when viewed from above.

In the second method, instead of mitering the seams with a saw cut, the bezel can be filed lower at each of its corners (to the level of the girdle) in a smooth,

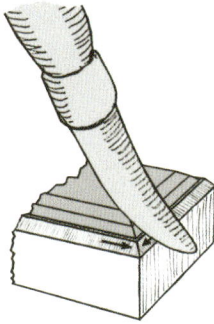

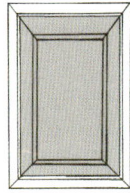

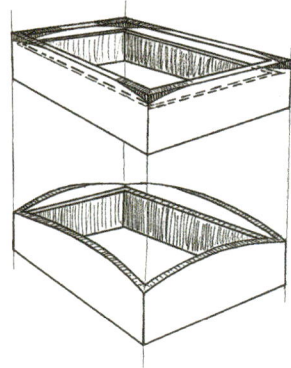

Use a burnisher to close and smooth the corners. When finished, the corners should be clean and crisp.

gradual slope from its original height in the middle of each side. No metal is actually pushed over the corners of the stone in this method. Rather, the stone is secured by the rest of the bezel (which should be of sufficient thickness to supply the requisite strength). A bezel set in this manner does not appear as a uniformly-wide, parallel band encircling the stone, instead tapering from narrow to wide to narrow in graceful "photo album tab" fashion, from corner to corner.

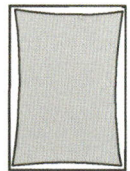

An alternate method is to file the top edge of the bezel into a slope that disappears into the corner. Note that these settings, when viewed from the top, reveal a tapering rather than a uniform strip. This method can be used on any stone with a corner, as seen in the teardrop above.

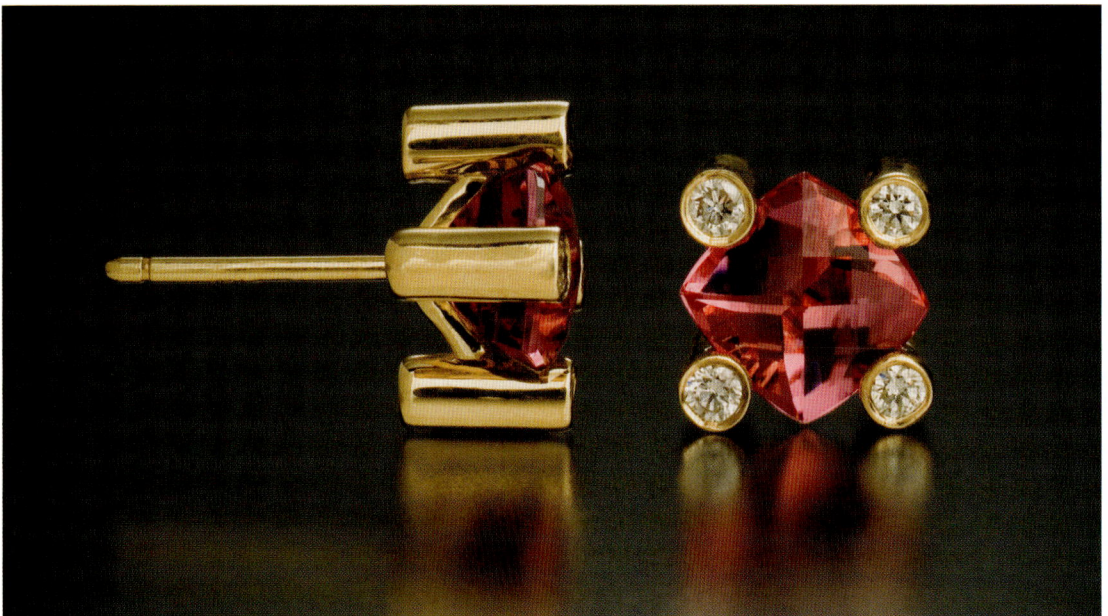

Julia Behrens | *Overlap* Stud Earrings
18K gold, tourmaline and diamonds

photo: Robert Diamante

Modified Bezels and Alternative Setting Possibilities

With careful consideration first given to strength and security, shoulder bezels can be altered in any number of ways to address specific setting problems or to enhance their appearance. Crystal clusters, for example, are occasionally cut and set as cabochons, flattened off on the backside and trimmed around the perimeter while leaving their irregular skyline intact. In a case such as this, the bezel may be cut to a similar, erratic contour, which both relieves it, allowing it to be pushed over selectively, and also, design-wise, reflects the eccentricity of the stone's surface.

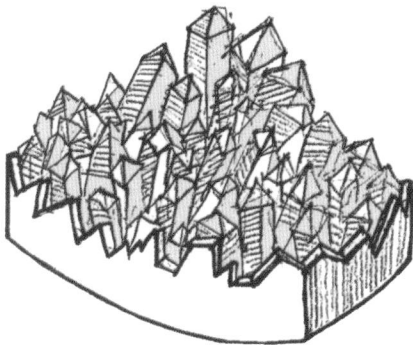

An irregular bezel works best for a crystal structure, both practically and aesthetically.

Certain other gem materials—turquoise nuggets, for instance—may be partially cut in such a way as to retain the unusual, irregular character of their surfaces. Though less craggy than crystal clusters, they do not have the consistent sloping profile of a standard-cut cabochon. In a situation like this, multiple saw cuts, made with a fine blade and extending down to the level of the inner bearing all the way around the setting, divide the bezel into little fingers that can be pushed over individually to accommodate the irregular contour of the surface.

Partial removal of the bezel wall can also radically alter its appearance. Non-essential bezel metal can be selectively sawed or filed away, creating a modified setting that often looks more like a prong setting than a bezel. Metal removed at regularly-spaced intervals can produce a crown-like effect while cuts made at random, or only at critical sites, create an entirely different effect. Or, portions of the bezel may be cut into prongs while other sections are left intact.

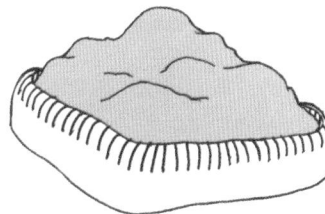

Use a thin sawblade to make many short cuts into a bezel. The result is easy to press over an irregular stone, and offers some interesting design details at the same time.

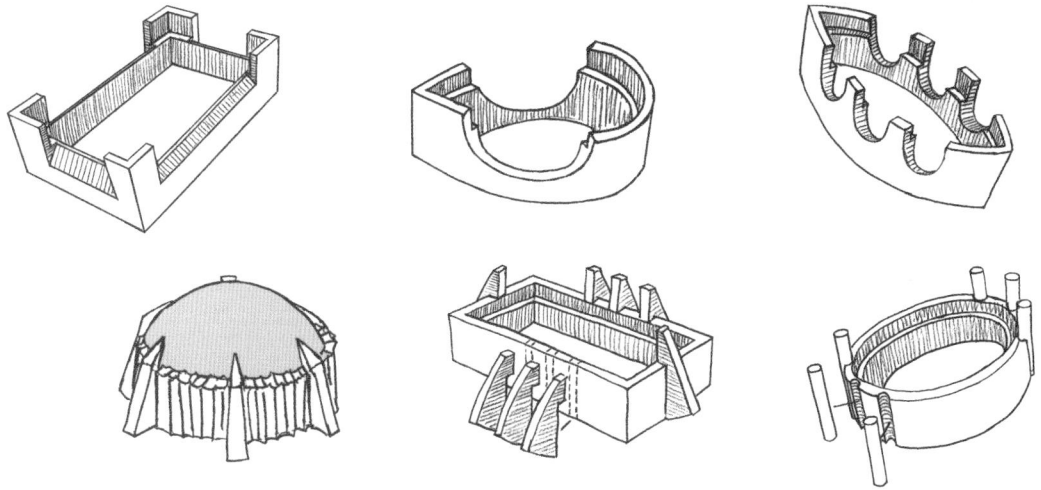

Here are a few of the many options for variations on bezels. Each of these sketches can point the way to an entire series of further options.

Hybrid prong/bezel settings are yet another possibility. Wire prongs of any cross section or sheet metal prongs cut to any shape can be soldered to the exterior surface of a bezel (the bezel in this case need only be slightly taller than the girdle of the stone). Once the stone is in place, the bezel, which is not actually pushed over the stone, prevents any side-to-side movement, while the prongs hold the stone in the setting.

With a little imagination, the possibilities are endless!

Specialty Bezels

In addition to the more familiar selection of standard bezels, there are a number of highly specialized bezel constructions whose distinctive designs address specific setting problems, accommodate unusually shaped stones, and attract attention. Generally, these specialty bezels are no harder to make than standard bezels and, in fact, some are actually easier to assemble. Their distinctive designs, however, often entail special planning, precise layouts and/or unusual constructions.

Tube Settings

As a general rule, the fashioning of bezels by conventional methods becomes more difficult as they get smaller in size. When it becomes impractical to shape and fit small bezels, tube settings offer a viable alternative. Seamless tubing, also called extruded tubing, is ideally suited to the production of small bezels. The outer dimensions of a stone must exactly match the inner dimensions of the tubing. Because tubing is commonly available in round and square cross-sections, it is most frequently used as bezels for round and square stones.

Until relatively recently, the only means of procuring tubing was to make it by hand. Producing a selection of various diameters and wall thicknesses represented a considerable investment of time. Today, seamless extruded tubing is available in a wide range of telescopic sizes and wall thicknesses. Tubing comes in a wide range of outer dimensions, many of which are also available in three standard wall thicknesses: heavy-wall, 0.020″ (±0.5 mm), medium-wall, 0.015″ (±0.4 mm) and light-wall, 0.010″ (±0.25 mm). Even thick-walled tubing is not particularly thick, so cutting a seat for a stone into the wall of a single tube with burs or gravers is not practical. Instead, select tubing into which the stone fits properly, then solder a short section of smaller tubing inside as a bearing. The entire assembly is fast, simple, and requires only one soldering operation. Setting a stone in a tube setting is done like any other bezel.

The next two types of settings, double bezels and cup bezels, are most often employed in situations where the completed assembly will hang freely such as earrings and pendants.

Double Bezels

Double bezels are shoulder bezels in which two cabochons are set back-to-back. The outer wall of this bezel must be tall enough to allow for an inner bearing plus sufficient material at either end to secure the stones. The construction of a double bezel is basically the same as for any other shoulder bezel, except that the bearing sits at the middle of the bezel, as shown. It can be as simple as a narrow shelf that will prevent damage that might otherwise result from the undersides of the stones rubbing against each other. Without the bearing, the stones would be free to move inside the bezel, and there would be no way to hold them in the proper position. Any jump rings or other exterior appliqués

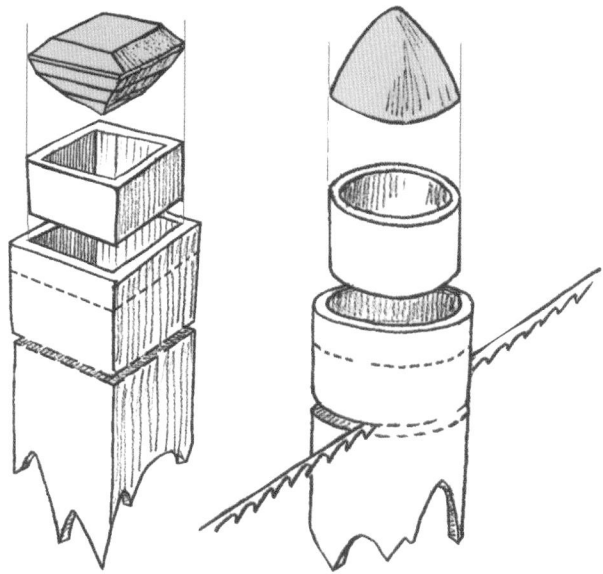

It is often easier and faster to insert a snugly fitted inner tube than to cut a bearing. Work on the full length of the tubing, then cut off the setting when the parts have been made.

should only be attached over the bearing so they do not interfere with the setting of the stones.

Double bezels are usually mounted on a shellac stick for setting. After the first stone is properly secured, the bezel is

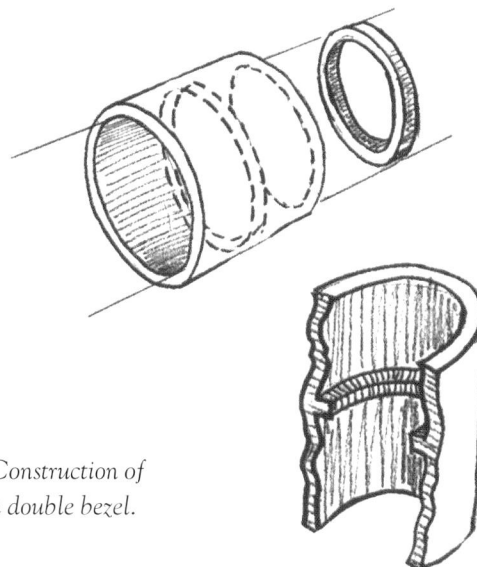

Construction of a double bezel.

A double bezel set into a shellac stick for setting.

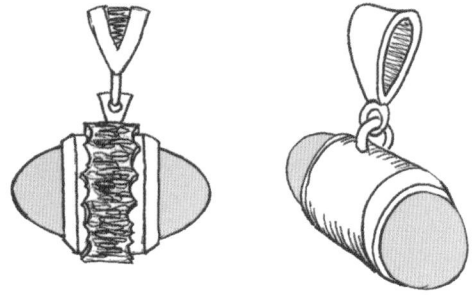

Here are a couple examples of how a double bezel can be used. It seems to lend itself particularly well to high cabochons.

removed from the cement, soaked in denatured alcohol to dissolve any residue, then remounted in reverse orientation to set the second stone.

Cup Bezels

Cup bezels are settings for round cabochons that incorporate a dapped disk as a primary component element. Depending on the degree of curvature of the disk and the corresponding contour of the stone, the profile of the finished setting can range from acorn-like to orb-like. Since they are normally viewed from the side when suspended, they are most effectively used with stones having a highly domed surface.

Cup bezels are usually made in one of two ways. In the first method, a disk of metal at least 24 gauge (0.5 mm) in thickness, and approximately one-and-a-half times the diameter of the stone, is dapped

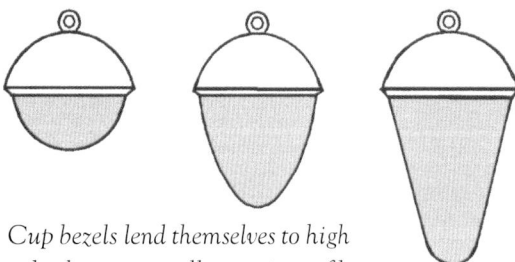

Cup bezels lend themselves to high cabs that are usually seen in profile.

in a steel dapping block, in progressively smaller holes, until it is roughly hemispherical and its circular opening is only slightly larger than the base of the cabochon. At this point, the stone should fit approximately 2–2.5 mm down inside the cup. The edge of the cup is filed smooth and burrs are removed.

Make a wire bearing with an outside diameter that is the same as the outside diameter of the stone. I find it easier to make the wire ring slightly undersized to begin with. After soldering, I carefully stretch it on a small mandrel, checking the progress frequently. If the wire bearing is too small, the stone will not fit in the setting; if it is too large, the stone will be loose, which makes it difficult to set.

When the fit is correct, solder the bearing ring inside the cup, parallel to the rim. The portion of the rim above the bearing will become, in effect, the bezel. Complete any additional soldering, pickle, and clean up the piece in preparation for setting. Because of its rounded contour, a cup bezel is also best secured in a shellac stick for setting.

Unless the cup has some sort of perforated design, it has the potential to trap water. To prevent this, apply a small bead of clear, jewelers' grade epoxy (not a cyanoacrylate glue) to the bearing just before you insert the stone to make a water-tight seal. The flat end of a broken sawblade, stuck into the eraser end of a pencil, makes a handy applicator).

After the rim of the cup is properly closed with a bezel pusher, set it aside (still attached to the end of a shellac stick) to allow the epoxy to cure. Most quality epoxies have an initial set time of an hour or less, but require a curing time of 12 to 24 hours to attain maximum strength. After the epoxy has cured, remove the cup bezel from the shellac stick and soak it in alcohol only long enough to remove any shellac residue. Prolonged immersion may attack the epoxy. The combination of hemispherical cup and domed cabochon give this final, assembled bezel an almost spherical silhouette.

The alternate cup bezel construction is particularly well suited to the setting of bullets or other high profile cabochons. The construction begins with a basic bezel that is eventually what will hold the stone. This bezel gets soldered into a dapped disk that is of slightly larger diameter than the stone. The curvature of this disk is much shallower than that of the more hemispherical cup in the previous example. No inner bearing is required because the stone sits in the cup. Solder a ring or loop to become the bail, then use epoxy as described above and press the bezel onto the stone. The ledge where the dapped disk extends beyond the bezel may be left intact, or filed flush with the bezel.

Setting Bullets and Tongues

Recently, these two styles of tall cabochons have become popular. Bullets are usually taller than they are wide, are circular in cross-section along a central axis, and taper in a reasonably uniform curvature to a slightly rounded point. Tongues are flatter and broader, typically oval in cross-section, and end in a curved, blunt tip.

The unique character of bezel settings for both of these shapes comes less from

Sequence for Making a Cup Bezel

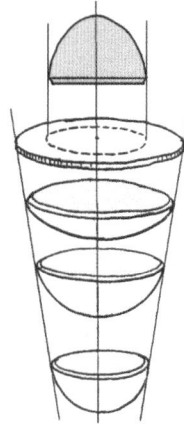

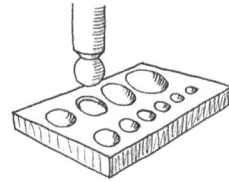

Set a disk in a dapping block and use a series of punches to form a dome that will contain the stone.

Depending on proportions of the stone, it is sometimes possible to simply set the stone into the cup.

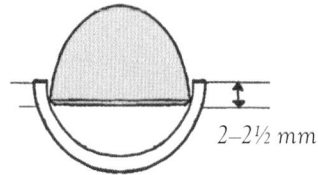

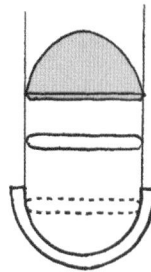

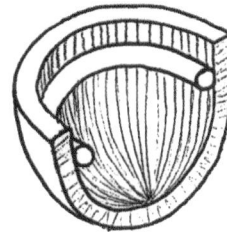

2–2½ mm

In other cases it will be necessary to solder a bearing ring inside the cup.

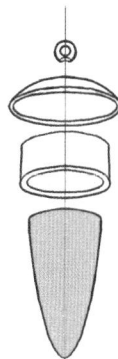

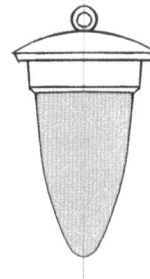

An alternate method is to solder a bezel into a shallow dome that is a little larger than the base of the stone. This provides an attractive overhanging rim.

their mode of construction than from the manner in which the stones are set. In fact, bezels for tongues and bullets are often standard cup bezel constructions. These stones are frequently cut in such a manner as to be almost straight sided, having little or no angle at their base ends. When a stone provides little or no slope against which the bezel can be locked the only solution is a tight-fitting bezel reinforced with epoxy. When being used as pendant forms, which generally take less stress than settings used in other high stress situations, this is an acceptable means of dealing with the problem. Because of the tall dome of these cuts, the rule of thumb proportion (bezels = ⅓ to ¼ the height of the stone) will not apply.

Setting Cone-Shaped Stones

Cone-shaped cabochons are circular

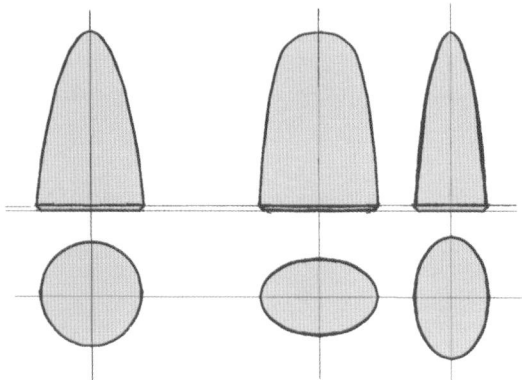

Bullets are tall round cabs, and tongues, shown on the right, have an oval cross section.

in cross section, triangular in side view, and decrease in diameter in a uniform, non-curving taper from a broad base to a pointed tip. Like bullets and tongues, they are frequently used in pendant forms. Because of their straight sided, steep conical taper, however, setting them presents a problem exactly opposite to that posed by bullets and tongues.

While parallel-sided cabochons provide little or no purchase for the bezel,

the conical cabochon has an excessive slope, creating a dilemma of a different nature. The difficulty arises when attempting to compact all of the metal of the bezel against the stone. The amount of compression required to draw the bezel down against the surface of the stone is often more than the metals plasticity can accommodate all at one time, without annealing. The bezel, unable to be further compacted, will fold and wrinkle, and the seam will crack. It is not possible to anneal the work-hardened bezel midway through the process with the stone locked in place.

There are several solutions to this setting problem. Selective removal of some of the metal at the bezel's edge reduces the amount of compression required. This relieved edge can be handled in different ways. Uniformly shaped and spaced, prong-like fingers of metal sufficient to hold the stone securely not only add a decorative touch, but simplify the closing of the bezel as well. A partial bezel created by the removal of certain sections of its wall while leaving other sections intact is another possibility. Yet another option might be the random sawing and filing of the bezel's upper edge to create an erratic, mountainous skyline. Reverse setting of the cone is still another possible solution.

In a reverse setting, the cone-shaped stone is inserted into a close-fitting bezel (which is open at both ends) with a matching taper from the larger side, and is then secured in place by a solid plate of the same exact size as the stones base. This plate, to

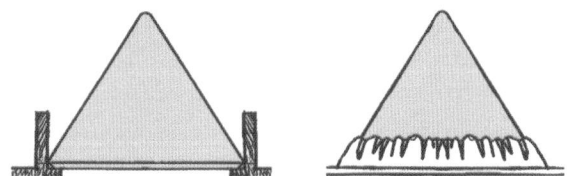

Cones can be set in a conventional bezel, but because of the steep sides, setting will be easier if you cut notches in the bezel.

which a loop or jump ring has already been soldered, rests directly against the stone, inside the bezel. The outer edge of this plate is slightly beveled before being fitted into position. The larger end of the bezel is filed back to a level slightly higher than the top surface of the backing plate. The edge of the bezel is also filed to a shallow angle allowing it to be closed over the corresponding beveled edge of the plate with a stone pusher. The bezel locks the plate in position which, in turn, holds the stone securely down inside the tapered wall of the bezel.

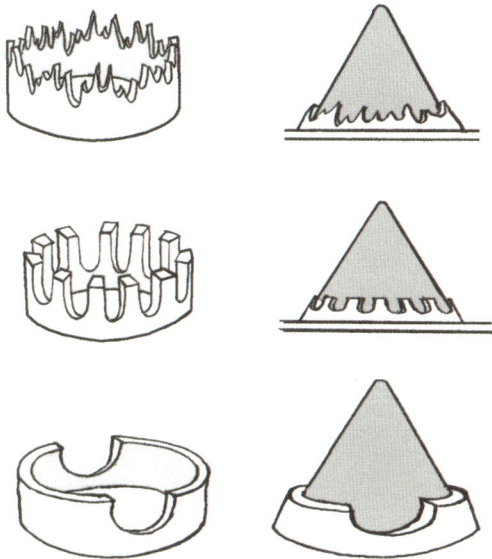

All three of these examples facilitate setting by removing a portion of the bezel.

Reverse Bezels

In certain circumstances, for either practical or aesthetic reasons, it may be appropriate to hide the actual setting structure. Take for example the case of a heavily textured surface. If a bezel is soldered onto such a surface, solder will almost certainly spill onto the surface where it would be highly visible, unsightly, and impossible to remove. In a similarly problematic situation, a shallow, low-profiled stone may require a bezel that is so short it presents little leverage for setting. Attempting to do so might damage the surrounding surface. In yet another case, it may simply be desired, as a visual special effect, that a stone appear to float on the surface with no visible means of attachment. In cases like these, a reverse bezel, soldered to the back side of a piece, can provide a viable solution.

Andy Cooperman | Skin & Bones
Gold, sterling, spectrolite, ruby, 5" high
photo: Doug Yaple

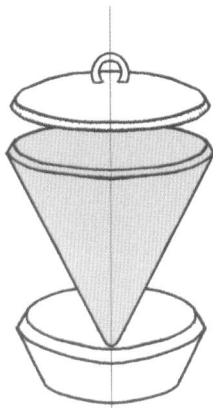

1. Make a collar and a lid to fit the stone.

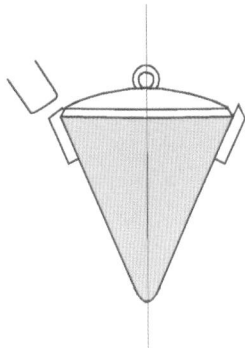

2. Press the edge of the collar over the beveled edge of the rim.

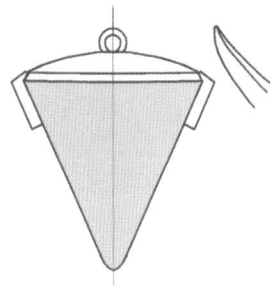

3. Smooth the edge with a burnisher to make it disappear.

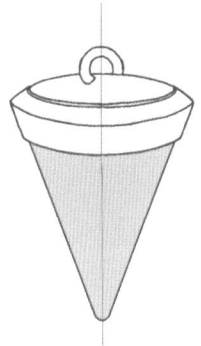

4. The finished piece.

A reverse bezel is a variation on a shoulder. It is attached on the back side of a piece rather than to the front and is fitted to the stone in a slightly different way. As usual, the bezel and bearing are first shaped and fitted to the stone, and to one another, but are not yet soldered together. The bezel strip is cut approximately 2.5–3 mm wider than the width of the bearing. It is very important that the inner bearing match the stone's base exactly in both shape and outer dimension. Use at least 16 gauge (1.3 mm) sheet or wire for the bearing. The inner bearing will reinforce the assembled bezel where the stone protrudes through to the front.

The inner edge of the bearing must be filed to the same angle as the slope of the stone. This tapering of the bearing's inner face is best done before it is soldered inside the bezel. When the bearing drops easily over the stone, the bezel and bearing can be soldered together.

The assembled bezel is soldered to the backside of the work piece. The metal inside the perimeter of the bearing is sawed out, leaving a slight rim. This projecting sawed edge is then tapered to the same angle as, and blended with, the previously beveled inner bearing (this operation is often most easily accomplished with a

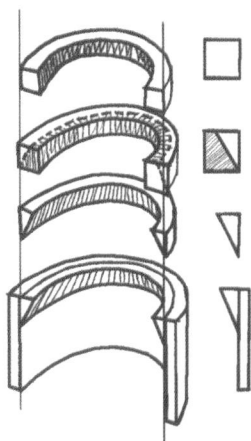

Steps in making an inner bearing. Start with a square wire, file it to match the slope of the stone, then solder into a bezel-like rim.

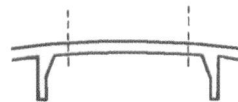

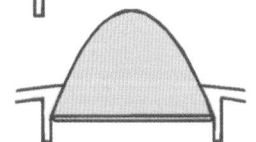

Solder that rim onto a base sheet, then saw away metal to make a hole for the stone. The angle filed here will match the angle already filed into the thickening rim. Check the stone frequently to establish a tight fit.

small inverted cone bur). Trial fit the stone in place, checking for accuracy, until the stone seats properly. The edge of the hole should meet the surface of the stone without gaps.

Closing the bezel from the back requires special techniques because the rim of metal being pressed against the stones flat bottom has so far to travel, and poses a much more formidable challenge. There are two solutions, both of which require adjustments to the bezel that should be performed before it is soldered in place.

The first involves making a wire ring (16 or 18 gauge round wire works well) that fits tightly along the inner wall of the bezel, flat against the cabochon. The height of the bezel wall should be filed back to approximately one-and-a-half times the diameter of the wire. This is most easily done with the stone and wire ring temporarily in place, but before the bezel is soldered into its final position (it may be difficult to get at after it is secured in place). Close the bezel in the usual way—it presses against the wire which, in turn, holds the stone into the bezel.

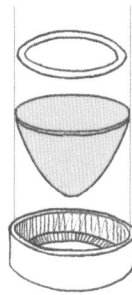

Make a bezel with a filed rim to match the stone, and follow this with a round wire that is the same size as the back of the stone.

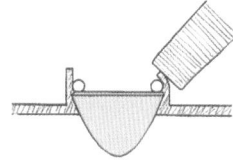

Press the bezel over as usual, but in this case you are pressing it against the wire.

The bezel can be left plain or decorated, for instance with openings like this.

In this variation, the wire is omitted. Mark the tabs, and score lightly to facilitate crisp uniform bends.

In the second method, the wire insert is optional. Sections of the bezel are carefully sawed away, leaving small tabs evenly spaced around the perimeter of the bezel wall. Temporarily seat the stone, and use a sharp scribe to mark a line indicating the bottom of the stone. Saw out the tabs down to this line. These tabs should stand no higher than 2–2.5 mm above the stone, and should be no wider than 3–4 mm (the wider the tabs, the more difficult they are to push over).

Though either method will secure the stone, the choice of which method to use depends on functional and aesthetic factors. Consider accessibility to the bezel: will it be hard to get at for setting and removal of any resulting marks? Also, think about how it will look when viewed from the back, remembering that the back side should be handled as carefully as the front.

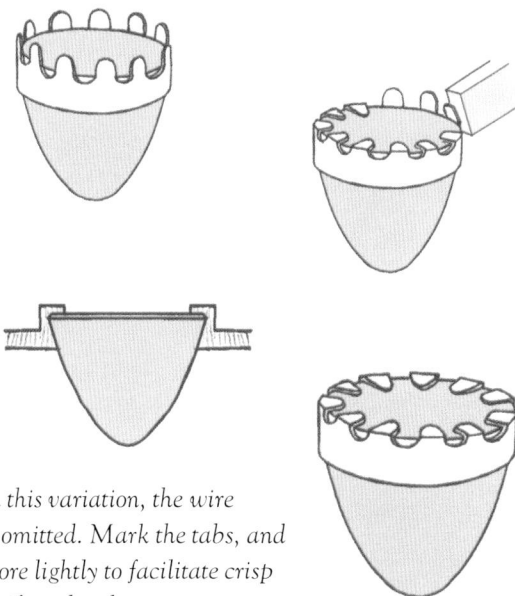

Bezels for Teardrop-Shaped Stones

A teardrop-shaped stone presents yet another setting quandary. Teardrops are elongated and circular in cross section; tall cones with rounded bottoms. The smooth-sided, conically-tapered surface of a teardrop-shaped stone offers no grip to a standard bezel or prong setting. Occasionally, the narrower end of some teardrops may be pre-drilled to accept a peg, but in the absence of one, other means of securing the stone must be devised.

Though stones like this are often cemented into commercial bell caps, this is never a truly acceptable resolution. An alternative solution requires some minor cutting into the stone, and while this is usually safe, there is a small risk that unseen faults inside the stone may cause it to break during this process. No cutting should be pursued without the consent of the stone's owner.

The first step is to draw a silhouette of the stone. Place the teardrop on a piece of paper and trace the pointed tip with a sharp pencil. Make a guess about how far down the taper the metal cap should reach, and draw a line at that point. The location of this line is a judgment call—the setting must cover enough of the stone to trap it, but should not hide the gem any more than it must. The setting can always be trimmed back if necessary.

Set the metal point of a pencil compass at the tip of the silhouette and position the pencil tip at the base line of the triangle. Describe an arc with the pencil point. Use the compass to measure the base of the triangle, and step off this length three times. Use a ruler to connect the point three steps out to the tip of the triangle. The result is a slightly oversize pattern for a cone that will be fitted to the stone and cut to size later.

Transfer this layout to a piece of thin sheet metal (22–24 gauge (0.6–0.5 mm), saw it out and file one side edge true (the other will be trued by sawing, later, after fitting). To aid shaping and fitting, saw off the last 1–2 mm of the pointed tip. Using round/flat forming pliers, carefully roll the fan-shaped piece into a cone, matching it to the tapered end of the stone as

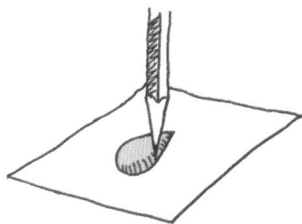

1. Trace the stone

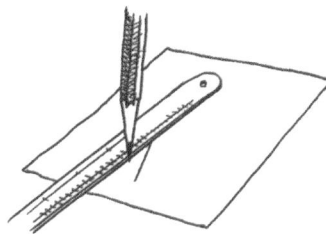

2. Determine the size of the cap.

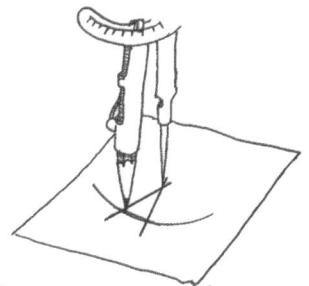

3. Use a compass to mark out dimensions.

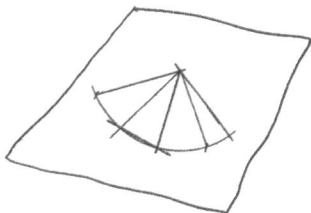

4. Layout the pattern for a cone.

5. Transfer to metal.

6. The cone pattern ready to be formed.

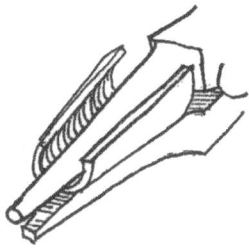

7. Bend the cone in pliers.

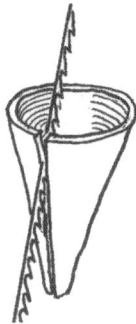

8. True the seam with a saw.

9. Hold in tweezers to solder.

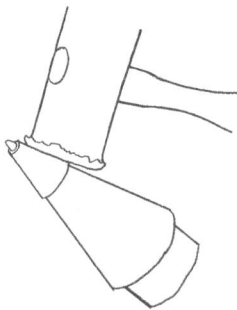

10. True up on a mandrel.

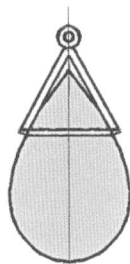

11. Test fit and mark the stone.

12. Secure the cone in shellac.

closely as possible. Mark where the edges overlap and remove excess. Bring the edges together and saw through the seam. Solder with hard solder and true up the cone with forming pliers or whatever small mandrels are at hand). Trial fit the cone over the stone. If it is too large, recut and resolder. When properly fitted, the stone should fit comfortably, with the cone's metal edge in continuous contact with the stone all the way around. Refine the cone and solder a ring or loop onto the end to provide a means of suspension.

The next step is to create a groove in the stone. To mark the location of this groove, draw a line with a fine-tipped felt marker on the stone along the edge of the cone. If the stone is nonporous, the ink can be dissolved later with denatured alcohol later. Because ink can stain organic materials like amber and coral, porous teardrops should be wrapped with a single layer of clear tape. Mount the metal cone on a shellac stick, point down, and set it aside while the stone is prepared.

Use a cut-off wheel (also called a separating disk), to cut a shallow groove all the way around the pointed end of the stone, approximately 1 mm above the line. Cut only a shallow groove, no more than 0.25 mm deep. A deeper cut may weaken the stone, causing it to break off during the setting of the bezel. Wash away the ink with alcohol (or remove the tape).

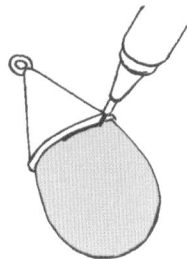

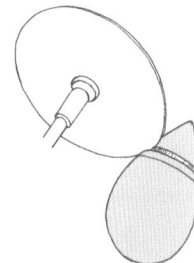

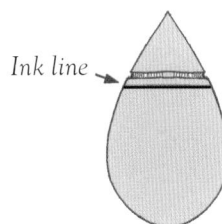

Ink line →

Press the stone into the cone and mark the edge. Cut a groove above this line with a separating disk.

Draw a short length of hard, springy wire 24 to 26 gauge thick and wrap it around a small cylindrical mandrel (e.g., a nail) that is slightly smaller in diameter than the groove. Do not cut the ring from the length of wire yet. Slide the loop down the stone until it snaps into the groove. Mark where the ends overlap, remove the wire from the stone, trim to length, and bring the ends into alignment. Do not solder or anneal this springy jump ring. It should fit securely into the groove (the combination of the springiness of the wire and the unsoldered seam allow it to flex past the rim of the groove and then snap into place).

With the ring in the groove, temporarily slide the cap over the stone. Center the ring on the cone's flat edge. A visible rim, equal in width to at least half the thickness of the gauge of the metal used to fashion the cone, should extend out beyond the jump ring. If there isn't sufficient rim visible, make a new ring of thinner gauge, or, cut the groove a little deeper (but only if it can be done without weakening the stone) and cut the ring proportionately smaller in diameter to refit.

Measure the diameter of the jump ring (still in place in the notch) with a sliding gauge or caliper. Select a straight-sided setting bur of the same diameter and use it to carefully cut a seat down into the open end of the metal cone, trial fitting the stone (with jump ring), until the ring rests barely below the level of the cones edge. Using a stone pusher, carefully and uniformly close the edge over the wire, locking wire and stone place.

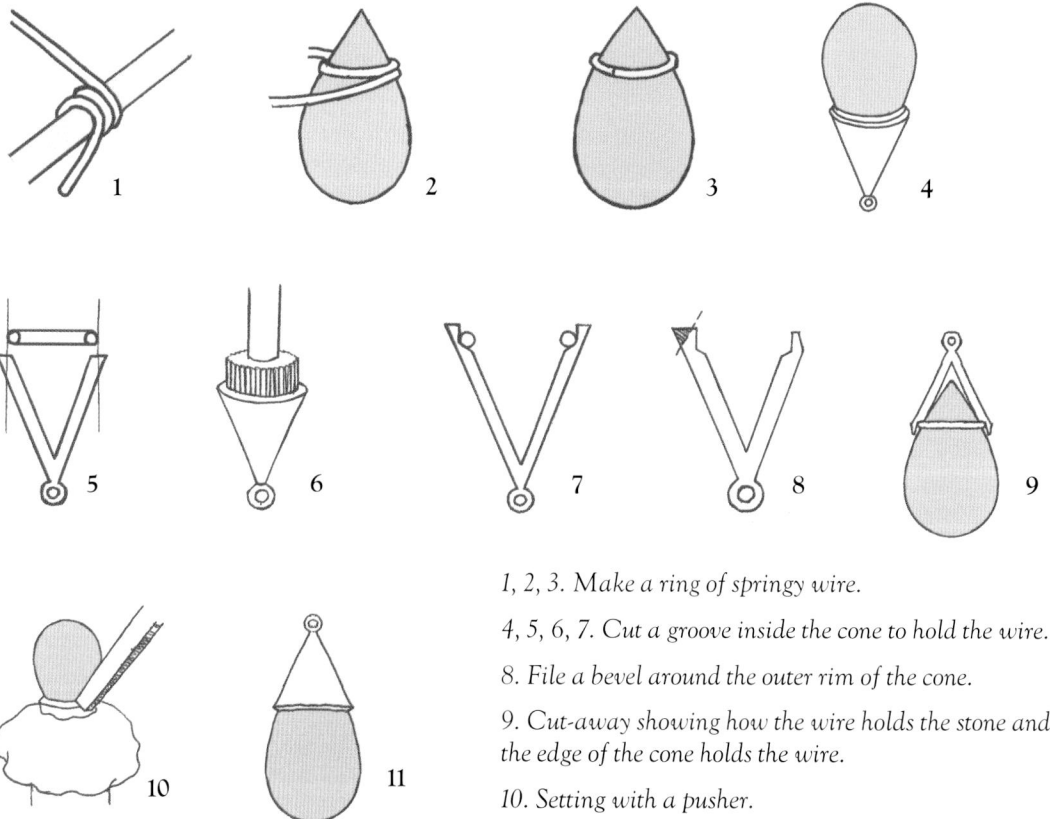

1, 2, 3. Make a ring of springy wire.

4, 5, 6, 7. Cut a groove inside the cone to hold the wire.

8. File a bevel around the outer rim of the cone.

9. Cut-away showing how the wire holds the stone and the edge of the cone holds the wire.

10. Setting with a pusher.

11. The end result.

Chapter 4
Prong Settings

Like bezels, the family of prong settings is large and diverse. The many different varieties of prong settings are generally grouped by mode of production: some are fabricated from wire; some are made from tapered, bezel-like tubes; some are assembled from cut-out, slotted units, and some, as described in the preceding chapter, are hybrids—part prong, part bezel.

Unlike bezel mountings, which trap stones with a solid band of metal, prong settings employ metal fingers. Because of their generally taller profile, more delicate appearance, and open structure, prong settings are most generally used to set faceted stones. Because faceted gems are usually transparent or translucent, and depend on the play of light to display their color and sparkle, prong settings are often the most suitable choice. However, as with bezels, there is no hard and fast rule, and both cabochons and faceted stones may be suitably secured in prong mountings.

Crown (or Coronet) Settings

This classic prong setting takes its name from its resemblance, in miniature, to its royal namesake. Commercial crown settings are available as four- or six-prong die-struck heads, generally gold, sometimes silver, in a range of sizes which will accommodate most small- to medium-size stones.

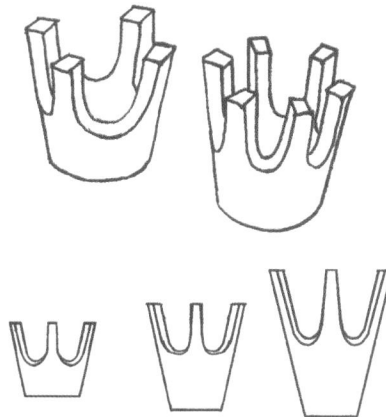

Typically, crown settings are made with four or six prongs, in low, medium, or tall versions.

This setting is easy to make and equally easy to customize. The commercial choice of four or six prongs is purely a matter of convention. A crown setting may have as few as three prongs, or, depending on its size, as many as desired. In profile, the crown setting is a truncated cone, with sections of the cone sides removed to create the prongs. The slightly tapered, basic cone section from which the setting is made can be produced by either of the following methods.

Making a Crown Setting
Method 1
The first method requires the development of a flat cutting pattern for the cone based on measurements taken from the stone. Using a sliding caliper or a spring gauge, determine the stones girdle diameter and overall height from table to culet.

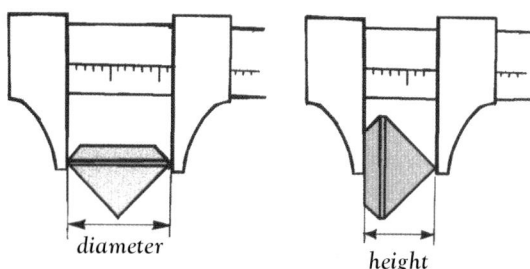

diameter   *height*

Transfer these measurements to a paper on which you've drawn axis lines. Sketch in the profile of the stone, centered on the vertical axis. Next, sketch a side-view profile of the crown setting you want to make, keeping the upper and lower edges parallel to the girdle line. The top edge should extend several millimeters above the top of the stone to provide sufficient prong height. The bottom should extend far enough below the culet to insure that it is safely contained within the crown. The taper is a matter of personal judgment, but it's wise to match the taper of an existing mandrel or cone stake. This will make it a lot easier to true up the cone.

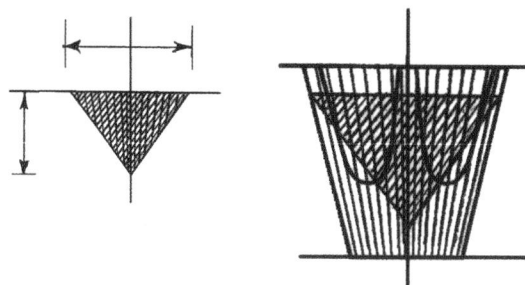

Draw a side view of the stone, using the actual measurements.

With a ruler and pencil, extend the sides of the setting until they intersect (A). Set the point of a pencil compass at this intersection, and adjust the other leg to touch the top of the setting. Swing an arc, reset the pencil tip to the lower corner of the proposed setting, and describe a second arc. Using the compass, or a small spring dividers, set to the larger diameter of the proposed setting, mark off three-and-a-half times this measure along the uppermost arced line. Connect this last point to the original intersection point (where the metal tip of the compass was located) with a straight pencil line. The area between the two arced lines (blue) is the cutting pattern for the metal blank from which the initial truncated cone for the crown setting will be made.

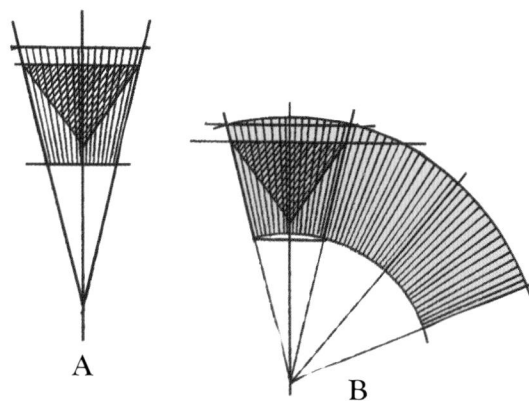

A   B

Work from the silhouette to layout a pattern for the cone that will become the crown setting.

Cut out this curved pattern and transfer it onto a piece of 16 to 20 gauge sheet. Use thinner metal for small settings and thicker for larger stones to achieve a practical and attractive proportion. Either trace around the paper pattern with a scribe or glue the pattern onto the metal. Saw out the curved blank, file the edges, and debar. Using round/flat forming pliers, carefully start shaping the blank, bending from both outer edges, and gradually working toward the center until the edges meet. While shaping, make sure the taper of the pliers jaws is aligned with the taper of the blank. Saw through the seam with a medium sawblade (e.g., #1/0) to produce a tight, gap-free joint. Flux and solder with hard solder. After pickling, remove excess solder that may have flowed onto the interior surface and true up the form on a mandrel with a rawhide mallet. Do not remove excess solder on the exterior surface at this time. File the top and bottom edges flat, then smooth them with fine abrasive paper, taking care that the edges remain parallel and that the tapered sides maintain a uniform slope.

James Kaya | Ring
Platinum, 18k gold, diamonds, peridot
photo: Robert Diamante

Sequence for Making a Cone, Method 1

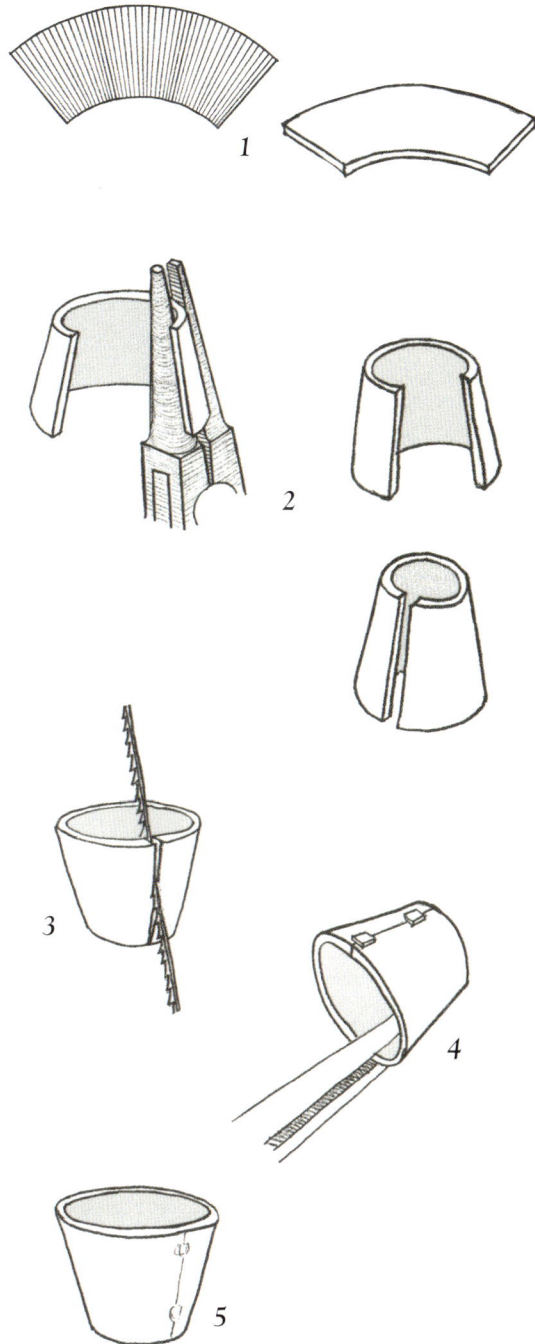

1. Paper pattern and resulting metal blank.

2. Bend the cone, starting at the edges and working toward the center.

3. Use a sawblade to clean up the joint.

4. Solder, often while holding the cone in tweezers.

5. Leave excess solder on the outside for now.

Method 2

The second approach to fabricating a crown setting is somewhat faster and more direct, but requires a keen eye and practiced hands. In this method, the setting is simply shaped from a strip of metal with forming pliers and is field fitted to the stone.

A crown setting fashioned in this manner requires a strip of metal of suitable gauge that is slightly wider than the desired height of the finished setting. First, curve the strip along its length into a gentle arc. This arc approximates that of the flat pattern described in the previous method. The strip must be several inches long, to supply the necessary leverage. The longer the strip, the easier it will be to bend.

Starting at one end, grip the metal in pliers jaws and pull it sideways. Gradually advance the strip in the jaws of the pliers, pulling it into the desired curve as uniformly as possible. It may prove necessary to flatten the strip with a rawhide mallet occasionally during this process. After the strip is suitably curved along its entire length, it will have become somewhat work-hardened and should be annealed.

Use round-nose pliers to roll one end of the strip into a tapered collar, matching its larger diameter to that of the stone. Position the pliers inside the curl so the taper of the developing cone coincides with the taper of the round jaws. Use the jaws of the pliers as fulcrums around which the metal is formed.

After the end of the strip has been rolled into a tapered tube of the appropriate diameter, saw off the cone and bend the ends into alignment. True the seam by sawing, then solder.

Whichever method you use to create the cone, the following process is the same for sawing out the prongs and refining the form.

Sequence for Making a Cone, Method 2

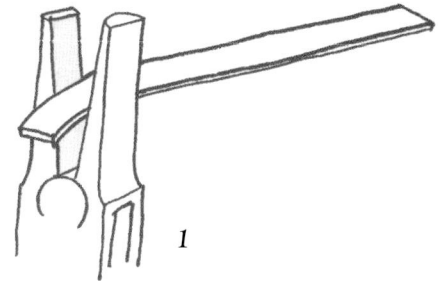

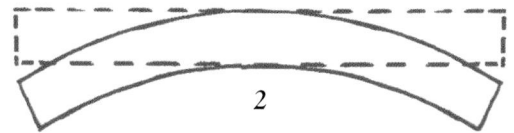

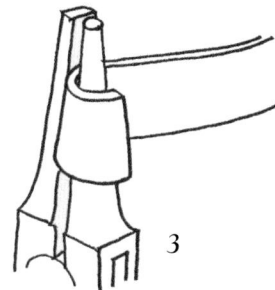

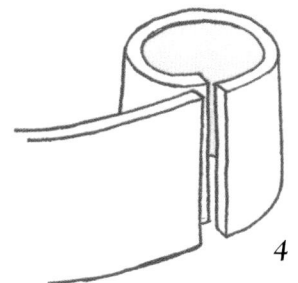

1. Start with an annealed strip wider than the intended height of the crown.
2. Bend it in forming pliers to a uniform curve.
3. Reanneal and form into a symmetrical cone on round-nose pliers.
4. Cut off excess material, file and sand the seam as needed, and solder.

Secure the smaller end of this tapered tube to a small shellac stick, and then darken its exterior surface and exposed upper edge with an indelible marker. Determine the number of prongs, and mark off the upper edge. Short segments will be the prong tips, and the longer segments show the bays that will be removed with a jewelers saw. Trace the top of the tube onto paper, divide the circle into the chosen number of segments, then transfer these measurements to the upper edge of the cone.

Use a dividers to lightly scribe a line parallel to the upper edge to mark the depth of the bays between prongs. Saw out the sections between the prongs. Be sure to leave sufficient metal for strength, but not so much that the setting will be visually heavy. Locate one bay over the seam—this will leave as little visible seam as possible. Placing the seam between prongs, rather than on a prong, also eliminates potential setting problems later on.

After the unwanted metal has been removed, use needle files to true up and refine the prongs. File carefully and shape the prongs as uniformly as possible. Either polish the filed edges of the prongs with a miniature buff, or smooth them with a small burnisher, The tip of a scribe buffed bright works quite well.

If desired, the lower half of the setting can be handled decoratively as well. After work on the upper prong section has been completed, warm the setting with a soft flame and remove it from the shellac stick with tweezers. Clean with denatured alcohol, and then reattach it, prong-side down, onto the shellac stick. Sculpt the base with saw and file, as desired. When decorative detailing of the base is completed, the finished crown setting is ready to be soldered in its permanent location.

Sequence for Creating a Crown Setting

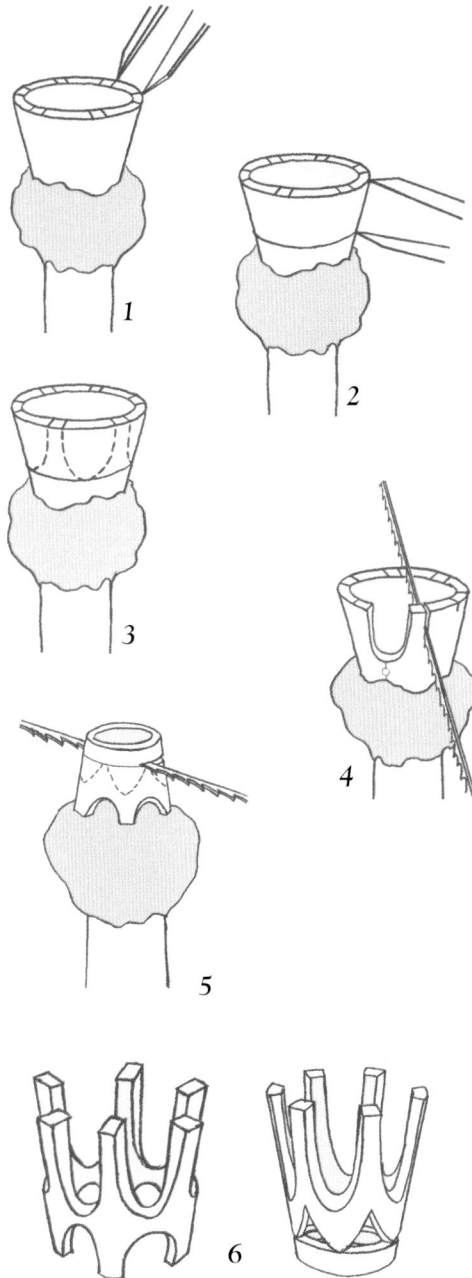

1. Secure the cone in a shellac stick, then lay out the location of the prongs.
2. Establish the depth of the prongs.
3. Draw the shape of each prong.
4. Use a fine sawblade to remove the sections between the prongs.
5. Cut away the bottom of the cone.
6. Finished, with and without the base reattached.

Wire (or Basket) Settings

The ubiquitous wire setting is perhaps the most universally recognized member of the prong family, and certainly one of the most widely employed. Its open wire construction requires very little material, is structurally strong yet delicate, and admits light from all angles. These attributes allow this setting to display a stone to advantage without overwhelming or detracting from it. Though most commonly encountered in its classic four-prong configuration, its appearance can be easily modified by increasing or decreasing the number of prongs, from as few as two, to as many as a dozen or more. In profile, the alignment of its prongs may vary from vertical and parallel to a maximum taper of approximately 30 degrees from vertical. The height can be increased or decreased, within reason, allowing a wide latitude of both visual profiles. It can also be fabricated to accommodate a wide range of shapes, cuts, and sizes of stones.

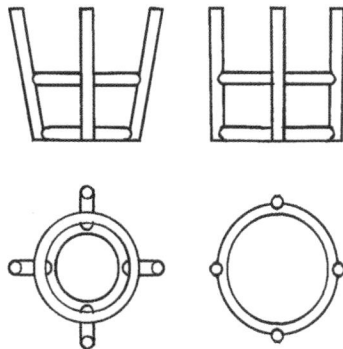

Wire settings can be made with angled or vertical sides. This drawing shows the profile and top views.

All wire settings, regardless of the number of prongs, share a similar skeletal system of two basic elements: the prongs themselves, and the inner wire supports, or bearings, to which they are attached. Though most wire settings have two bearings, an upper and a lower, this is more a matter of convention than of function. A wire setting may be fabricated with one bearing, and when practical, additional bearings can be added for design purposes.

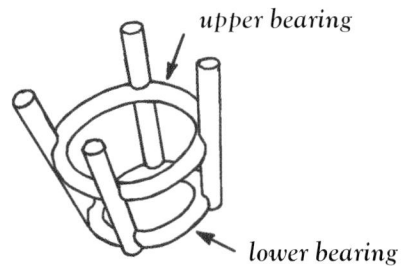

The basic skeleton of a wire basket setting.

Wire settings are most commonly constructed from round wire, but square and half-round wire also work well. The prongs and bearings are usually made of the same gauge. For stones in the range of 4–6 mm, 18 gauge wire is sufficient. For larger stones, 16 gauge wire is recommended. Because of the complexity of their construction—a standard four-prong wire setting requires ten solder joints in close proximity—wire settings are rarely used for stones smaller than 4 mm in diameter. Fabrication of wire settings for stones smaller than this is exceedingly difficult.

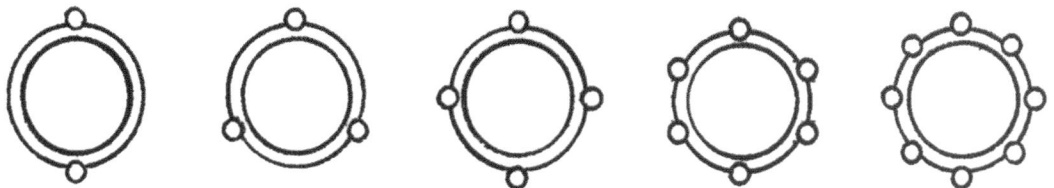

Depending on the size and shape of the gem, this basic wire basket setting lends itself to almost any number of prongs.

Before fabricating a wire setting, consider practical, structural, and functional factors. For example, wire settings are commonly used in simple earrings—nothing more than the setting and an ear post. If the settings are too tall, the weight of the stone, magnified by leverage, can cause the earring to flop forward. The solution is to set the stones as low as possible. Particularly in the case of prong settings, form should follow function.

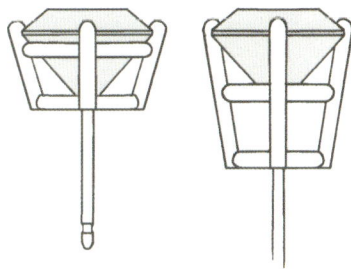

The earring on the left will sit better on the earlobe because of its low profile. The taller basket will droop forward on the ear, which is rather inelegant.

The length of a setting's prongs also affects its overall strength and security. The taller a prong, the easier it is to bend or loosen (again, a consequence of leverage). Rings, for example, must withstand the rigors of daily wear, so low profile settings with short, stout prongs are most practical.

The first two settings are good, both in terms of function and aesthetics. The tallest basket, though, counts too heavily on the strength of the prongs, and is an accident waiting to happen.

Patty Bolz | Brooch
22k gold, opal, emerald, yellow sapphire.
photo: Robert Diamante

Making a Basic Four-Prong Wire Setting

An average four-prong wire setting will require about six inches of wire. Select a length of annealed wire of the appropriate gauge and straighten it by clamping one end in a vise, gripping the opposite end with a pliers, and pulling firmly. This will stretch the wire slightly as it eliminates minor irregularities. Once straightened, it is important that the wire be handled carefully during subsequent operations, keeping it as straight and mar-free as possible. A bent, irregular wire will yield a bent, irregular setting.

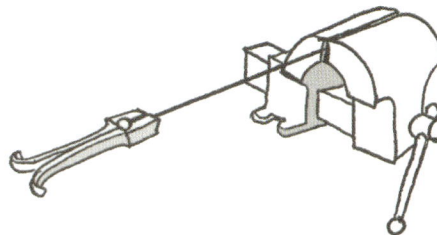

It is critical to start the construction process with wire that is perfectly straight. To accomplish this, grasp as shown, and pull backward until you feel the wire stretch.

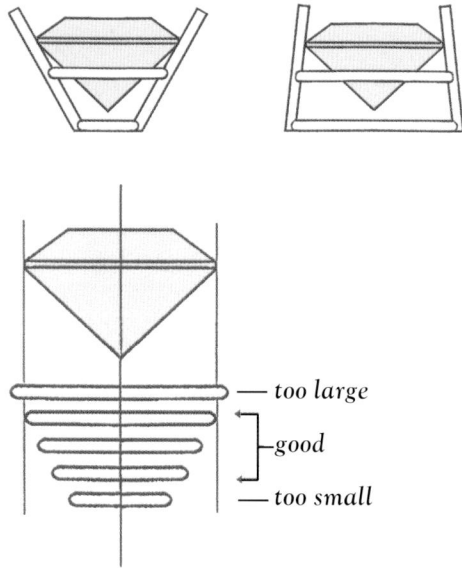

The size of the two wire rings will determine the angle of the prongs. Avoid both situations shown at the top.

Make the two inner bearings, starting with the upper bearing, where the size is critical. The outer diameter can be exactly the same as the stone or a little bit smaller, as long as it doesn't extend beyond the girdle of the stone. This would position the prongs too far away to grip the stone securely. Conversely, if it is made substantially smaller, the stone will either have to be set excessively high in the prongs, or the prongs will have to be splayed out to allow seating of the stone closer to the upper bearing.

Bend the wire into a ring. Accurate fitting at this point will eliminate time-consuming corrective measures later on. Before cutting the ring off, check the size by holding it over the inverted stone. When properly adjusted, the stone's girdle should be barely visible when viewed directly above, extending out slightly beyond the wire loop. Adjust as needed, then saw the ring off the wire, align the ends neatly, and join with hard solder. Avoid the temptation to use successively lower-melting grades of solder. As mentioned earlier, there are ten

solder joints in a four-prong wire setting. Using lower-melting grades of solder may actually make fabrication more difficult. Remember that the finished setting still needs to be soldered to a piece of jewelry. If lower-melting grades have already been used during the assembly, it may fall apart during this final attachment. Not a happy scenario!

After soldering and pickling, gently true the bearing on a small mandrel with a rawhide mallet, taking care not to stretch it. Flatten the ring on a surface plate if necessary. If the seam is properly soldered, filing and sanding are not required. We want to be able to locate the seam later so it can be strategically situated where it will be hidden and reinforced.

Make the lower bearing in the same way. The outside diameter of the lower bearing determines both the profile of the setting and the level at which the stone will be set. The lower bearing can be exactly the same diameter as the upper bearing (a straight-sided setting), or the lower ring may be made smaller (a tapered setting). The smaller the lower bearing (within reason), the greater the taper. The lower bearing should not be larger than the upper bearing, or the prongs will angle inward, making it impossible to seat the stone. If the lower bearing is too small, the prongs will slant excessively outward, which tilts the prongs so much that it will be difficult to pull them down onto the stone.

With a scribe, mark off four evenly spaced points (i.e., north, south, east, and west) on the lower bearing, with one of the marks placed on the solder seam. It may be helpful to draw crosshairs on paper then transfer the location to the ring. It is important that these marks are accurate—if the spacing of the prongs is irregular the setting will be crooked.

File shallow notches into the bearing at the marks to create seats for the prongs. The seats increase surface contact, which will insure strong joints, and at the same

Sequence for Creating a Crown Setting

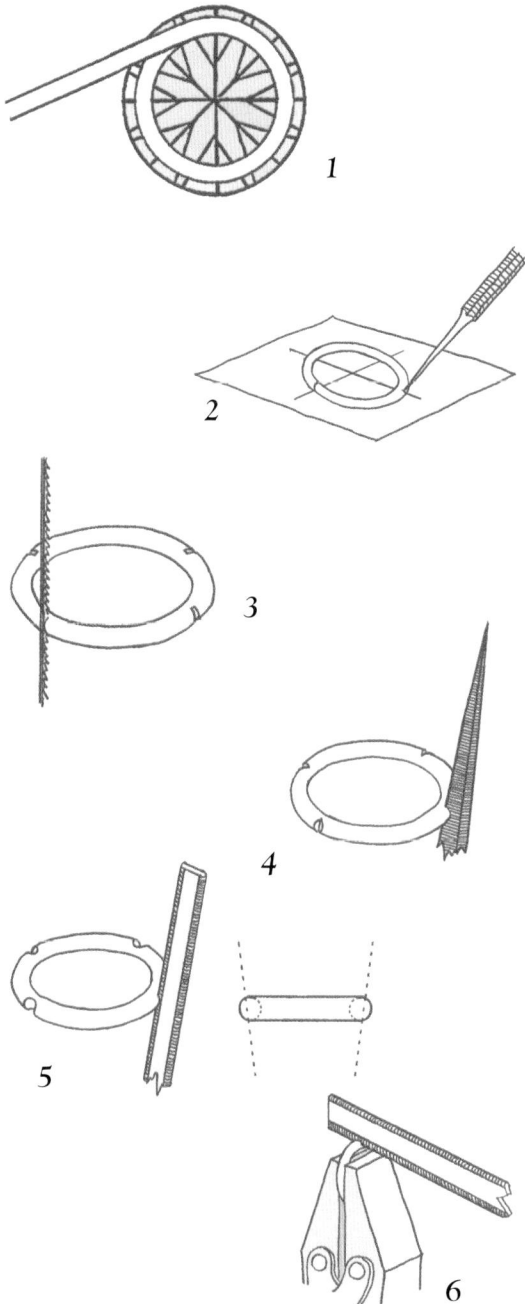

1. Bend the wire into a symmetrical circle, solder, then true up on a mandrel.

2. Carefully lay out the location of the prongs.

3. Make a starting cut with a sawblade...

4. ...then follow up with a triangular file.

5. Convert this angled notch to a round groove with a joint file.

6. Use the same file to refine the angle of each notch.

time they provide locators for the prongs so they can't slip around during soldering. Since one of these notches is situated on the seam in the ring, that prong camouflages and reinforces the joint. Each notch is created in the following, three step sequence:

1. Use a jewelers saw to make a shallow cut on the outer surface of the bearing at each mark, just deep enough to allow a file to bite without slipping.

2. Use a triangular or square needle file to cut notches in the bearing, no deeper than one-third its thickness.

3. Use a joint file (a flat needle file with teeth only along both of its rounded edges) to round out the notches. Each notch should be filed at a slight angle that corresponds to the taper of the setting. Mark one side with ink so that if you drop the ring you'll be able to quickly tell which side you were working on. Take care that all the notches are filed at the same angle. Again, symmetry is important in this setting, both for looks and strength. A flat-nose parallel-action pliers provides the ideal means for holding the bearing while filing.

Instead of cutting four separate pieces of wire for the prongs, use two longer pieces, each bent at mid-point. Carefully adjust the angle of the legs to match the taper of the setting, trial fitting the notched lower bearing down inside each U-shaped wire until it can be tension-fitted into position. When properly seated, it should stay in place when the assembly is inverted. Make sure the bearing sits level.

Position the notched bearing in one of the U-shaped wires, using the modified cross-lock tweezers to clamp the parts together. The tips of the tweezers should point toward the curved end of the U, in line with the leg/prong being gripped. The tweezers tip with the lengthwise groove is positioned to the outside of the basket, cradling the prong, and the tip with the cross-wise notch is clamped over the bearing, on

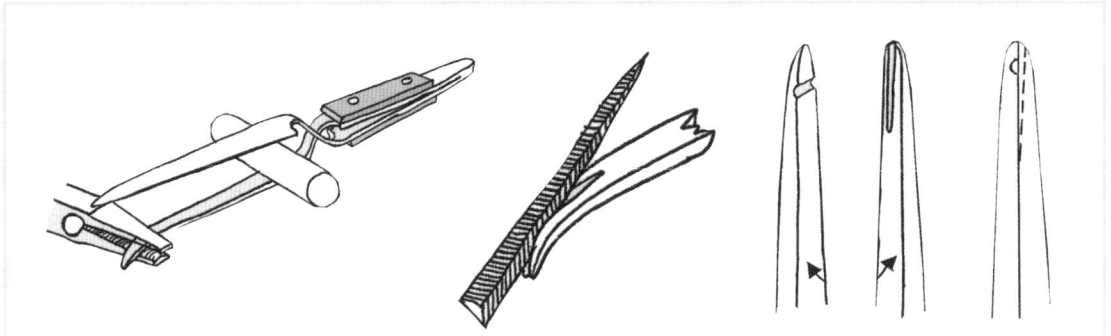

Binding the wire elements together is impractical, if not impossible, and ritual sacrifice to the solder gods in hopes of securing divine assistance is frowned upon nowadays. Holding the parts together during soldering is made a lot easier with a pair of tweezers that have been modified just for this purpose. Heres how to do it:

• Temporarily wedge the jaws open with some small object so youll be able to work on the inner surfaces of the tips. To make it easy to file a groove lengthwise along one tip, bend a slight curve. With a triangular needle file, file a lengthwise groove on the inner face of this curved tip.

• With the same file, file a notch across the inner face of the other tip, several millimeters in from the end. Both notches should be well defined, but neither should be deep enough to weaken the tips.

• Once the inner faces of both tips are notched, use a flat-nose pliers to straighten the temporarily curved tip. Make sure that the tweezers jaws are properly aligned so the tips meet properly. These notches will hold the prongs and bearings in alignment during soldering.

the inside. The tweezers function as both an aligning and clamping jig, as well as a handle that helps you hold the setting while soldering.

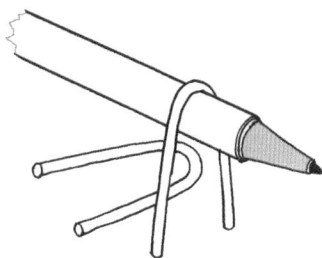

Solder two prongs at a time by forming them as tall staples. It is critical that the rings and prong wires meet at exactly 90°.

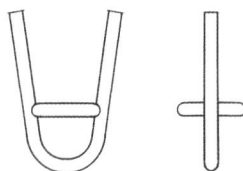

Once this initial assembly is secured in the tweezers, solder the two opposing joints individually. Though it might seem counter-intuitive, it's best to solder each of the eight prong-to-bearing joints in separate operations. As mentioned before, use hard solder for all of these joints.

To localize heat, aim the torch tip vertically, with the flame directed straight up. Use a standard-size torch tip, adjusted to a soft, somewhat bushy flame. In this situation, a soft, diffuse flame provides a non-directed, gentle heating environment that is far safer than a sharp, concentrated flame. Remember, it is the heat of the parts being assembled that actually melts the solder, not the flame.

To avoid soldering the tweezers to the setting, work on the joint opposite the tweezers. Apply a small amount of flux to

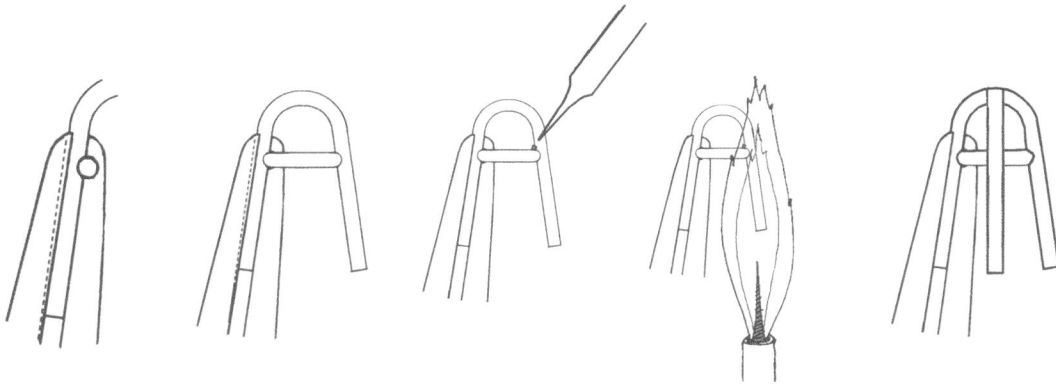

Assembly sequence, using prepared locking tweezers. Left to right, lock the first U-shaped prong element against the ring and be sure the pieces are perpendicular. Lay a small piece of solder in the oppose joint, then warm it until the solder flows. Regrip and solder the opposite side. Pickle, clean, and repeat to attach the other prong element.

both joints (even though only one joint is soldered at a time, fluxing the opposite joint prevents oxidation), and preheat it to the glassy stage before applying the solder. Pass the prong being soldered sideways in and out of the side of the flame. Use a rhythmic motion, bathing the area in heat, and bringing both the bearing and the prong up to the melting temperature of the solder. Try to heat only the immediate area surrounding the joint. Only the part of the assembly that you're working on should go in the flame—never direct the tip of the flame directly into the basket.

Use a pair of fine-pointed tweezers to place a small piece of hard solder at the joint. Place the solder inside the assembly, leaning against the inner surface of the prong and resting on the shelf formed where bearing and prong cross. When it melts, gravity and capillary attraction will pull the solder neatly into the joint. Use only enough solder to fill the seam—avoid flooding the joint.

When the joint is soldered, dip the basket, still locked in the tips of the tweezers, in water to cool it so that it can be inspected safely. Check to see that the bearing has remained level and true between the legs of the 'U." Correct its orientation at this time, if necessary. If the joint is sound, re-position the tweezers, clamping the just-

soldered joint, and repeat the process with the opposite, unsoldered joint. No pickling is normally required between these steps. Simply re-flux and solder. Pickle briefly after this soldering operation, and brass brush with soapy water. Fit the second U-shaped wire unit into position in the other two notches and repeat the process. Check the angle of all four prongs with respect to both the lower bearing and the assemblys imaginary vertical central axis. Adjust for uniformity.

The upper bearing is left unnotched until this point for good reason. Despite your best efforts to measure as accurately as possible, minute differences in the spacing between prongs can result in a slightly skewed arrangement. If the upper bearing had been filed before now, the location of the notches might not fit the prongs. Making them fit only magnifies the misalignment, so its better to let the prongs dictate the location of the notches on the upper bearing.

Use a marker to temporarily darken one surface of the bearing and then position it, dark side up, inside the prongs. Adjust the prongs with chain-nose pliers until the bearing rests only very slightly higher than its desired final level. Remember, the minimum depth of the finished setting must be sufficient to allow clearance for the culet of the stone. As before, the seam on the bearing should be aligned with a prong. With a scribe, lightly mark off the contact point of each prong on the darkened bearing. Notch the upper bearing at these points as you did for the upper bearing. When properly fitted, solder it in place. It is a good idea to first solder only one joint, quench to cool, and inspect for accurate alignment. Adjust if necessary, reflux, and then sequentially solder the other three joints. Pickle the basket, then shine it with a brass brush. Clip or saw off the two U-sections below the lower bearing, and trim the prongs to a uniform length.

Sequence for Fitting the Second Bearing

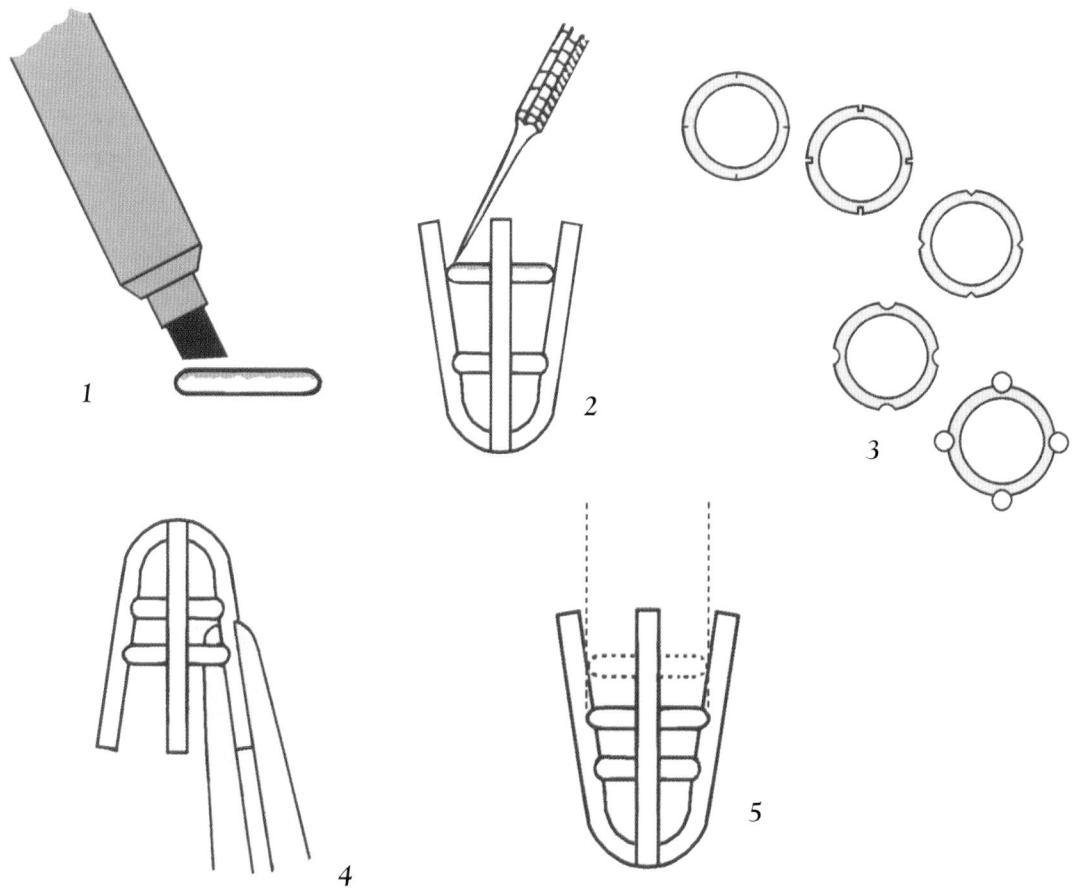

1. *Paint the second ring with a permanent marker.*
2. *With the ring in position, mark the points of attachment.*
3. *Follow the previous sequence to notch and then file perfectly fitted round grooves for each prong.*
4. *Check the fit and angles.*
5. *Grip as before and solder.*
6. *Cut away the excess portion of each prong.*

Patty Bolz | Brooch
22k gold, steel, tsavorite garnet, diamonds

photo: Robert Diamante

Variations

Four- and six-prong settings are most common but, baskets with more or fewer prongs are equally secure and, because they are less familiar, they are often more interesting. In a two-prong wire setting, the simplest of all to assemble, the stone rests directly on the upper bearing and is clamped securely in place by the prongs at opposite ends of its imaginary midline. Locked rigidly atop the bearing, the stone cannot tip.

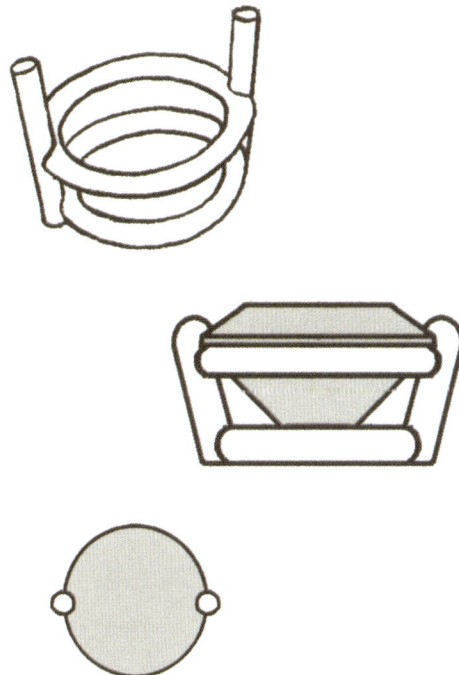

The trick to a two-prong basket setting is that the girdle of the stone sits firmly on the upper bearing. The two prongs must be exactly opposite each other, where they will clamp the stone down into the setting. The top view is elegantly minimal.

The construction of a three-prong wire setting differs only slightly from that of a four-prong. The prongs are pre-assembled flat from two lengths of straight wire, one twice as long as the other. The longer wire (which will yield two of the three prongs) is bent at its midpoint, then the shorter wire is soldered to the point of the bend, creating a three-spoked, equally spaced unit. Bend the legs over a dapping punch or similar form. The subsequent notching and fitting of the bearings to the prongs is done in exactly the same fashion as described for the four-prong basket. Combine the descriptions of three and four prong settings to make 5, 7, and other settings with odd numbers of prongs.

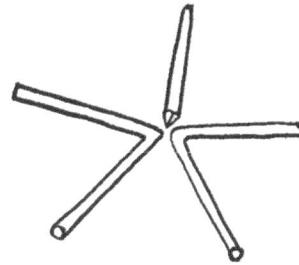

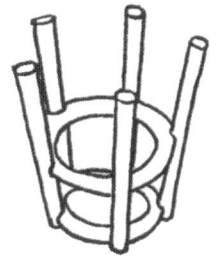

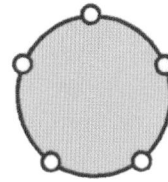

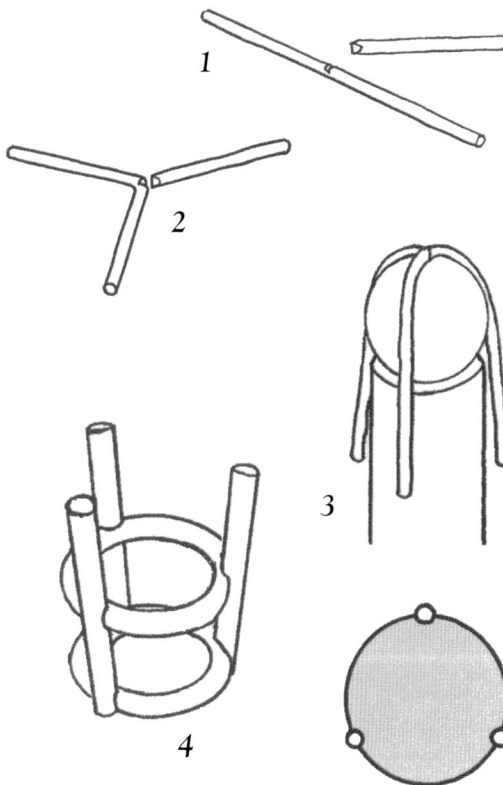

To make a five-prong basket, start with the three pieces shown above. The assembly sequence is the same as described for other numbers of prongs.

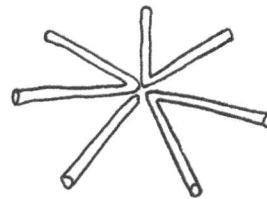

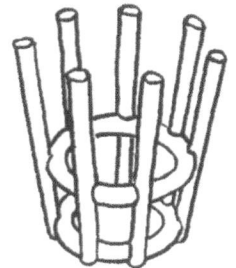

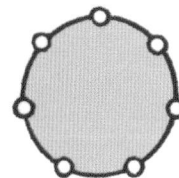

1. *To make a three-prong basket, notch a wire, then soldered a pointed piece into the notch to make a symmetrical tripod.*
2. *Press this over a dapping punch to form, notch as before, and solder as described earlier.*

A six-prong basket starts with three pieces of wire bent into "V" shapes. From these examples it should be possible to figure out any other number of prongs.

Setting a Stone in a Prong Mounting

In preparation for setting the stone, each prong must be notched on its inner face. These notches, all cut at a uniform level, equidistant from the top of the setting, form a shelf upon which the girdle rests. The notches make it possible to bend over the stone without putting dangerous pressure on the girdle.

Before flexible shaft machines became commonplace in jewelry studios, seats were cut in prong heads with a flat graver or needle files. Both methods have their advantages and disadvantages, so I'll describe both.

Cutting a Seat with Needle Files

Needle files can be used to cut seats efficiently and effectively in most prong settings. The exceptions are very small settings, and prong settings made from angular sheet metal prongs, because those styles have limited accessibility. One advantage of needle files is that they require no flexible shaft or other power equipment. Though a little slower at cutting seats than burs, they can produce results every bit as crisp and professional.

Three specific shapes of needle files are required for cutting seats by hand: a round, a crossing, and a barrette. A #4 cut is ideal—sharp enough to remove the necessary amount of metal, but fine enough to prevent coarse scratches that will be difficult to remove later. The round and crossing files are ready to use, but the barrette requires minor modification. The edges of most barrette files are rough from the grinding manufacture. These rough edges are almost as abrasive as the teeth, and can scratch some gemstones. Smooth the edges by rubbing on a piece of fine abrasive paper.

Adjust the prongs until the stone fits snugly into the basket, making full contact with each prong. Ideally, the fit should be just tight enough that the stone must be pressed into place with slight pressure, and then be held there by the tension. I use a plastic toothbrush handle with the head sawed off to gently press the stone into place. Check from several angles to insure that the stone is level and that the portion of the prongs that extend above the girdle will be sufficient to secure the stone.

Coat the interior faces of the prongs with a marker—this will make the marks easier to read. With a scribe or needle, mark the upper edge of the girdle on each prong. Remove the stone and check to be sure that all the prongs have been marked.

The notches will not be cut on the marks, but, rather, slightly below them. If the notches were filed exactly at the scribed points, the stone would fit loosely because of the material cut away. Instead, file the notches about a millimeter below the scribed marks. File the notches with a round needle file, no deeper than one-third the thickness. Temporarily insert the stone to check the fit and to make sure the notches are all filed at the same level.

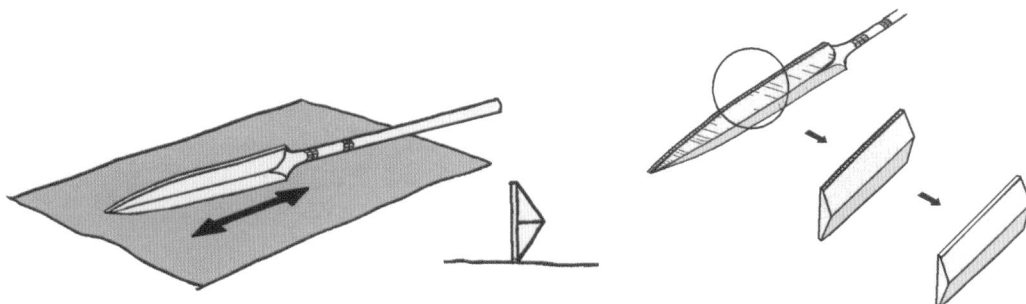

Rub the edge of a barrette file on abrasive paper like this until the small vertical edge is completely smooth.

You should hear a slight click as the stone snaps past the upper edge of the notches and into the filed grooves. Adjust, re-file, and refit as necessary until the stone rests snugly within the prongs.

Remove the stone and use a crossing needle file to remove the slight edge at the upper half of each notch. These edges would prevent the tips of the prongs from lying flat against the stone. File carefully to create a flat, vertical inner wall. File back no deeper than the original depth of the notch. Use the crossing file to remove any rough edges or burrs.

Sequence for Cutting a Seat with Files

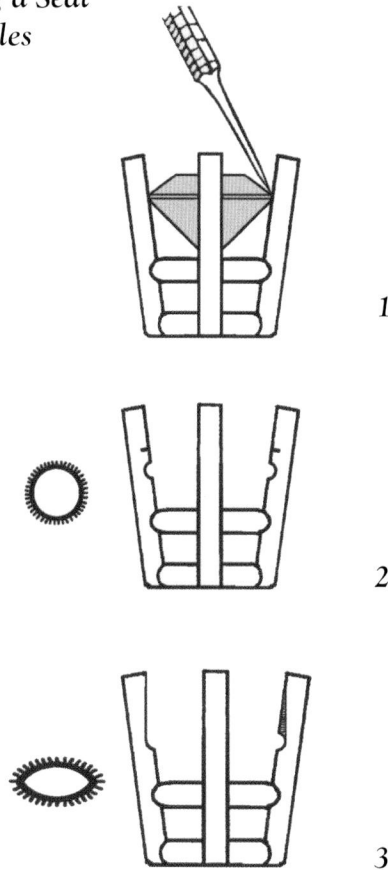

1. *Mark the places where the stone touches each prong,*
2. *Uuse a round needle file to cut notches below these points.*
3. *Cut away the metal above the notch to prepare the prong to be pressed against the stone.*

Cutting a Seat with a Bur

Using a bur to cut a seat has several advantages. The process is much faster than using a graver or needle files, and, especially in the case of small settings, the bur can fit into tight spaces with relative ease. There are, however, a number of limitations. A set of good stonesetting burs is expensive and requires a flexible shaft machine. Because burs rotate in a circular path, they only cut circular seats. Though fine for round stones, they are of little use when cutting seats for other shapes. Burs can also cut too efficiently—they can cut too deep and too far, even cutting prong tips off. The bottom line: even though burs are faster and simpler to use than gravers, their proper use still requires practice, a steady hand, and constant monitoring.

Setting Burs

There are several families of specialized burs that are used for setting stones. Of these, Hart burs and stonesetting burs are most common. Hart burs have a sharp, angular profile, tapering conically on either side of the cutting edge. Hart burs are available with 45° or 90° cutting edges, the choice of which to use usually depends on the shape of the stone and individual preference. Stonesetting burs have vertical sides above a conical tip that mimics the silhouette of the pavilion of a round, brilliant-cut stone. Standard stonesetting burs are designed to cut straight down into a setting, in line with the axis of the bur's shaft. They are less inclined to wander and are easier to control. For most prong settings, and especially for beginners, stonesetting burs are probably the best tool for the job. Some stonesetting burs are designed with a built-in depth control that limits the depth to which the bur can cut. This may be helpful for commercial settings, but it limits the use of these burs in other situations on hand-fabricated settings. I prefer plain setting burs that allow me to control the depth and angle of a cut.

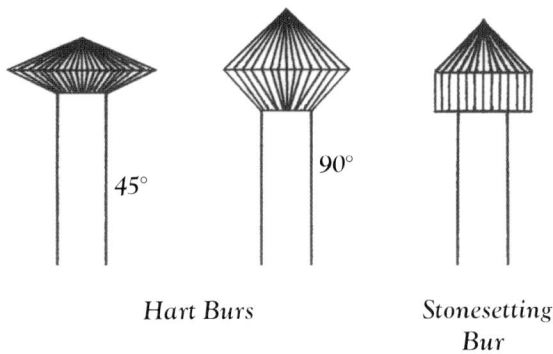

45°   90°

Hart Burs   Stonesetting
                         Bur

Though in skilled hands either type of bur may be used interchangeably, Hart burs are specifically designed for cutting sideways, and are usually reserved for cutting seats that employ some lateral notching or undercutting of the setting wall (or prongs) to help secure the stone. Because of the sideways cutting action and the directional rotation of its toothed edge, a Hart bur can easily jump sideways and cut a notch around the tip of a prong. In the case of delicate prongs, a sharp bur can even cut the tip off completely. Needless to say, great care and control must be exercised when using Hart burs to cut seats in prongs.

Burs are sold singly or in sets. If you only set faceted stones occasionally or, if the stones you set are of specific sizes, it might not be necessary to buy a complete set. Setting burs are available in three grades: carbon steel, tungsten vanadium steel, and high speed steel. Carbon steel burs are the least expensive, but they are heat sensitive. To prevent overheating, they must be kept lubricated and run at moderate speed. Even with care, carbon steel burs wear out faster than the other two types.

Tungsten vanadium burs achieve their hardness from the alloy rather than from heat hardening and tempering, as in the case of carbon steels. Though generally more forgiving of higher temperatures, they are brittle and a little more expensive than carbon steel burs.

High speed setting burs cut more efficiently and last longer than either carbon steel or tungsten vanadium burs. They are also specially alloyed to withstand the high temperatures. Though the cut of the teeth of high speed burs is noticeably coarser than that of the other two types of burs, they produce a smooth cut and resist clogging. They are more expensive than either of the other two varieties of burs, but if you plan to do a lot of stonesetting, these are the burs of choice. They can be purchased individually as a need arises, which distributes the cost over several orders. Their greater initial expense will be quickly offset by their long life and efficiency.

Selecting the Proper Size Bur

The ultimate goal is to select a bur that matches the diameter of the stone. Burs range from smallest to largest in increments of a millimeter (increments of 0.25 mm., 0.3 mm. and 0.5 mm. are most common). To select an appropriate bur, use a stone gauge (either a spring gauge or a sliding gauge) to measure the girdle diameter. Place the stone table-side-down on a flat surface and check the diameter at several locations—round stones are not always round. If the readings are consistent, use the same gauge to select a bur of the same or very slightly smaller diameter. If the diameter varies, use the smallest reading to select a bur. Try to avoid using a bur that is larger than the stone. All burs cut a path slightly larger than their own diameter; this allows them to cut without binding or stalling.

Before putting the bur in the flexible shaft, first hold it to the prongs to check for proper alignment. The bur should fit snugly inside the prongs, making contact with each one. Visualize the path the bur will take as it cuts into the setting, and, visualize the amount of metal that will be removed. Picture the thickness of the prong after the seat has been cut and be sure it is thick enough to secure the stone. Use chain-nose pliers to make adjustments, moving prongs in or out until the alignment is correct. Remember that no more than one third of the thickness of each prong should be cut away.

Controlled cutting requires that the setting is held steady. If you can't get a solid grip on it with your fingers, mount it in a ring clamp, on a cement stick, or in a gravers block. Because the progress of the bur must be closely monitored, the actual cutting is best performed as close to the face as is feasible. It is customary to do this with the work supported at mid-chest height, often on or near the benchpin, where it can be easily and constantly inspected. Wearing a loupe or an optical magnifier of some sort is helpful. Eye protection is an absolute must because of the rotational spinning action of the bur, close proximity to the face, and the possibility of airborne metal debris.

Burs should be lubricated to reduce frictional heat and help clear chips from the cut. Any light oil will suffice, but oil of wintergreen is a traditional choice because of its refreshing fragrance and because residue washes away easily. Put a small piece of sponge or a wad of cotton in a small lidded container and saturate it with oil. Touch the bur to the oil-soaked material (not while spinning) to pick up a thin film of lubricant.

The actual cutting of the seat is done in stages to insure both a level seat and to prevent over-cutting. The flex shaft should be running at a medium speed before the bur actually engages the prongs. If the bur is placed into position before the flexible shaft is running, or if the bur is rotating too slowly, the cutting edges may grab and distort the prongs. If it is running at too high a speed, it may be difficult to control the cutting action, causing you to remove too much metal too fast.

As the bur begins to cut into the prongs, visualize a central axis running through the center of the setting. Keep the shaft of the bur in alignment with this imaginary line. It may be helpful to position the setting in such a way that one of the settings prongs is centered in the direct line of vision, and is in turn lined up with the shaft of the bur. When the cut is about half way to the required depth, remove the bur, rotate the setting 90°, and resume cutting. Viewing the advance of the bur from several angles makes it easier to keep the cut perpendicular.

Securing the Stone

When the bur has reached the appropriate depth, temporarily place the stone into position. Make sure it rests squarely on the seat. If the stone is at all loose within the setting at this point, remove it and gently adjust the prongs inward slightly with chain-nose pliers. Do not force the stone into the setting. If the seat is not level, or not deep enough, remove the stone and carefully continue cutting.

Once the stone rests level on its seat within the prongs, remove it and use a half-round or crossing needle file to smooth away any roughness at the edges

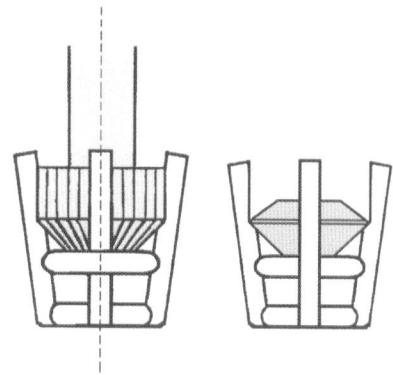

Be sure the bur enters the setting vertically. Check frequently by placing the stone into the crown.

of the cuts left behind by the setting bur. These are easily removed at this stage, but are significantly more difficult to deal with when the stone is in place and the prongs have been closed. Unless the prongs are extraordinarily stout, no additional filing or removal of material from the prong tips is necessary at this point. It is easier to adjust the size and shape of the tips after they have been partially forced over the girdle.

Half-Setting the Prongs

When the stone is seated firmly and squarely within the prongs, begin closing the prongs against the stone. This may be accomplished with a stone pusher or with a chain-nose pliers. Regardless of which method is employed, it is important to note here that the closing of the prongs is accomplished in two stages. In the first step, the prongs are only partially closed, or half-set.

Half-setting allows the progress of the closing of the prongs to be monitored carefully, and, when necessary, for adjustments to be made. As the process of temporarily locking the stone in position progresses, the setting is examined continually to insure that the stone remains true and level in its seat. Only after the stone is satisfactorily and firmly secured, in a second operation, are the prongs permanently tightened against the stone.

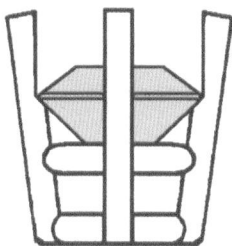

It is critical that the setting bur enters and remains precisely centered and level in the basket. The stone should drop into a level and snug seat.

Using a Bezel Pusher

To use a bezel pusher to close the prongs, place the flat end against the outer surface of the tip of the prong, and rotate the handle of the pusher forward and upward in a smooth, swift motion. As long as you have complete control of the pusher, a reasonably fast motion makes it easier to bend the prong tip. Keep the flat face of the pusher in full contact with the outer surface of the prong during this operation. This will insure that the inner face of the prong stays straight and flat, and can later be pressed into full contact against the stone from girdle to tip. If, instead, the pusher is held against the prong at an angle, the prong may curl instead of bending at the girdle. Although the tip may touch the stone, there will be a gap between stone and the prong. Imagine holding a baseball in your fingertips instead of by pressing it into the palm of your hand and you'll get the idea. Clearly, this tips-only setting is much weaker and must be avoided.

Do not push the prong all the way onto the stone at this time. Instead, stop when the prong is about halfway down. Repeat the same operation on the prong directly opposite the first, working back and forth around the setting until all the prongs are half-set. Inspect the setting to make sure that the stone rests true and level in its seat, and that the prongs maintain proper alignment. If the stone has shifted or tilted, use a knife blade or a flat graver to gently lift the prong enough to readjust the stone. Do this only when necessary—if the prong is bent back and forth very much, it may fatigue and break off.

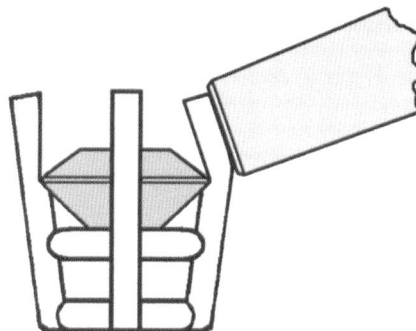

Lay the flat face of a bezel pusher against the prepared prong and lean against it with slow even pressure.

Sometimes, especially in the case of delicate settings, the force of bending over one prong pushes the prong across from it backwards, and out of alignment. To prevent this, support the opposing prong with a small piece of wood. File a shallow groove into the end of a dowel to cradle the prong. Or, if the piece youre working on is in a ring clamp, brace it against the wooden benchpin. File a shallow groove in the side of the pin to stabilize and support each prong as the one on the opposite side is being set.

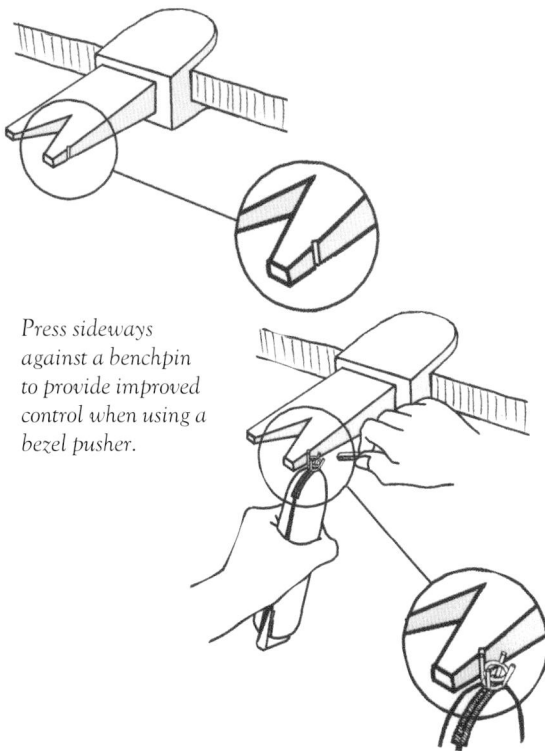

Press sideways against a benchpin to provide improved control when using a bezel pusher.

Using Pliers to Half-Set the Prongs

An alternative to setting with a bezel pusher is to use a chain-nose pliers. This requires less physical force (ah, leverage), and because of this, some people feel it offers better control. Position the pliers so that the inner face of one jaw lies flat against the entire length of a prong, with the other jaw resting on the tip of the op-posing prong. As the handles of the pliers are gently closed, the jaw resting squarely against one prong supports the setting and prevents it from distorting, while the other jaw pulls the tip of the opposing prong in over the girdle. After bending a prong to its halfway position, flip the pliers around and do the same to the opposite prong. Repeat this sequence on the other prongs until the entire setting is half-set. Inspect for sym-metry, make adjustments if necessary, then press the prongs down onto the stone.

Because the lever action of the pliers magnifies the force you are applying, even a small change in pressure or angle can have quick and dramatic effect. If the jaws are closed too forcibly, both stone and setting can easily be damaged. You might want to hold back on the coffee before this one.

Using pliers to press prongs over a stone.

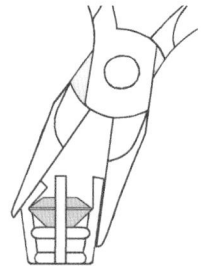

Shaping the Prong Tips

The length and shape of the tips are ad-justed when all prongs have been half-set. A prong tip should be of sufficient size and mass to insure safety and durability, but should never be so long or clumsy that it overwhelms or otherwise detracts from the beauty of the stone. The primary function of a setting is to safely secure, enhance, and display a stone to advantage. Exactly how much prong tip to leave intact, or what shape it should be, is a matter of balance between pragmatic function and the aes-thetic sensibility of the setter. A prong tip should be long enough, but not too long; strong but delicate; substantial but unobtrusive. It should look nice and there should be enough of it—no more, no less.

Several factors influence the size and shape of prongs. Consider the total number of prongs—the more prongs there are, the more delicate each individual prong can be. Also consider the thickness of each prong. The thicker the prong, the shorter or narrower it can be, mass replacing width or length, The size of the stone is also a factor because smaller stones can be overwhelmed by too many prongs, or prongs that are unnecessarily chunky.

Each case should be considered individually, but these guidelines generally hold true:

• Prong tips should not extend beyond the stones girdle facets (the small triangular facets closest to the girdle).
• Shape prongs by reducing width rather than thickness for durability and strength.
• There should be no undercuts, overhangs or sharp projections that could snag.

Four Basic Shapes

(1) Domed (often achieved by the use of concave cutting bur instead of filing).

(2) Triangular or wedge-shaped.

(3) Chisel-ended.

(4) Split (when the tip is large enough)

John Cogswell | Ring
Sterling, ruted iron disk
photo: John Cogswell

If prong tips need to be shortened, they can be trimmed with a flush cutter, or they can be cut with a fine sawblade. If you use a saw, exert as little pressure as possible as the blade nears the bottom of the cut. When the section being removed is nearly severed, stop sawing and run the blade backwards in the cut several times. The tip will break off at this point, or you can flick it off with a fingernail.

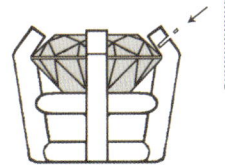

Shape the prong with a #4 or #6 cut barrette file, the edges of which have been polished with fine abrasive paper. If you use a light touch and avoid scraping the stone with the teeth of the file, the smooth, polished edges will slide safely over the faceted surface without damaging the gem.

Wedge-shaped, chisel-ended, and split prong tips require hand shaping with the barrette file after the prong has been half-set, but before it is completely tightened against the stone. For rounded, hemispherical tips use a commercial concave cutting bur. Select a bur that fits comfortably over the unshaped prong tips. If too large a bur is used, its interior cutting surface will not contact all areas of the prong tip uniformly, and the result is a, misshapen tip instead of a smooth hemispherical one. Also, the edges of an oversized bur are more likely to touch the stone, and that's not good. If you use a bur that is too small, it will cut overlapping circular grooves in the prong tip.

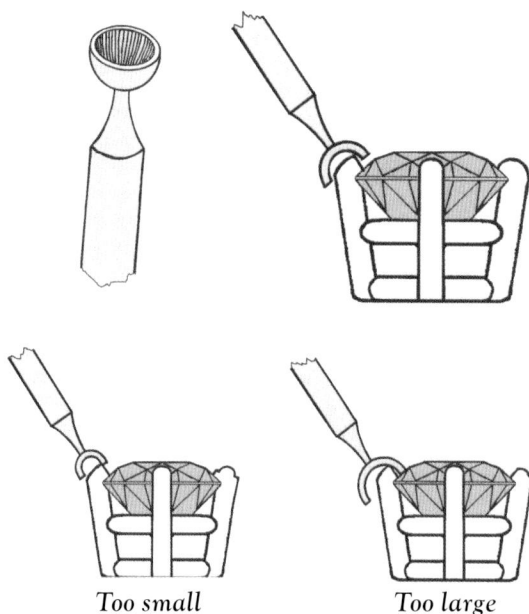

Too small   *Too large*

When using a concave bur to shape prong tips, it is important to select the correct size.

To prevent the cutting bur from clogging with metal debris, run it against a small piece of chalk. The chalk dust will fill the grooves between the teeth, preventing the removed material from glazing the burs interior surface. If necessary, brush out residue with a stiff brush.

To shape the tips, hold the bur over the tip of the prong with light pressure, its shaft in alignment with the axis of the prong, while rotating the handpiece in a circular motion. Run the bur at a slow speed, taking care not to tip the bur against the stone when rotating forward or to the

sides. Also take care not to rock the hand-piece backwards too far, where the bur could cut a notch into the outer surface of the prong. Check the progress often. Since the prong tip itself is hidden from view by the cutter, it is possible (especially in the case of a new, sharp bur) to overcut quickly. Re-chalk the concave cutting face of the bur after each inspection. Final touch-up or shaping at the point where the prong lies against the stone is done with the safe-edged barrette needle file.

After the tips are shaped, they may appear to be pressed against the stone, but this is often an illusion caused by the thin metal burr created during the shaping process. The tips require a final tightening.

Though some setters may also do the final closing and tightening of the tips entirely with the chain-nose pliers, the danger of crushing or distorting a setting is so great that I recommend that final tightening be done with the stone pusher. It is actually much easier to monitor and control the force being exerted by the stone pusher, because that force is transmitted directly from the hand.

Place the end of the pusher on each tip with its shaft perpendicular to the slope of the crown, and push firmly while slightly rocking the tool side to side. Remember

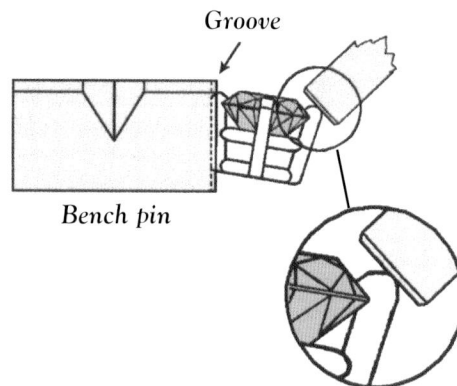

Groove

Bench pin

Support the setting against a prepared face on the side of the benchpin and secure the prongs with a bezel pusher.

to brace the opposing prong to prevent misalignment. As each prong tip is pressed against the stone, the small burr left from filing will be pushed outward, creating a ragged border. Carefully cut this rough edge with a flat graver, an X-Acto knife, or (my favorite) a single-edged razor blade.

After the burrs have been removed, inspect the finished setting to make sure there are no gaps or snags—use an Optivisor or loupe and silhouette the setting against a strong light source. Rub the tips of the prongs briskly on cloth, such as a T-shirt. If the prongs snag or pick up bits of fibers after rubbing, further tightening is needed. When you are satisfied that the prongs are properly secured against the stone, inspect the surfaces of the prongs and polish off any marks that were made during the final setting. Use a light touch so you don't remove any more metal than necessary.

Polishing Prong Settings

Because the tips were shaped with a fine-cut needle file, only light polishing should be needed to smooth and brighten the prongs. Excessive buffing can thin and weaken the prongs, or even round off facet edges on soft gemstones, so care must be taken at this step.

Buff prong settings with a small diameter muslin buff or a circular soft-bristle brush, lightly charged with rouge. A 2.5" or 3" diameter is ideal; a buff or brush of this size has a lower surface speed than a larger buff. The tips should require only brief contact with the buff to smooth and brighten their surfaces. The manner in which each prong tip is gently and lightly presented to the buff is sometimes referred to as kissing the buff. Each prong should be polished individually, positioned so the direction of the spinning buff as it passes over the tip of the prong rotates away from the stone. Avoid direct contact with the buff, and use only the light charge of rouge.

If the buff or brush becomes overcharged with rouge, scrape off the excess with a hacksaw blade or the tines of an old fork. After buffing, inspect the prongs one last time. If all marks and any roughness from the setting operations have been removed, the surfaces of the prongs are suitably lustrous and the buffing has not revealed any loose tips or gaps, wash the finished setting with soapy water and dry it with a soft cloth.

Specialized Prongs

Wire settings designed for stones with corners usually use sheet metal rather than wire for the prongs. Though it is possible to seat an angular corner in a round wire prong, this is generally not the sturdiest solution. Rectangular, square, and marquise settings are often constructed exclusively

Stephani Briggs | Necklace
22k gold, pearls
photo: Robert Diamante

with sheet metal prongs. Octagon and oval settings are often made with only wire prongs, and pear-shaped baskets usually combine both.

Because sheet metal prongs are small and difficult to hold, I recommend working off a larger piece. Cut a strip of 24 gauge sheet about a half-inch wide and at least an inch long. With dividers, mark off two lines parallel to one end of the strip; one line should be approximately 2 mm in from the edge, the other approximately 4 mm. Use a medium sawblade to make short, shallow cuts at each end of the scribed line closest to the end of the strip. These shallow cuts will provide a starting point for the edge of a square needle file. Use the needle file to cut a groove about two-thirds of the thickness of the sheet.

Work alternately from both edges, filing in towards the center until the two opposing grooves meet and form a single trough. Be careful that you don't file too far, and avoid bending the strip as you handle it. Use a pair of flat-nose pliers to bend up the narrow end of the strip into a "V," then, saw along the other line to cut

the folded prong off the strip. If the scored groove was not filed too deeply before bending, and the prong is handled gently, it is usually possible to refine and shape it without soldering the scored joint (the seam will automatically be soldered later when the bearings are soldered in place). If, however, there is any doubt regarding stability, solder the seam with hard solder. To file and shape the prong, grip one flat side with a flat-nose pliers while filing the edge of the other side. Often, to make the prong more delicate and graceful, its edges are filed back to give it a taper, larger at the top, and smaller at the bottom.

The tapered prong will be longer than actually needed, but this helps in the assembly process. The smaller, lower end can be anchored into a soft firebrick or soldering block to hold it during soldering. Any wire prongs are soldered, as usual, while clamped with the notched cross-lock tweezers. Angular prongs are set in exactly the same manner as described in Angular Bezels.

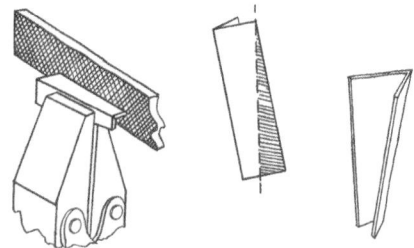

Hold the prong element in pliers and file to achieve an angled profile.

Wire Settings for Pear- and Marquise-shaped Stones

Wire bearings for pear-shaped and marquise-shaped stones are made like bezels of the same shapes. Pear-shaped bearings are the easiest to make because both the upper and lower bearings can be made in a single opera-

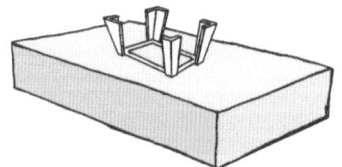

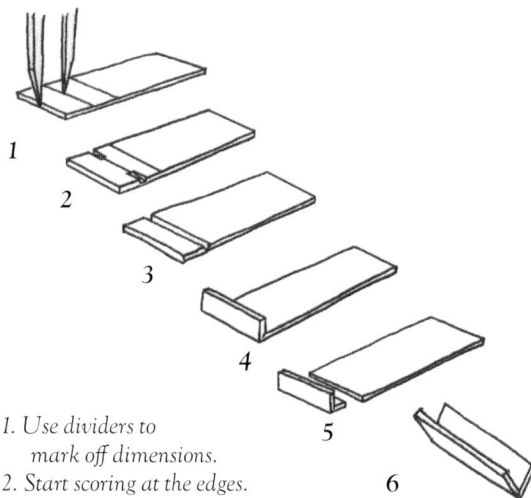

1. *Use dividers to mark off dimensions.*
2. *Start scoring at the edges.*
3. *File a notch almost all the way through the sheet.*
4. *Bend in your fingers to 90°.*
5. *Cut off the angled piece.*
6. *Solder the scored line for strength.*

tion. Start with a length of annealed wire slightly more than twice the circumference of the stone. To determine this length, bend a piece of thin binding wire to the approximate size and shape of the stone, mark the size, then straighten it. Cut the bearing wire a little more than twice this length, adding extra to allow for trimming and fitting. Bend the wire sharply at the midpoint with flat-nose pliers. Keep the legs of this "V" straight. Pinch the bend firmly with pliers so the legs are parallel and in contact along the entire length. This doubled wire can now be handled and shaped as a single unit, producing two identical bearings in a single operation. The two bearings will be separated later by clipping off the connecting bend, and their individual sizes can then be adjusted as needed. Locate the new midpoint of this doubled wire and mark it with a fine-tipped marker.

Form the preliminary curve of the bearings by bending the doubled wire around a cylinder. Select a round mandrel that is 2 or 3 millimeters smaller in diameter than the width of the stone. I find that the shank of a drill bit or the barrel of a ball-point pen works well, and both come in assorted diameters. Center the curved, doubled wire over this form, and with finger pressure alone, squeeze it around the mandrel. Continue squeezing, bringing the ends together, then allow them to slightly cross. Make sure the two wires stay together along their length during bending. If the shaping was done uniformly and carefully, the double-wire unit should be pear-shaped and close to the correct size. The size of each bearing will be fine-tuned individually after they are separated. When the fit looks good, clip the original bend that is holding the wire. To adjust the size of each individual wire, squeeze its sides together to make it smaller, or pull in opposite directions to make it larger. Like the round wire setting described earlier, the lower bearing can be the same size as the

upper, or smaller, depending on whether or not the setting is to be straight-sided or tapered. Either way, the upper bearing should be slightly smaller than the stone. Saw through the crossed ends of each wire to miter them, align the tips, and solder.

I think it's best to make bearings for marquise-shaped wire settings individually. Select a piece of straightened wire long enough to make both bearings, plus an extra half inch or so for good measure. Cut it in half and bend each piece to match the curve of the stone. Make sure the curvature is uniform from end to end.

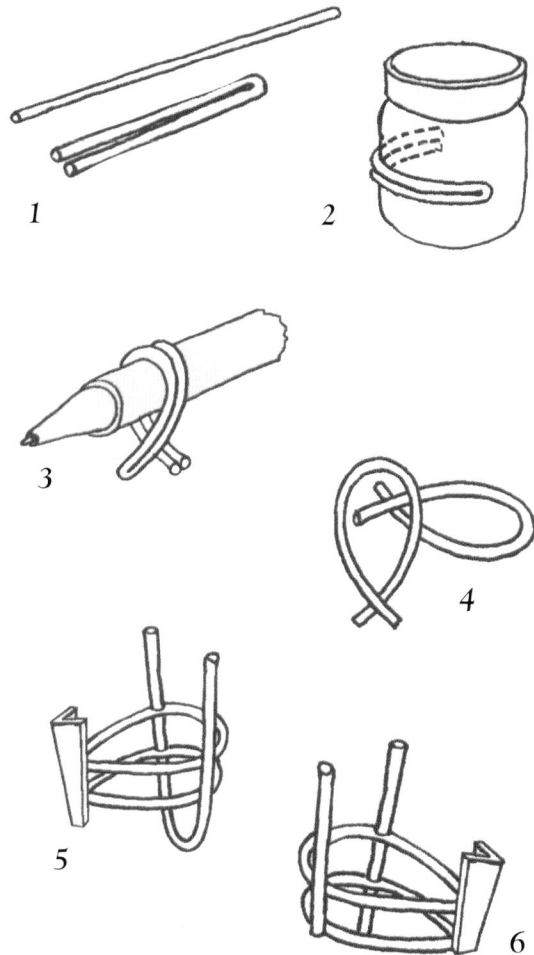

Hold the prong element in pliers and file to achieve an angled profile.

Either make the bend with a flat/half-round pliers or press the wires against a dowel, small jar, or similar cylinder. Attempting to score these wires to create the sharp, angular bend at one end is a waste of time. Instead, mark the center of each of these two curved halves, and then cut each of these halves in half. All four of the resulting wire elements should be the same length, and identically curved. File a steeply angled bevel at one end of each wire, such that when the beveled ends of two wires are placed face-to-face they form a mitered joint that matches the point on the stone. Do not miter the opposite ends yet; this will be done later, when the size and fit of each of the bearings has been adjusted. Solder the mitered joints and then

adjust each bearing to fit the stone. It will probably be necessary for the unsoldered ends of the curved legs to cross over one another to do so. Saw through the "X" formed by the crossed wires to miter the joints, then align and solder. Notch the lower bearing where each prong will be soldered. Make two U-shaped prong units and solder them to the lower bearing.

Square, Rectangular, and Triangular Wire Settings

Wire settings for square, rectangular, and triangular stones are assembled with wire bearings and chevron-shaped sheet metal prongs. Before starting to construct any of these settings, determine the desired profile of the finished setting. If both bearings

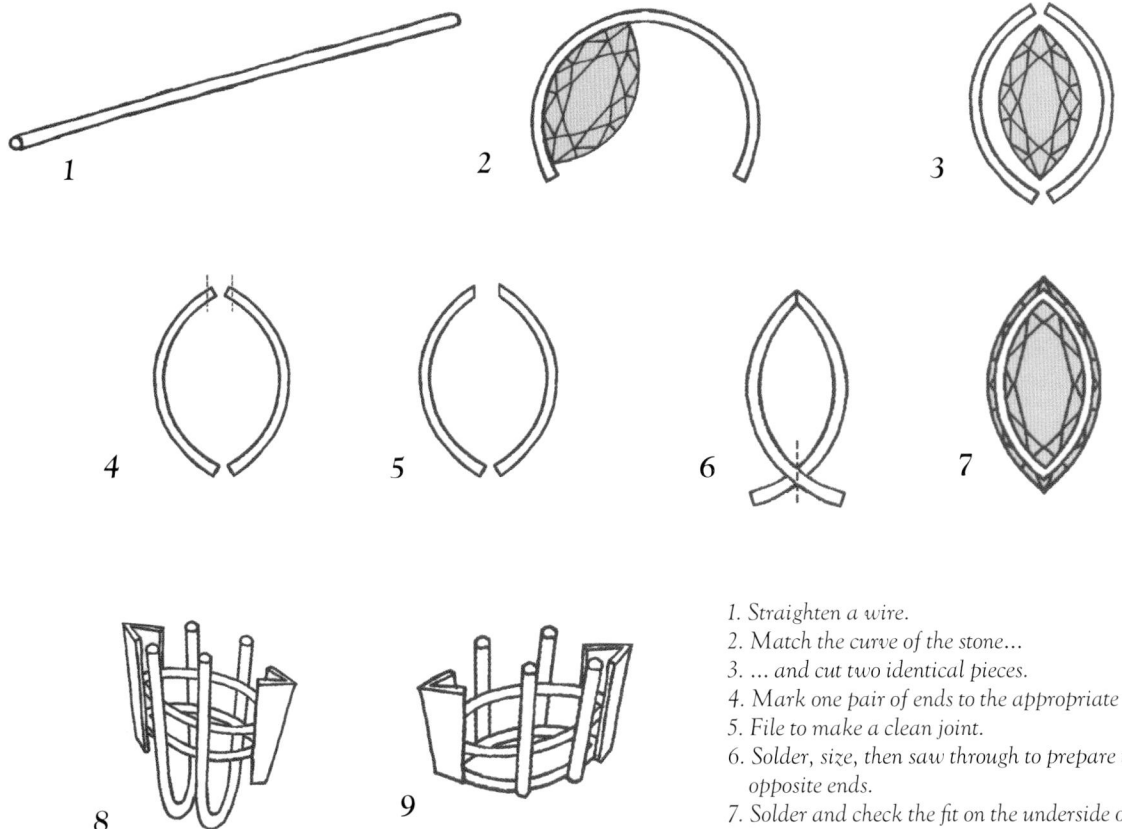

1. Straighten a wire.
2. Match the curve of the stone...
3. ... and cut two identical pieces.
4. Mark one pair of ends to the appropriate bevel.
5. File to make a clean joint.
6. Solder, size, then saw through to prepare the opposite ends.
7. Solder and check the fit on the underside of the stone.
8. Make angled sheet prongs and "double-prong" wires as described earlier.
9. Check the joints, then trim to complete the setting.

are made to the same size, the setting will have straight sides. If the upper bearing is slightly smaller than the stone and the lower bearing is smaller yet, the setting will have a tapered profile.

Start with a straightened wire long enough to make the required number of sides. It's a good idea to allow at least several millimeters, just to be safe. Carefully measure the sides of the stone with a sliding caliper. Because the sides of a square or equilateral triangle are all the same length, you can use a single divider to hold this dimension. If the stone is rect-

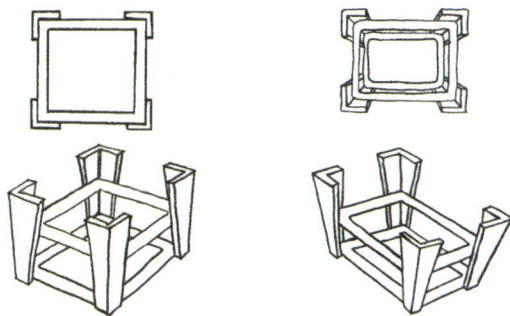

If top and bottom bearings are the same, the setting will have straight sides (left). If the lower bearing is smaller, this will give the setting a tapered profile (right)

Christopher Hentz | Ring
Palladium, 14k gold, garnet
photo: Ralph Gabriner

angular, use two dividers—one for the long side and the other for the short side. Open the dividers to slightly less than the actual measurement of the stone. This will make the resulting frames a bit smaller than the stone, creating the bearing.

If the setting is to be straight-sided, make two frames that are the same size. If the setting will be tapered, measure off shorter increments onto the lower bearing wire. Score both wires at the marked locations, first with a shallow saw cut, then with a square needle file. Bend and solder the corners. Notches made with a square needle file will yield sharp square corners, but a square file does not remove enough metal for triangular corners. To bend acute angles, first score with a square needle file and bend the sides to make a 90° corner. Carefully saw into the joint with a fine saw blade. This will remove a little more metal, allowing the bend to be closed a bit further. Repeat the sawing and bending as needed to produce the proper angle. Score and bend all interior corners, but leave the ends until last. If one end is a little too long, trim it to exact length now. Carefully saw and file the inner edges of each end until they are properly mitered.

Remember, the scoring of the interior corners will have substantially weakened the bearing, so it must be handled gently to prevent it from breaking during this operation. If the bearing seems overly fragile, the interior corners can be soldered as they are created.

After all corners of each bearing have been soldered, attach the chevron-shaped sheet metal prongs. Solder these to the lower bearing first, then adjust for alignment and solder the upper bearing in place. On a tapered setting, the slightly larger dimensions of the upper bearing, plus slight adjustment of the prongs, is usually sufficient to create and maintain the spacing between the bearings during this final assembly. On straight-sided settings, make a U-shaped wire spacer. Place this between the two bearings to maintain a uniform spacing while the upper bearing is being soldered in position.

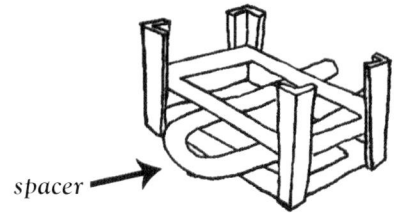

Here's a handy trick for any of these constructed settings that involve two levels of frame. Make a U-shaped spacer from copper or brass wire of the appropriate size. Heat to oxidize before using, and it is unlikely that solder will stick to it.

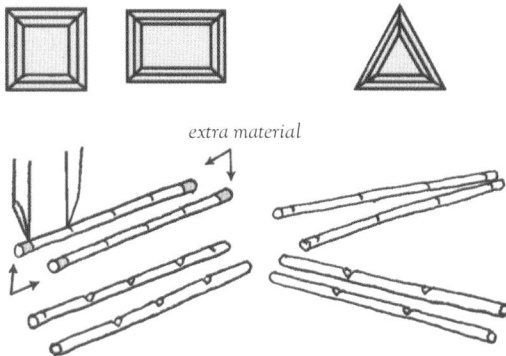

extra material

Constructing settings for almost any shape of angular stone follows the same princples.

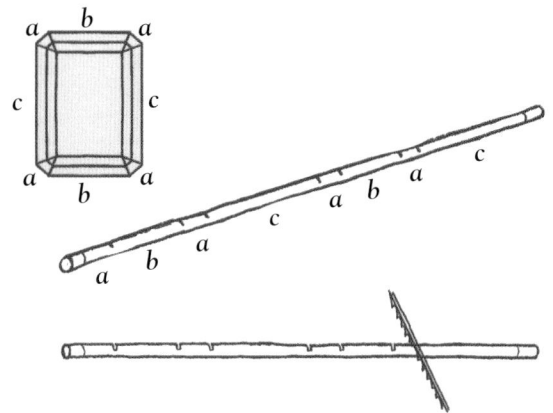

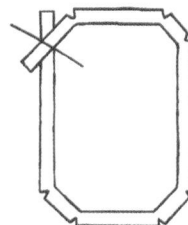

Octagonal Wire Settings

The construction of the bearings for an octagonal or emerald-cut setting is similar to that of square, rectangular, or triangular settings. However, the specific locations on the wire where the notches are made, and the manner in which the corners are scored and bent is quite different. Normally, when a sharp, angular bend is required, a V-shaped notch is cut into the inner face of the sheet or wire at the location of the desired bend. Once sufficiently

Make careful measurements of the three lengths that make up the girdle, then mark them onto a straight wire. Saw partway through, then bend as shown, creating notches on the outer circumference.

weakened by this notch, the metal is bent, closing the notch. This joint, which opens to the inside of the bend, is then soldered to close and strengthen the cut. In the case of octagonal settings, however, the bearing wires are not scored with angular notches, but with simple saw cuts. Furthermore, these cuts are made on the outside surface of the wires, directly opposite the side where an otherwise normally scored cut would be made.

Mark off the three interior bend locations on a piece of wire. As mentioned before, its a good idea to start with a wire slightly longer than the actual length required. Make a shallow saw cut no deeper than one-third of the diameter of the wire at each bend location. To make each bend, hold the wire with a flat-nose pliers and bend the wire at the cut in such a way that the cut opens, rather than closes. Do not rotate the pliers to make the bend, but rather push against the base of the wire, at a point close to where it protrudes from the jaws. Carefully adjust each angle before moving to the next. Avoid bending back and forth during adjustment or the wire might break. As each saw cut is opened up in the course of making the bend, it will automatically create a V-shaped notch. Later, these notches will be rounded out with a joint file to accept the wire prongs. After the three interior bends have been made and adjusted, the ends should come together. Saw or file the tips to create a mitered joint. If a slightly over-length wire was used to begin with and all sides were measured from one end, one of these legs will be a little too long. Cut off the excess. If both ends were cut squre, they will form a right-angled notch at the corner. Saw or file this contact point to create a mitered seam. It is not necesssary or desirable to completely miter this joint. Rather, stop when the inner edges meet for about two-thirds of the diameter. The area that was not filed will form a shape that matches the other corners.

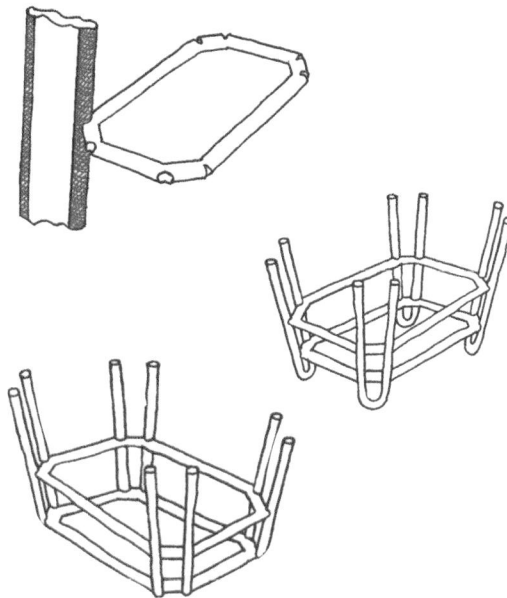

Shape the notches with a joint file to be a perfect fit with the wire being used for prongs. Bend U-shaped pieces for each corner, solder in place, then trim.

Setting Angular Prongs

The sharp pointed corners of an angular stone are fragile and easily chipped, so you must exercise great care when enclosing these points with sheet metal prongs. It is neither necessary nor advisable to force a prong directly onto the tip of a gemstone. Rather than focusing attention on the corner of an angled stone, think instead of bending the sides or legs of an angled prong onto the stone. There are two ways to close these prongs, each yielding a slightly different appearance.

The Mitered Prong Method

First, adjust the height of the prongs. Place the stone in the setting, make sure it is level, and look at it closely from the top and the side to determine exactly how much metal will be needed to hold the stone securely. I usually err on the generous side, knowing I can file material away later if I need to.

Visualize where tht top edge of the girdle rests inside the prongs, and with a fine-tipped scriber, lightly make a line

Patty Bolz | Earrings
22k gold, aquamarin cabochons.

photo: Robert Diamante

where you plan to trim off the excess. As described earlier, I darken the prong with permanent marker so the scribed line will show up clearly.

Remove the stone, saw off the excess, then sand the edges to remove burrs. Put the stone back into the setting and double-check the height of the prongs. Unlike wire prongs, it is difficult to remove extra material from these prongs after the stone has been set, so it is important to find the perfect height now.

With the stone back in place, carefully saw down the vertex of each chevron prong to the top of the girdle. Use a fine sawblade (4/0 to 8/0) and hold the saw at an angle so the blade is parallel to the slope of the stone. Use a light pressure and stop when you feel the blade meet the stone. Usually any stone you'd chose to set in this type of setting will be harder than a sawblade, so if you use a gentle touch, you won't hurt the stone.

The saw cut has now created two flaps separated by the kerf of the sawblade. Push these flaps toward each other with a bezel pusher, stopping as soon as the edges of the flaps meet. Saw through this point of contact; this will create another gap. Press the flaps in again until they touch, then repeat. The repetitive sequence of sawing and pushing results in a crisp, tight, and neatly mitered corner. Remember to work back and forth across the stone to keep it level as you close the prongs.

Once all the prongs have been tightened against the stone, use a safe-edged barrette file to smooth and refine the upper flat planes of the prong tips, then rub the outer edges toward the mitered seam with a burnisher to close any miniscule gap. When done properly, the saw cut will be virtually invisible. As a final touch, use a #42 flat graver to bright cut the inner edge of each leg of the prong, cutting from the outer corner to the center of the "V." When viewed from above, a mitered prong is a simple "V" with legs of uniform width that parallel the edge of the stone.

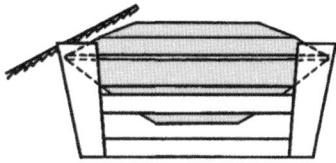

Saw through the corner of each prong with a narrow sawblade.

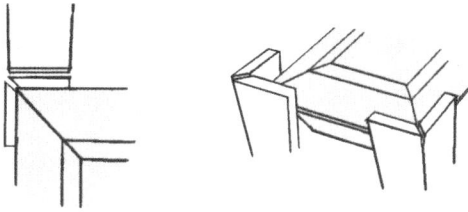

With a bezel pusher, press the flaps of the prong sides together just until they touch.

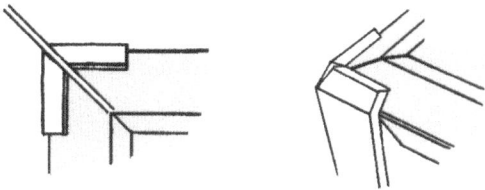

Saw again to create another small gap, then press the flaps together until they touch. Continue this process until the top plane of each prong lays firmly on the stone.

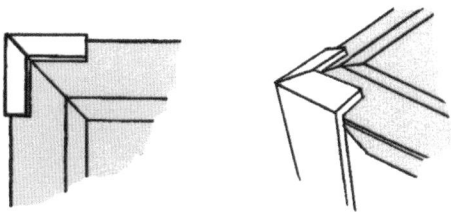

File and burnish to yield a crisp corner with an almost invisible seam.

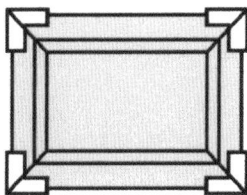

Top view of the completed setting. It is important that all planes of the prongs match in length and width.

The "Picture Tab" Method

In this method, no saw cut or mitering is required. Instead, the prongs are filed in such a way that the legs are shaped into triangular flaps that are pressed over the girdle of the stone. The first step, as just described, is to adjust the prongs to the proper height. Once you have done this, darken the exterior corner of each prong near the top so scribe marks will be clear. With the stone temporarily in place, mark the location of the top edge of the girdle on each prong. Remove the stone; filing with the stone in place might cause damage.

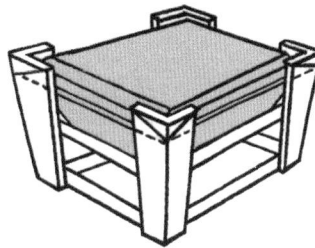

With the stone in place, mark the place where the top of the girdle hits each prong.

Use a flat hand file held at a steep angle to carefully lower the corner of each prong down to the mark you've just made. This will create a V-shape on the top of each prong with the outer ends of the legs left at their original height. Sand these sloping surfaces to remove the file marks and deburr. Place the stone back into the setting and check that the inner corner of each prong is at the same level as the upper edge of the stone.

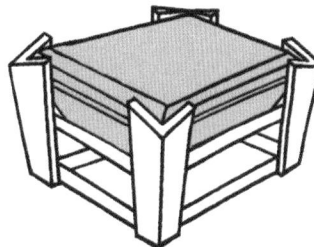

File to top of each prong at an angle so the the corner is even with the girdle and the "wings" are taller.

The goal of this filing is to create slightly elongated triangular flaps that rise above the girdle. Since the lowest point of each prong is level with the upper edge of the girdle, there is no metal to push over at these fragile locations. As with the mitered prongs, file the flat surfaces of the tabs after they are in place to add crispness to the shape.

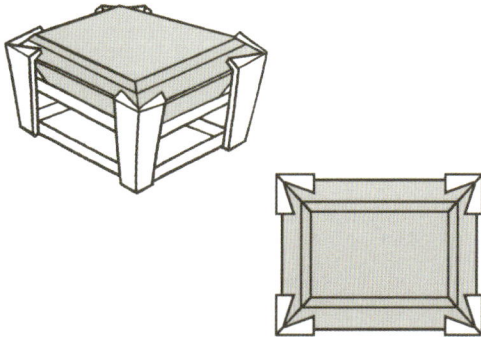

Press the triangluar wings onto the stone, working sequentially around the setting to keep things symetrical. The lower drawing shows a top view of the finished setting.

William Richey | Ring
gold, diamonds
photo: Robert Diamante

Slotted Modular-Assembly (or Cut-Card) Prong Settings

The cut-out, slotted construction of this modular unit resembles the manner in which cardboard displays are assembled, which explains why this style of setting is often referred to as cut-card assembly. The best-known example of this design is the standard, commercial Tiffany setting, but this versatile style permits great variation in appearance, and accommodates almost any cut of stone.

Construction

Cut the components of this setting from flat sheet metal, usually working in 20 gauge or larger to provide both structural

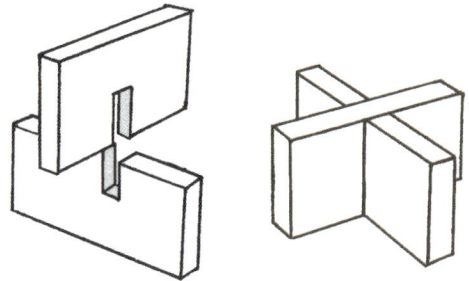

In its simplest form, this is the concept of a cut-card construction. As the following drawings show, however, the simple idea can lead to intricate forms.

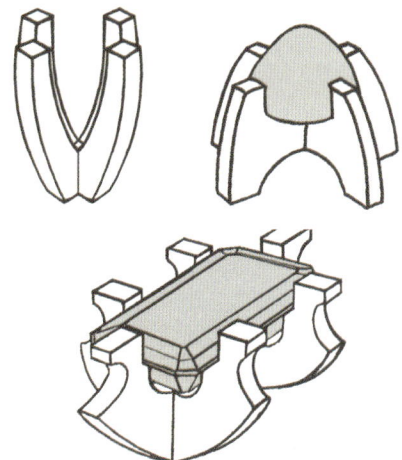

Here are a few examples of the possibilities of cut-card settings. In addition to their attractive appearance, these have the benefit of requiring no special equipment. They are made with a good eye, a good ruler, and a sawframe.

and visual strength. I use 18 gauge for most stones, but often go up to 16, 14, or even 12 gauge for larger stones. The goal is that the setting should appear in proportion to the stone. The layout and sawing of the parts requires precision because the seat for the stone is created in the individual units prior to assembly, rather than cut with burs later. This setting can be used for cabochons or faceted stones, the only difference being the shape of the bearing—flat for cabochons and angled for faceted stones.

Measure the height, width, and depth of the stone carefully. All subsequent layout for cutting and fabrication will be based on this information. If the stone is

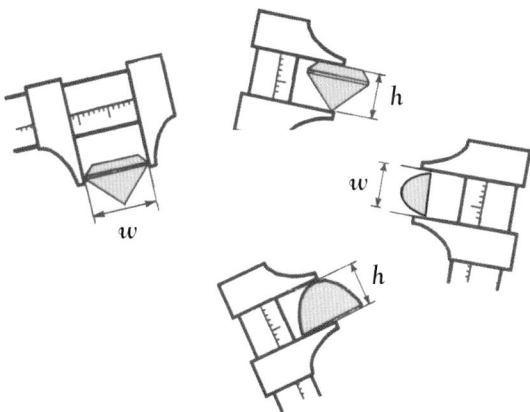

The first step in this setting is to gather careful and precise measurements.

circular, the width and depth will be the diameter; for all other shapes, these will be distinct measurements. For faceted stones, measure the height from the table to the tip of the culet. For cabochons, measure from the top of dome to the base.

Mirror-Image Elements

Slotted settings for round and square stones use two pieces that are identical except for the location of the slots that link the two pieces. Oval, rectangular, and irregular stones will require a long and a short (or sometimes two short) pieces. To make two identical shapes, score a V-

groove perpendicular to its lengthwise axis into a strip of metal that is large enough to produce two units. When the groove is filed to about half the depth of the piece, fold the strip so that the groove opens up (the reverse of most corner-making bends). The faces of the sheet should come completely together. I often glue this interface with a quick-setting cyanoacrylate adhesive for reinforcement at this point.

The folded unit must be a perfect rectangle. All future measurements and layouts will be done from these exterior edges. The idea is to fold a piece that will make it possible to work on two units at once. This means that work is done first on the open sides. When the form is nearly done, the folded edge is filed off and the pieces separate.

I like to paint the sheet with a black marker. This makes the scribed lines show up clearly. Position the sheet so the folded edge is at the top. Use dividers to mark off

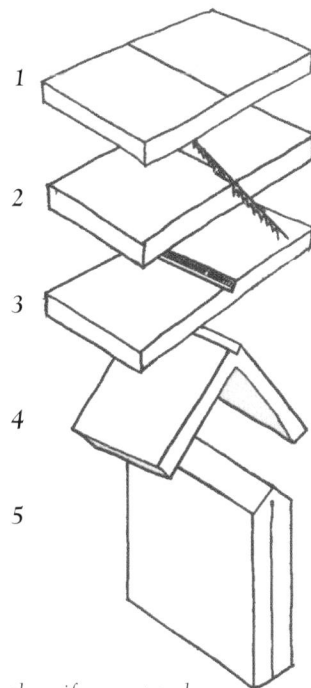

1. Start with a perfectly uniform rectangle.
2. Saw a line down the center.
3. Score the line with a triangular file.
4. Bend the panel precisely and mallet closed.
5. File the edges even and the top (folded) edge to a crisp angle as shown.

a horizontal line indicating the level where the girdle will rest in the finished setting. Make sure to allow sufficient material above this girdle line for the prongs, and also enough below the line to accommodate the lower half of the stone and room for the slots where the units will be fitted together.

With a dividers, ruler, and scribe, lay out the silhouette of the stone, using the measurements taken earlier. Mark off the stones girdle diameter, height, and table, then connect the dots to define the profile of the stone. Draw vertical lines upward from the edge of the girdle. These lines will later become the vertical inner faces of the prongs. Draw a line that will cut away most of the area below the stone, leaving just enough to provide a secure bearing for the underside of the stone. Be sure to allow ample material from the bottom of this area to the lower edge for the slots that will be cut later.

Sequence of Steps for Making a Cut-Card Setting for a Faceted Stone

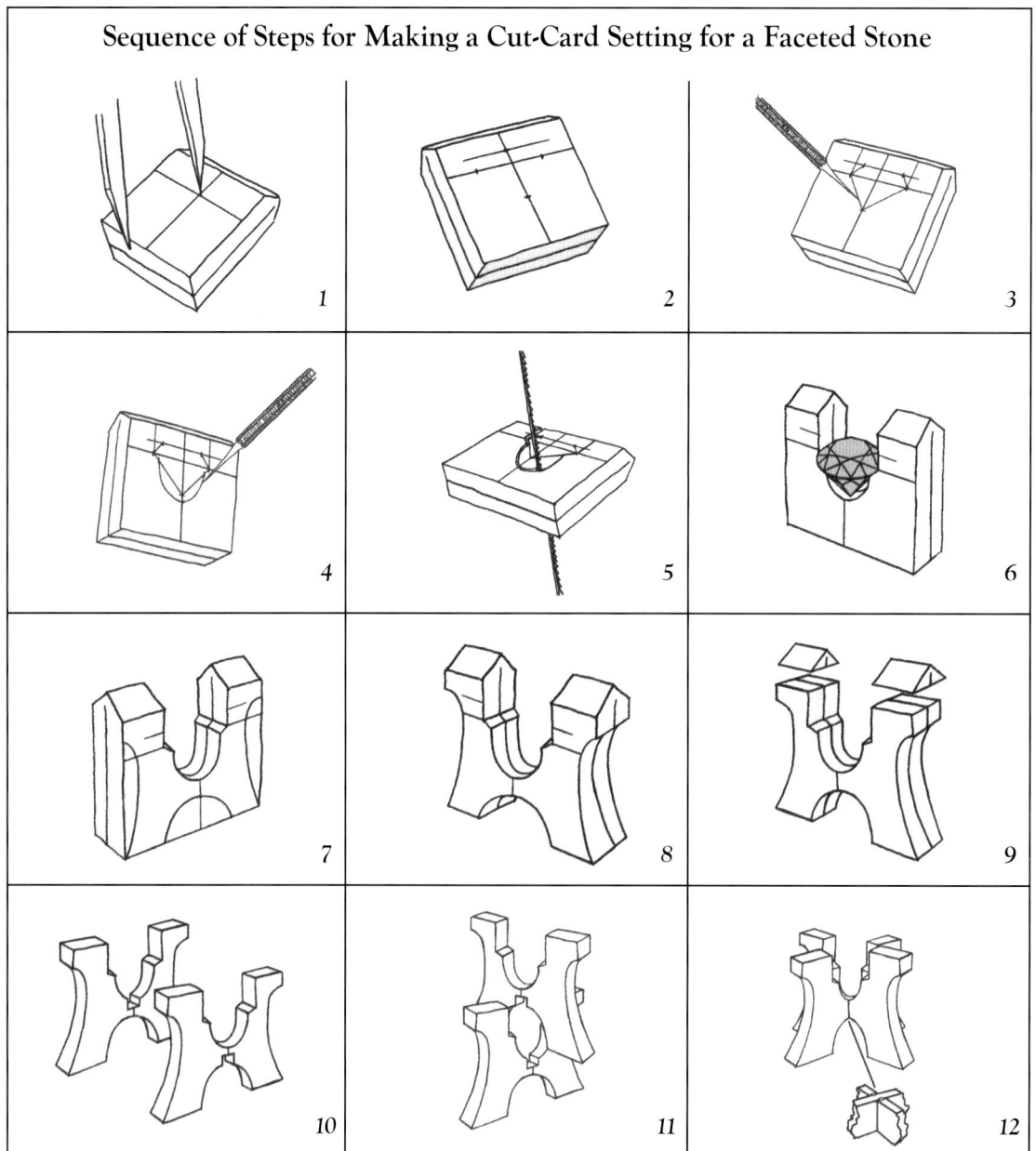

Sawing very carefully, remove all metal inside the lines just drawn. Cut just to the inside of all scribed lines, and file very accurately. Don't file away too much because a tight fit is very important. Temporarily trial-fit the stone into the cut-out. If the layout, sawing, and filing have been done properly, the stone should fit snugly on the seat. Check that the table is level. When the stone fits properly, use the tip of a polished scribe to burnish these interior cut edges smooth and bright. It will be impossible to finish these surfaces after the setting has been assembled. Draw and then saw the outer shape of the setting.

File away the scored bend at the top of the sandwich to separate the two halves into matching units. If the sandwich was glued for reinforcement, heat the sandwich with a soft flame to burn away the cement. Using dividers, locate and mark the halfway point on the vertical center line, between the bottom of the interior cut-out and the lower exterior edge on each plate. Cut a slot on each plate, only as wide as the gauge of the metal, to this halfway mark. The slot on one plate should extend *down* from the interior cutout to the midway mark; the slot on the other plate should extend *up* from the edge.

Carefully slide the slotted units together. One nice feature of this setting is that it holds itself in position for soldering without the need for soldering jigs or bindings. Temporarily insert the stone to see that it seats properly. If not, separate the halves and adjust as needed. Reassemble, and place the setting, upside down, on a flat soldering surface. Flux, and place small paillons of hard solder on the intersection of the two plates. Heat with a soft flame until the solder flows.

Setting Methods

If the tips of the slotted-assembly setting are small and tapered, as in the Tiffany-style setting, the prongs can be pushed over the girdle like other standard prong settings. However, larger, more decorative prongs require special handling. Instead of trying

Patty Bolz | Brooch
22k gold, slate, pearls

photo: Robert Diamante

to force the entire tip of a large ornamental prong over a stone, cut a small slice from the inner face of each prong and press this smaller finger down onto the stone. These smaller split prongs require far less force to push against a stone, hold perfectly well, cover less stone surface and are protected by the mass of the larger prong from which they were cut.

I make split prongs with the stone in place. I use a very fine sawblade (#6/0 or #8/0), and make a cut approximately one milllimeter in from the inner face of each prong. These cuts should extend down to the level of the upper edge of the girdle. These cuts will create miniature, free-standing slabs which can be pushed against the stone with a small, wedged-shaped tool like the blade of a penknife. When these prongs have been half-set, trim and shorten them as needed. Use a small, safe-edged barrette file to refine. For the final tightening, I use a homemade pusher, fashioned from a heavy nail, secured in a graver handle. Saw the head off the nail and then file it to a 45° angle, which allows it to fit into tight spaces such as this. No hardening or tempering is required.

Multiple Settings

Although prong settings can, and often are, designed and constructed individually for a specific stone, in many instances it is useful to be able to produce multiple settings for multiple, same-sized stones all at one time. This is usually accomplished by one of two methods: the duplication of one original setting to produce second generation copies, or, by means of a special construction which can be subdivided into individual settings. The advantages of multiplicity are obvious: since each replica doesn't have to be built from scratch, there is a substantial savings in time, and the clones of well-designed, unique settings can enjoy lives of their own, being incorporated into many new and different designs.

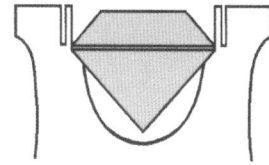

Make a thin cut inside each prong with a fine sawblade.

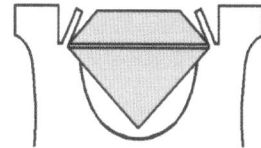

Tilt the prongs partway over the stone to lock it in place.

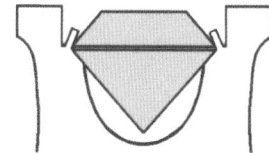

Trim the prongs as needed...

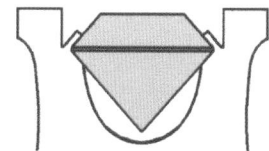

... then seat them properly onto the stone.

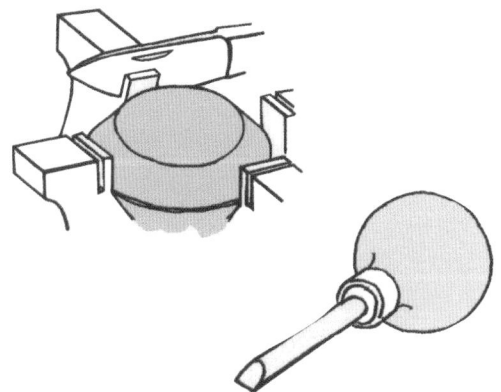

A dulled knife blade makes an excellent tool for this job. It is also possible to sharpen the tip of a bezel pusher, which will provide greater pushing power.

The replication of an existing setting is a relatively simple casting-related process, which begins with the production of a flexible mold. Since the primary focus of this book is on fabricated, not cast, settings, only a brief description of this molding process is provided here. A more detailed explanation of this process can be found in many of the casting textbooks or manuals which are currently available.

A heavy metal wire (i.e., a sprue) is attached to the original metal setting, which is then encased in layers of raw latex or silicon rubber packed inside an aluminum frame. This sandwich is then heated (vulcanized) under pressure in a special press. After an appropriate period of time, the cured mold is removed from the press and the frame, cooled, and the original model is cut free from the mold. When the halves of the mold are reassembled, wax is injected into the cavity left behind by the removal of the original metal model. These injected waxes, when cast, yield virtually identical replications of the original model, very slightly reduced in size, and absent the solder seams of the original.

If the original model was finished properly, minimal clean-up of these castings is required. After a little filing and sanding to remove the stumps left behind where the sprues were clipped off, the castings usually need only a quick tumble with steel shot to burnish smooth and brighten. The molding process is relatively fast, easy, and one well made mold can yield thousands of copies. This method is particularly well suited to the generation of large numbers of settings that will be used for stones of the same size. The drawback to the molding system of duplication is the need for expensive equipment. You must either have a vulcanizing press, a wax injector and the casting equipment (vacuum investor, burnout kiln, and centrifugal casting machine) to do it yourself, or you must entrust your one-of-a-kind model to another party, which entails some degree of risk, more time and greater expense. Fortunately, for most studio jewelers who are not doing mass production, there is an alternative means for producing smaller numbers of simple prong settings.

Fabricated Multiple Settings

Multiple prong settings for small round stones, faceted, or cabochon, are easily constructed in a simple process. These prong settings are best suited to small stones, generally in the range of three to six millimeters in diameter. The settings are constructed from round wire and round tubing, either handmade or extruded, and are constructed as one single assembly, which is later subdivided into individual settings.

I usually use 18 gauge round wire for the prongs of settings at the larger end of the size range mentioned above, and 20 gauge round wire for smaller ones. For the bearings, I use heavy gauge extruded (seamless) tubing, which is widely available in a respectable range of sizes. Handmade (seamed) tubing can also be used so long as care is taken to insure that the seam and one prong are aligned during soldering to both hide and reinforce the joint.

Before the actual construction of the setting begins, it is necessary to first make a simple little soldering jig that will hold all the parts in position for soldering. This jig consists of two small square plates of the same size, which I usually fashion from brass, or nickel silver. I cut two identical squares, approximately 10-12 mm on a

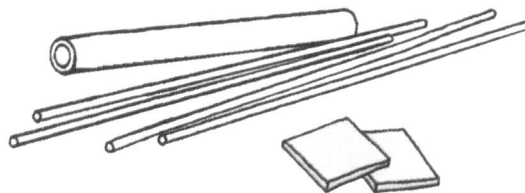

The parts for this multi-section setting include tubing, straightened wires, and two pieces of brass or copper.

side. After filing and checking to make sure that each plate is truly square, I use a ruler and fine-pointed scriber to draw diagonal lines between the opposing corners on both plates. The intersection of these lines defines the exact center of each of the squares. I center punch these intersection points. With dividers adjusted to the radius of the tubing I am using, I now describe a circle (which is exactly the diameter of the tubing) on each plate.

On each plate, these circles cross the diagonal lines at four points. I center punch and drill each of these locations with a drill bit exactly equal in diameter to the gauge of the wire I am planning to use for the prongs. I de-burr these holes, then set the plates aside while I prepare the bearings. (Note: By changing the number of holes in

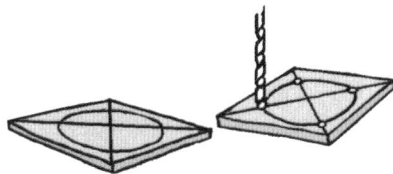

the jig plates, I can create settings having anywhere from three to six prongs.

The bearings (i.e., inner support structure to which the prongs will be soldered) for these small settings are sections of tubing of exactly the same diameter, or very slightly smaller, than the stones to be set. Generally, because these settings are used for small stones, and will be low in profile, the height of these bearings will be only about two or three millimeters. Using a tube-cutting jig with an adjustable length guide set to the desired dimension, I saw the desired number of tube sections. I sand all cut edges to remove saw marks and burrs, then set these aside and prepare the wire for the prongs.

Although in theory it is conceivable that an assembly of any length is possible, in reality, I find that a maximum length of about 8" (approx. 200 mm) or less is usually

more practical. I select a piece of wire of appropriate gauge, slightly more than four times the length of the assembly that I plan to set up. I straighten the wire by securing

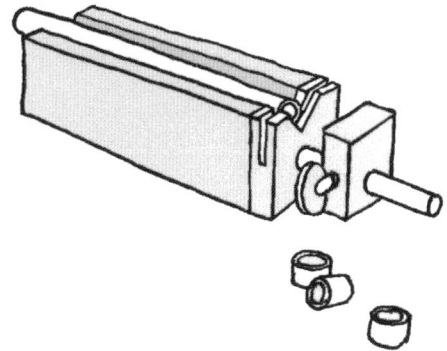

Use a tube cutting jig to insure that each section of tube is uniform and square.

one end in a vise and, while holding the other end with stout pliers, pulling firmly and steadily until I feel the wire stretch very slightly. After removing the wire from the vise, handling it carefully to prevent bending, I clip off the flattened ends, and cut it into four equal lengths.

Now I'm ready to assemble all the parts for soldering. I carefully insert the ends of three of the wires into the corresponding holes of the two plates, so that the plates are positioned at opposite ends (here, again, I usually find it helpful to put a drop of quick-setting cement on each wire tip, where it projects out from the plate, for stability). Using pointed tweezers, I gently place the tube sections inside these three wires. I don't worry about the spacing of the tube units at this point. Once all the tube sections are cradled inside the three

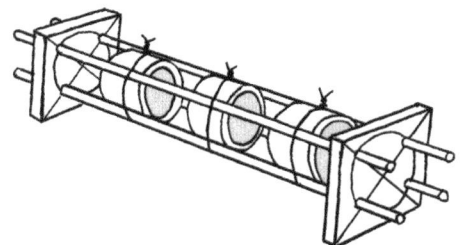

The various parts assembled for soldering.

Hughes-Bosca | Leaf Pin
18k, platinum, carved drusy leaf, white diamond, Tahitian pearl.
photo: Dean Powell

wires, I gently insert the fourth wire into the plates. I use the tweezers to slide the tubing units as needed to space them evenly. Now I gently tie each tube or wire location with a piece of 28 or 30 gauge binding wire, handling the assembly with great care.

The soldering of this assembly is done in one continuous, sequential operation. I flux all joints with a small pointed brush. Starting at one end, I use a small, soft flame to preheat each tube module to pre-melt the flux, then place a single paillon of Hard or IT solder on each of the two uppermost joints, away from the binding wires, and I heat to flow the solder. I repeat this sequence as I advance toward the other end.

When both of the uppermost wires are soldered at each tube section, I carefully invert the assembly so that the two lower (as yet unsoldered) wires are now on top. I repeat the solder sequence. After all soldering is completed, I quench the assembly in water and inspect to insure that all joints are complete. I remove the jig plates and reserve—they can be reused repeatedly. I pickle only after I am sure that all joints are properly soldered and all bindings have been removed. After the assembly is

pickled, rinsed, and dried, I use a fine saw blade to separate the assembly into individual settings by cutting the prong wires where they meet the next tube section.

If the tubing used for these settings is exactly equal in diameter to the stones being set, no scat cutting is required. The stone simply rests directly atop the edge of the bearing (this is true for both cabochons and faceted stones). If the tubing is slightly smaller in diameter than the stone, it is necessary to use a stonesetting bur to first cut a seat.

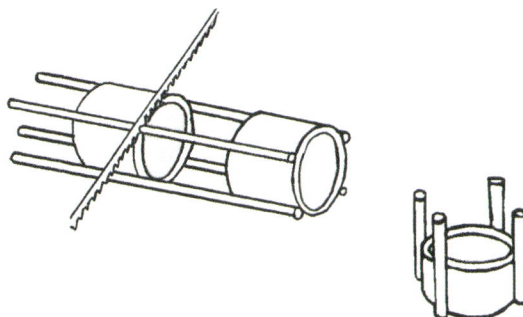

Cut the setting apart and file any rough edges.

A Simple Little Prong Setting Made from Square Wire

One of my favorite prong settings for small stones (2–4 mm) requires no solder fabrication at all. I make this setting by splitting a piece of square wire into four prongs with two cuts of a jewelers saw. Start with a two-inch length of 10 gauge square wire. Thinner gauge wire is too flimsy, and heavier gauge wire overpowers small stones. Although the finished setting will only be a few millimeters high, the extra length provides a handle that makes the sawing process much easier than it would be if I were trying to hold the small piece of wire.

Secure the wire in a ring clamp and file the end flat and true. With dividers, lightly mark off the depth of the prongs. The trick to splitting the wire into four equal prongs is to work on only one face at a time. To control the cut, angle the sawblade at a 45° angle, and reverse from side to side as you cut down to the scribed lines. Once the wire has been split into two equal halves, turn the piece and repeat to divide the halves into quarters.

Use a dull knife or similar tool to open the prongs. To check the accuracy, set the stone on top of the prongs and adjust them until they are properly aligned. If the angle of the prongs is awkward, it might be necessary to saw the cuts a bit lower.

Once the prongs have been sufficiently opened and adjusted, clean up the cuts to remove irregularities left by the sawblade with a square needle file. The taper of the file aligns with the tapered "V" of the prongs and produces a uniform taper that makes the prongs graceful and delicate. After the filing, use a knife-edged pumice wheel in a flex shaft to remove file marks.

It is sometimes convenient to cut a seat for the stone before cutting the setting off its length of wire. If the stone can withstand the heat of soldering (e.g., diamonds, rubies, and sapphires, most synthetics, etc.), it is even possible to set the stone completely before cutting it free. If I have any doubts about the stone's durability, I know that I can always cut the seat and set the stone later, after the setting has been separated from the length of wire and has been soldered into its final position.

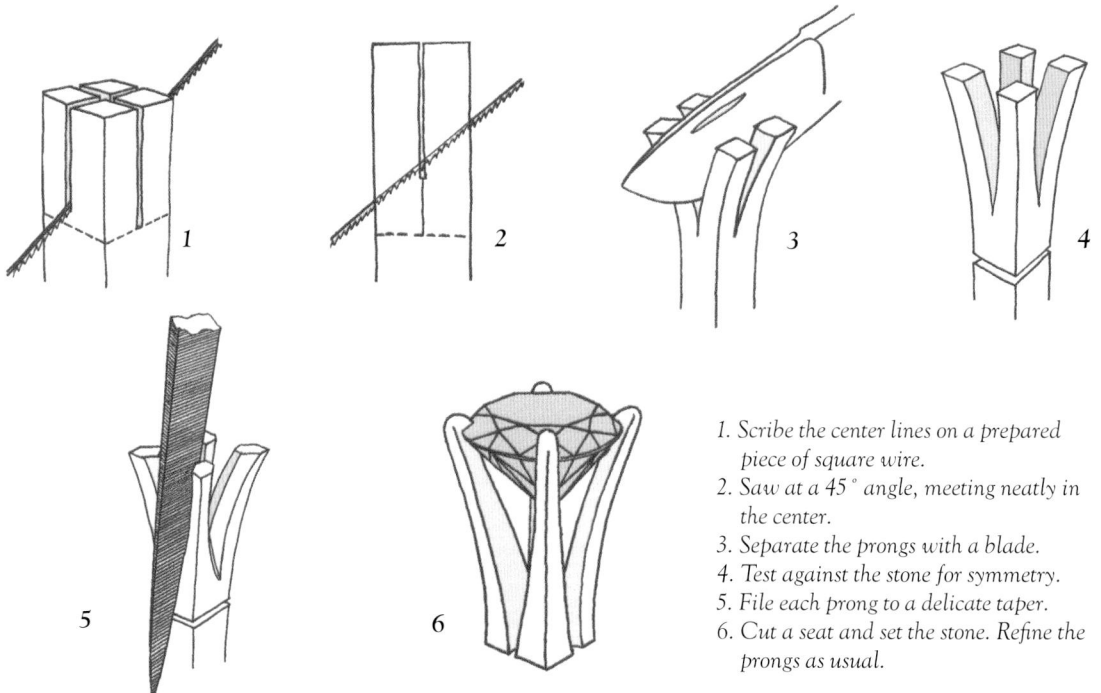

1. Scribe the center lines on a prepared piece of square wire.
2. Saw at a 45° angle, meeting neatly in the center.
3. Separate the prongs with a blade.
4. Test against the stone for symmetry.
5. File each prong to a delicate taper.
6. Cut a seat and set the stone. Refine the prongs as usual.

Chapter 5
Graver Settings

Traditional graver settings, including bead, plate, illusion, and pavé settings, epitomize the narrow-focus specialization characteristic of the commercial jewelry trade. The professional stonesetters who do this type of work devote many years of practice to master the techniques, and as a general rule, because this type of work is so precise, and demands such a high level of expertise, they usually do nothing but set stones. This highly skilled handwork is expensive, since it cannot be done by machine, nor by less skilled craftsmen. Also, these graver settings are used most often for setting diamonds, which most of us do not use on any grand scale. Most small-scale production and non-commercial studio jewelers can afford neither the time nor expense involved in learning how to do this type of setting, and, when we might need a diamond set this way, we send it off to a professional.

Don't pack away your gravers just yet, though! There are, in fact, several types of graver settings that are well within the grasp of anyone with a moderate level of skill, a few sharp gravers, and a little practice. These graver settings will accommodate cabochons and faceted stones, are fast and simple, and don't require solder assembly. These simple graver settings offer a good alternative to fabricated settings, particularly in the case of smaller stones. All you need are a few basic gravers and a sharpening stone to keep them honed.

Gravers

The graver itself is a steel blade with a sharpened, angled cutting tip on one end, and a wooden handle on the other. The blade and the handle are purchased separately, and the blade length is adjusted to fit your hand before being mounted in the handle. Gravers come in a wide range of sizes and styles, of which round, knife, flat, lozenge, anglette (or onglette), oval, square, and liners are most common. The settings which are described in this chapter require only three gravers. Once you learn how to fit, mount, and sharpen a graver, you can expand your collection as desired.

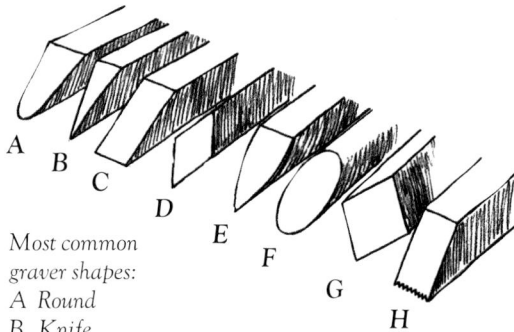

Most common
graver shapes:
A Round
B Knife
C Flat
D Lozenge
E Anglette (onglette)
F Oval
G Square
H Liner

Graver Blades

Graver blades are usually supplied four or five inches long (10–13 cm). They are available in two grades of steel. Carbon steel is easier to sharpen, but requires more frequent sharpening. High speed steel is a harder, tougher alloy that holds an edge longer, but it is more difficult to sharpen. There is only a modest difference in price, so the choice of which to use is one of personal preference. I have both, and use them interchangeably. If you only plan to use your gravers occasionally, I'd suggest carbon steel, because it is a bit easier to sharpen and maintain.

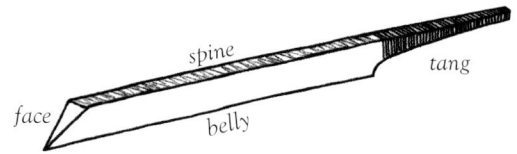

Parts of a graver.

New blades arrive with a 45° angle at the tip. Though pointed, they are not yet ready to use. The first three-quarters of the blade, from the tip, back, is uniformly wide. The back end, called the tang, is tapered to a blunt point to accommodate insertion into a handle. The angled plane at the front is called the face, the upper edge of the blade is called the spine, and the lower edge, from the pointed tip, back, is called the belly.

Before a new blade is ready to use, its working end needs to be reshaped to allow easier access into tight spaces and

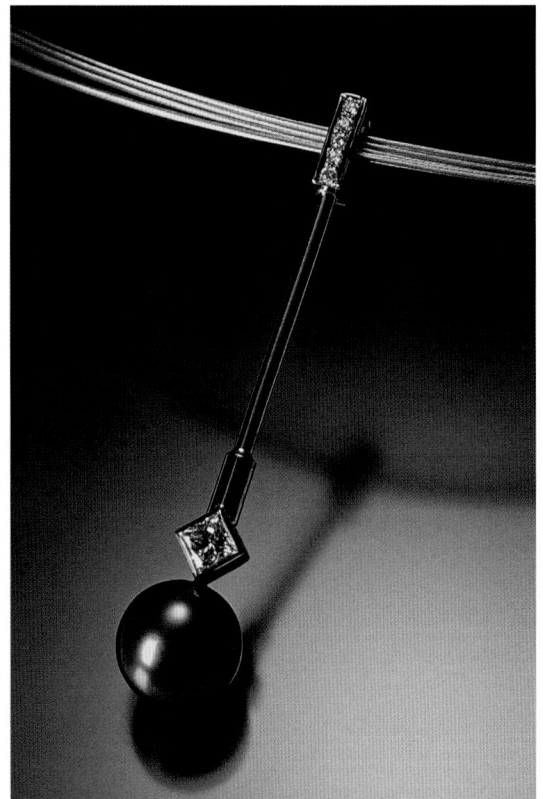

James Kaya | Pendant
18k white gold, black pearl, diamonds.
photo: Robert Diamante

to make it easier to sharpen. Unless your hand is quite large, the new blade will require shortening before being fitted with a handle so that it will fit comfortably in the hand. This reduction in length is done at the tang end. The modification of blade length occurs first.

Graver Handles

Just like blades, graver handles come in a wide assortment of profiles and lengths. The names of various handle shapes often reflect their silhouette-shape resembling those of fruits or vegetables—mushroom, pear, and gourd, for example. There are also oval, round, and vase-shaped handles. Some of these are completely round, and some have a flat plane on one side. The handles with the flat plane are referred to as half-headed where the flat plane is a safety feature. It prevents the graver from accidentally rolling off the workbench, and possibly falling, point first, into your lap. Ouch. I personally prefer half-headed mushroom handles, as I find them most

Nicole Jacquard | Bride Earrings
22k and 18k gold, diamonds, and pearls.
photo: Kevin Montague

comfortable. However, your choice of handle style is largely a matter of personal preference—select whichever style feels best to you. I recommend that if the style you settle on doesn't come half-headed, you file or sand a flat plane on the side of the handle for safety's sake.

The other reason that I favor half-headed mushroom handles is because they are commonly available in three different lengths. Over time, a graver blade gets shorter as a result of continual sharpening. When setting up a new graver, I always mount the shortest length handle. As the blade gets shorter, I simply replace the original handle with the next longer one. This greatly extends the useful life of your graver. The handles are often recyclable, and the replaced handles can often be re-mounted on other gravers. Once you have selected your handle(s), you are ready to adjust the length of the blade in preparation for mounting in the handle.

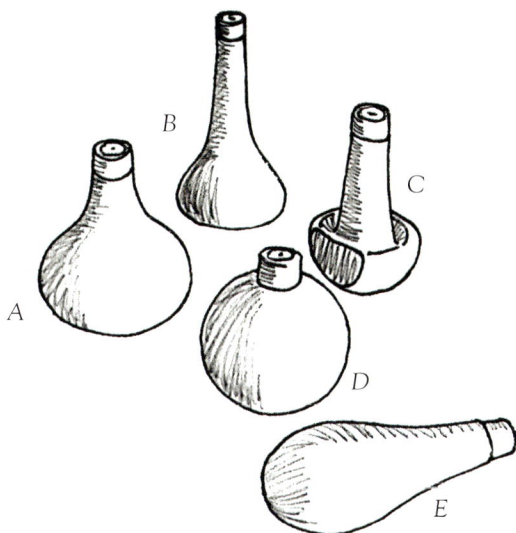

Graver handles are available in these standard shapes:
A Mushroom
B Gourd
C Half-headed mushroom
D Round (Ball)
E Pear

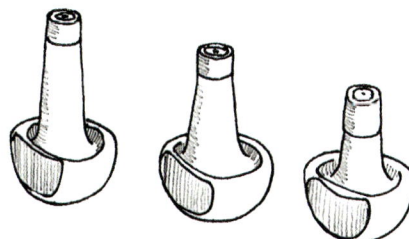

Gravers are made in three lengths, which allows for the fact that gravers get smaller through repeated resharpening.

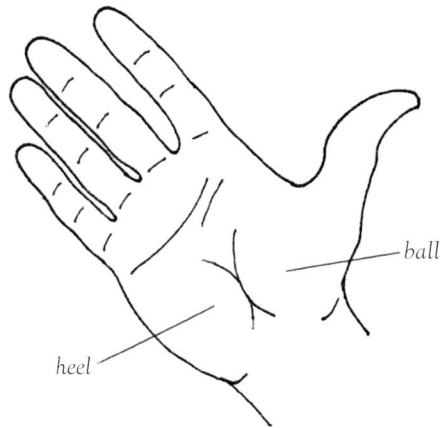

A properly fitting graver is essential for comfort and control. The first step is to identify the heel and ball of the hand.

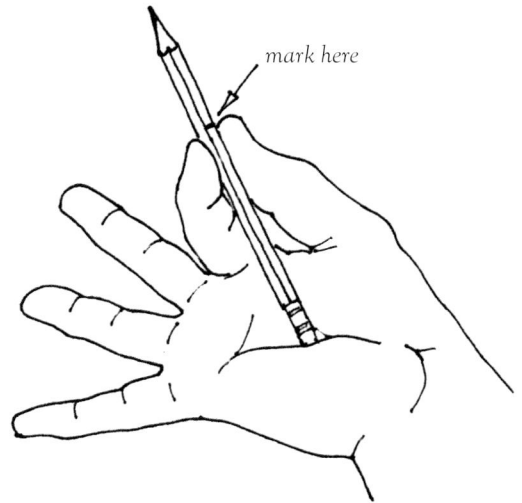

To determine the proper graver length, press a pencil firmly into the heel of your hand and mark the spot where your fingers comfortably meet.

To determine the ideal length (which will include the handle), place a pencil on the heel of your hand where the two curved lines converge. Reach up the shaft of the pencil as far as you can comfortably reach with your thumb and forefinger and pinch the shaft in such a way that the tips of both are exactly opposite one another and mark that spot. The distance from the end of the pencil to this mark is the ideal length for your assembled graver. Over the years, I have noted with some interest that despite the wide range of hand sizes, for most people this length almost always falls between 3¾" and 4" (9.5 cm–10.2 cm). This is the overall length of the assembled graver—now you need to determine how much of that length is blade and how much is handle.

Adjusting Blade Length

On a piece of paper, use a pencil and ruler to draw a straight line a bit longer than your desired graver length. Transfer the predetermined measurement of the ideal length of your assembled graver with two marks placed at opposite ends of the line. Place your graver handle on the line with its back end aligned with one of the marks. Make a light mark where the front end

of the handle lies. From this new mark, measure back ¾" (2 cm) on the handle end to allow for the portion of the graver that will be embedded in the handle. Transfer this intended length of the graver blade and mark with a fine-tipped indelible marker.

To remove the excess from the end of the tang, cut a notch across the tang with a cut-off wheel mounted in a flex shaft. The groove will weaken the tang sufficiently to cause it to break at that point. Secure the

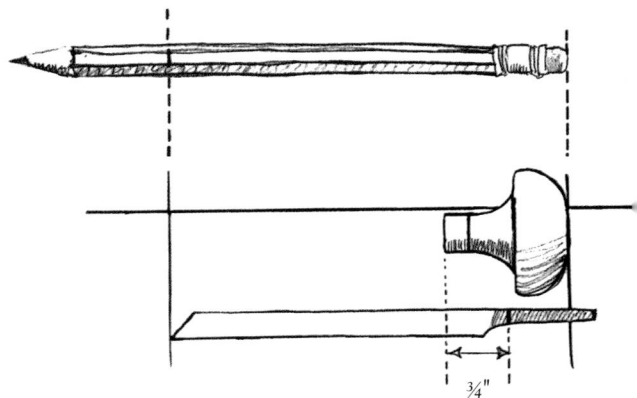

Transferring length markings from the pencil to the graver. Remember to account for the handle and for the tang.

blade, pointed tip down, in a vise so that the groove is level with the top of the vise jaws. I always use protective jaw liners to prevent marring the surface of the blade. Place a rag or old hand towel over the projecting tang and strike the tang sharply with a hammer. The tang tip will break off cleanly and the rag will prevent the broken piece from shooting dangerously across the room. Sometimes it takes several blows from opposing directions to break off the excess. Retain the tip you have just removed, and use it as a guide as you establish a new taper on the shortened blade. Even after it has served in this capacity, I still save it. It is high quality steel, and can be reshaped into some new tool.

Use the coarse wheel of a bench grinder to regrind the tang to match the original. Do not taper the tang to a sharp point. In the unlikely event that the handle should ever split during use, an overly pointed tang could be harmful. Have a container of water nearby for dipping and cooling the metal during grinding to prevent burning your fingers. This is mainly a matter of comfort. It doesn't harm the tang if it should get a bit overheated while grinding, because the tang is annealed anyway to eliminate any brittleness. Now that the blade length has been adjusted, and a new tang established, the blade is ready to be fitted with a handle.

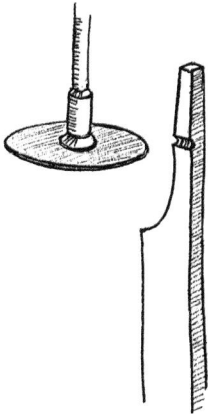

Grind away excess.

Notch the graver with a separating disk, grip in a vise, and give a sharp blow with a hammer. Catch the flying tang in a wad of fabric to prevent injury.

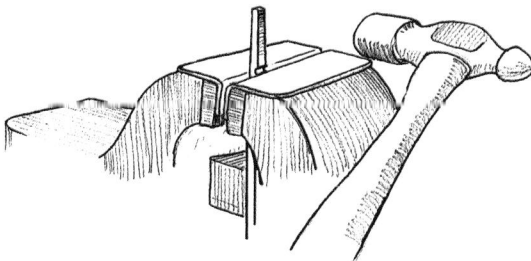

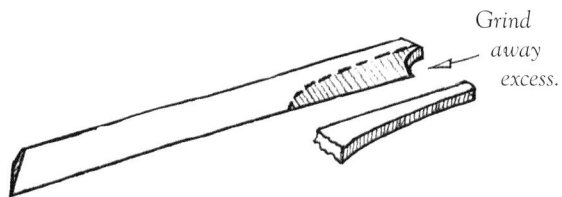

The tang should be tapered but it should not have a sharp end. When the shape is correct, anneal the tang by heating it to blue in a soft flame.

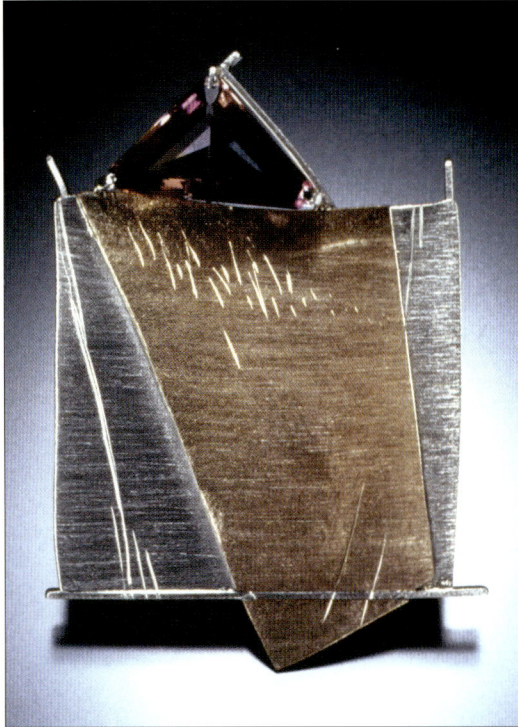

Bruce Anderson | Brooch
14k gold, sterling, amethyst.
2" tall
photo: Ralph Gabriner

Mounting Blades in Handles

The tapered neck of a handle is fitted with a metal ferrule that reinforces the area around the blade and prevents the handle from splitting when the tang is driven in. Never use a handle that is missing its ferrule. Inside the ferrule is a small indent left from the lathe on which the handle was made. Many people see this tiny hole and wrongly assume that this is sufficient for driving in the tang. Attempts to do so will split the handle.

Wrap a ⅛" drill bit with a small piece of masking tape about ¾" back from the tip to act as a depth gauge. Drill straight into the handle at the small indent until you reach the tape. With a marker, measure and mark the tang ¾" in from the end. Secure the blade, tang up, in a vise (use jaw protectors) and use a small hammer or mallet to tap the handle down until you reach the ¾" mark. I like to align the flat plane

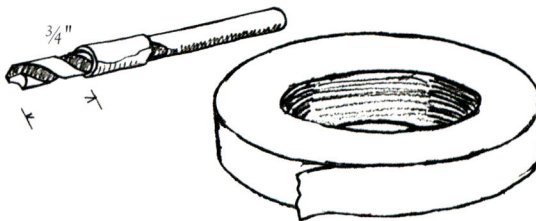

Use a bit of masking tape to mark the depth of a drill bit. When the hole in the graver handle has been enlarged, grip the tool in a vise and tap the handle with a mallet.

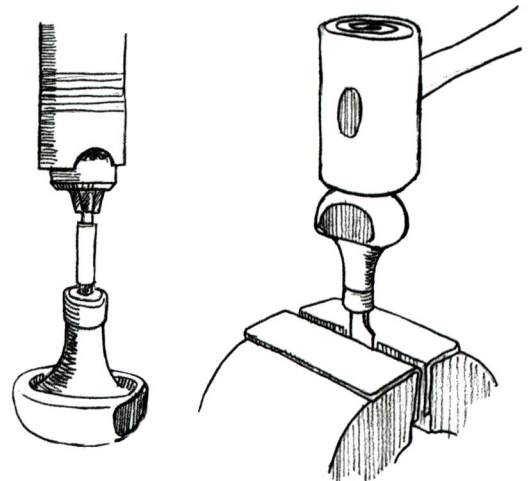

on the side of my handles with the flat of the blade (it doesn't matter on which side, since you don't feel the flat when you are holding the graver). This way, when the graver is lying on the bench, it rests on the side of the cutting tip, not directly on it, which helps keep it sharper longer.

Reshaping the Cutting End

To enable a graver's cutting tip to fit into tight spaces, and to make it easier to sharpen, reduce the height of the angled cutting face by removing excess material from the spine with a bench grinder. Because each of these three gravers you'll be using performs a different function, each is shaped slightly differently. When performing this reshaping operation, remember that you will only be grinding metal away from the blade's spine, never from the angled face. Any shaping or sharpening of the face is done later, and always by hand. Use a bench grinder or a flex shaft to remove the excess. Traditionally, this tapering of the working end reconfigures the tip to one of two profiles.

In the first, the extraneous metal is ground away from the spine in a smooth, concave arc starting about an inch back from the point at which the angled face meets the spine. Grind slowly, using light strokes, always dipping the blade into water after each stroke to keep it cool. Use a coarse wheel (which produces less frictional heat than a finer grit, and light pressure. As the tip gets thinner, the dipping becomes even more important. If the blade develops a blue color, it is an indication that the blade's temper has been lost (if this happens, all is not lost, however, and I will explain how to deal with this later on). After dipping, keep the end of the blade tilted down slightly, so that water on the shaft will slide to the tip, helping to keep it cool. Watch closely, and re-dip as soon as the droplet evaporates.

The other style of reshaping the blade involves grinding the spine in a straight taper, beginning at a point about 2–2½" (50–65 mm) on the spine. Both methods reduce the size of the cutting tip effectively. The difference between the two methods is mainly cosmetic, neither producing any noticeable difference in efficiency or workability. Regardless of which style you choose, remember to follow up with a sanding belt or sanding stick to remove sharp edges. The finished blade should feel comfortable in your hand, and the blade should slide smoothly against your fingers.

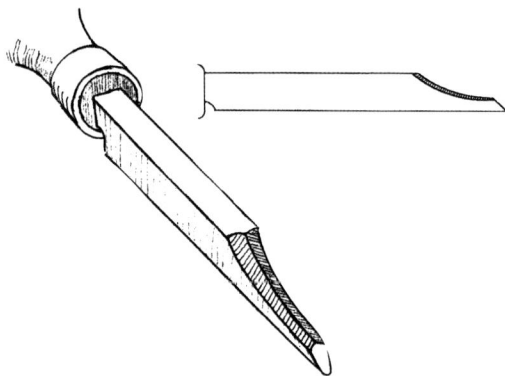

In this style, the shaft of the graver remains untouched except for the last inch or so.

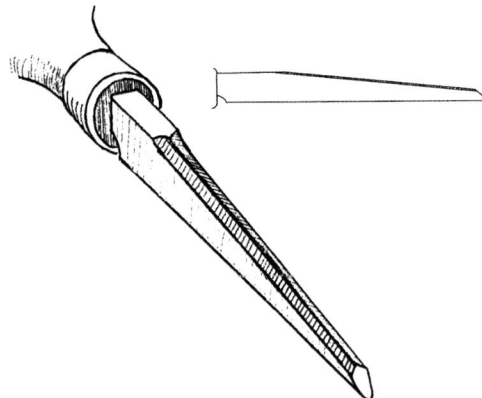

In this style, the shaft is ground to a slow taper for most of its length.

The settings described below require only three gravers. You will need a #52 round graver, a #42 flat graver and a #4 anglette graver. The numbers assigned to gravers identify both the type and size of the blade. The 50s are all round gravers, the narrowest being a #50, and the widest being a #59. The 40s are flat gravers, with #40 being the narrowest and #49 the widest. The single digits are assigned to the anglettes. The specific sizes that I am recommending reflect my personal preferences, but there is some leeway here and you can substitute other sizes to suit your own tastes. Round gravers in sizes #50, #51, or #52 are all commonly employed interchangeably for the same tasks with only slightly different results. The same is true for #40, #41 or #42 flat gravers, or #2, #3, or #4 anglettes. Experiment.

The #52 round graver is the workhorse of the three gravers that you will be using. It is used for digging down into the metal and raising spurs, or stitches, that will later secure a stone. Because it is used with some degree of force, the cutting tip must be stouter than the other two. Stop grinding when the height of the blade from belly to newly ground spine is 2 to 2½ mm high. If you grind it thinner than this, the tip will not be strong enough for the rigors of the job it has to do. The angle of the cutting face will also need adjustment. The narrow, relatively fragile 45° angle of the graver's tip, as it comes from the supplier, would soon chip or break from the force and pressure exerted during the raising of the stitch. To prevent this, it must be reground (by hand) to a somewhat steeper angle—about 60°. I will discuss regrinding the graver face and sharpening a little later.

Like the round graver, the anglette is ground back to a height of 2 to 2½ mm at the tip. This graver is used to incise linear cuts into the surface. Because these cuts are relatively shallow, little pressure is required, and the original 45° angle of the face does not require alteration.

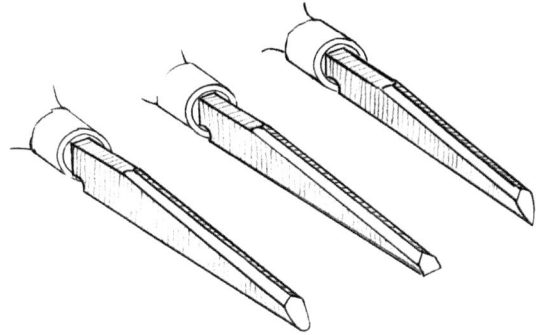

These are the three gravers used most often in stonesetting. From left-to-right: Round, Flat, and Anglette.

The #42 flat graver looks like a miniature woodworkers chisel, but is used more like a woodworkers plane. It is used to trim and refine, shaving metal away in very thin layers with repeated light strokes. It is never used to dig deep into the surface, nor with any pressure. As it glides along the surface of the cut, it trims away any irregularities, leaving a bright, shiny

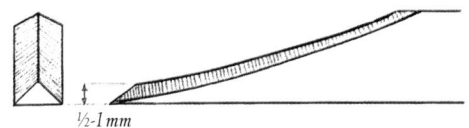

Proper face shapes and angles for three common stonesetting gravers.

Steve Midgett
Shield Form Pin/Pendant
*Platinum, paladium, silver mokume,
shakudo, and diamonds.*
photo: Steve Midgett

surface in its wake. Because this graver is never used with any force, its spine can be ground down to a very thin point. Generally, the tip is tapered down to 0.5 mm – 1.0 mm. Because it is so delicate, grinding must be done with great care so as not to overheat the tip. Take your time—do not try to rush the grinding operation. Use very light strokes and dip in water often.

Damage Control
(What To Do if You Lose Your Temper)

Sometimes, despite your best efforts, you might overheat the tip of a graver during the grinding operation. Though this is a nuisance, it is easy to fix. If during grinding you observe a bluish discoloration at the tip, it means you have lost your temper, so to speak. Because the steel has now been annealed, it will not hold a sharpened edge. You must re-harden and re-temper the blade, which at this scale is a relatively simple operation. Carbon steel tools are hardened in two steps called hardening and tempering. In the first process the tool is heated to approximately 1450° F, and then immediately plunged into a cooling bath. The steel becomes hard, and unfortunately, as brittle as glass. Any attempt to use the tool at this stage will result in a broken tool. To reduce the brittleness, the tool must be subjected to a second, much lower temperature heating called tempering. This eliminates the brittleness while only slightly reducing the hardness.

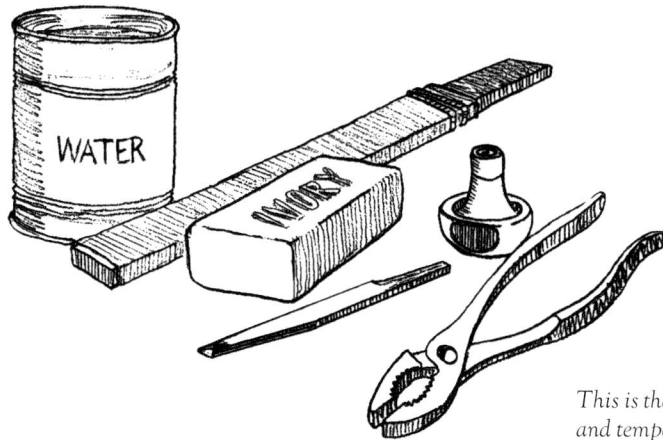

This is the equipment you'll need to harden and temper small tools like gravers.

Hardening and Tempering

Before heat-treating a blade, remove it from its handle. Secure the blade in a vise, and tug firmly on the handle to remove it. You will need a pair of utility grade pliers or vise grips, abrasive paper, a bar of hand soap (I prefer Ivory), and a container of room temperature water, deep enough to submerge the blade.

Before the re-hardening process begins, first use a sanding stick to remove the bluish discoloration from the sides of the tip. Do not sand the belly or the angled cutting face. Once the sides are bright and clean, coat about 2" of the blade with soap. Moisten the surface and scrape the blade over it, molding the soap with your fingers to coat the blade. This waxy layer will keep the blade from turning dark and scaly from the heating.

Hold the blade in pliers with the pointed end straight up. Heat the end of the blade (1"–1½", 25–38 mm) with a torch flame until it reaches approximately 1450° F. You will recognize this temperature when the steel shifts from bright red to incandescent yellow-orange. The steel will glow as if lit from within. Immediately plunge the entire blade, point first, into water and swirl it around. When you withdraw the blade from the water and wipe off the remaining carbonized soap residue, the blade should be flat, dull gray, the same color as a file. If it is, the blade is now glass hard, and very brittle (handle carefully at this stage). You can test the hardness by stroking the surface with an old file. If the file slides over the surface without biting, you're ready to proceed. If the steel has not

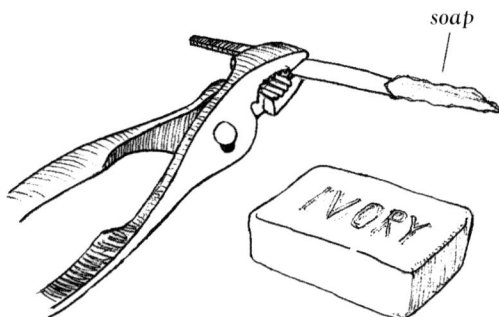

soap

Paint the tool with a layer of soap to protect the steel froma discoloring oxide scale.

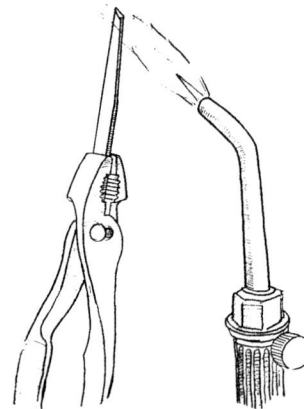

Heat the last inch or so of the tip to an incandescent yellow-orange glow, then plunge quickly into water.

been suitably hardened, you will need to repeat the hardening sequence.

Use a sanding stick to re-brighten the sides of the blade in preparation for the tempering process. For this second step, use a very small, soft torch flame, or an alcohol lamp flame. Hold the blade with utility pliers, but this time hold it horizontally, with its tip slightly lower than the tang end. This positioning will ensure that the flame will not flow up the tip of the blade, possibly overheating and annealing it all over again. Your goal here is not to heat the tip directly, but rather to heat the blade about an inch or so back from the tip, and to allow heat to move slowly, and controllably, toward the tip. Hold the blade above the flame; do not move it around. Be patient, and watch for oxide colors to develop. These colors will allow you to monitor the progress of the tempering.

the tip. The color bands will slow slightly, making it easier to watch the progression. A split second before the brassy yellow reaches the tip, I plunge the blade into the cooling bath and swirl it around. In that split second, the brassy yellow will have reached the tip, producing the desired degree of temper. Dry the blade and check it carefully. If the color at the tip has progressed beyond brassy yellow, the blade should be re-hardened and re-tempered. If its OK, use the sanding stick to remove the discoloration on the sides of the blade.

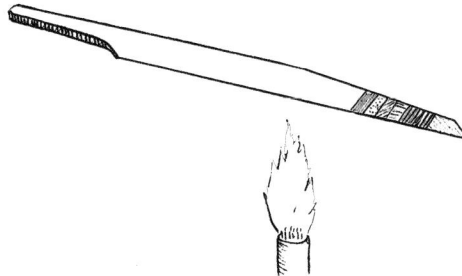

Hold the graver so the flame is behind the section you want to temper and allow the heat to slowly travel toward the tip.

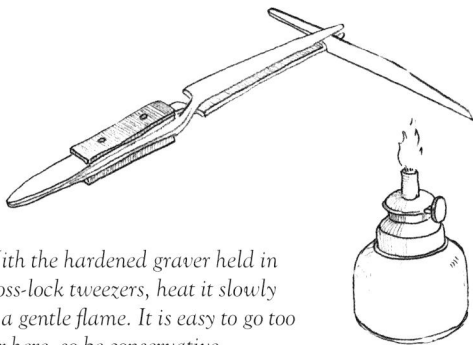

With the hardened graver held in cross-lock tweezers, heat it slowly in a gentle flame. It is easy to go too far here, so be conservative.

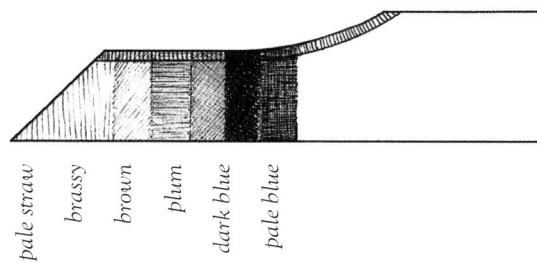

pale straw *brassy* *brown* *plum* *dark blue* *pale blue*

The colors that appear on the blade will begin to move in bands along the blade from the hottest spot directly over the flame. These colors always appear in the same sequence: pale straw yellow, brassy yellow, brown, plum, dark blue, then pale blue. Quench the blade immediately, as soon as the brassy yellow color reaches the tip. I move the blade completely out of the flame as the pale straw color approaches

Sharpening
Sharpening Stones
There are four types of surfaces that are used for sharpening gravers: oilstones (commonly called India oilstones), Arkansas stones, ruby slips, and diamond impregnated blocks. Of the four, the first two are the most common and the least expensive. The latter two are used to sharpen high speed steel gravers.

Michael Boyd | Brooch   photo: Tim Brown
18k and 22k gold, magnasite, shale, emerald, black jade. maw sit-sit, dumorderity, tourmaline.

India oilstones are double-sided, man-made abrasive blocks that are made of aluminum oxide or carborundum, with a darker, coarse-grit side, and a paler, fine-grit side. The coarse side is used for reshaping or regrinding broken tips, and the fine side is used for sharpening. To prevent particles of steel from clogging the surface, apply a small amount of light oil (I use 3-in-1 Oil) to the surface of the stone before each use. Most oilstones are about 5–6" (13 cm–15 cm) long, 2–3" (5 cm–7.5 cm) wide, and about 1" (2.5 cm) thick. Most blades require only a few strokes on the fine grit side for re-sharpening (usually, only the #42 flat graver needs further attention).

Arkansas stones are made from natural, fine-grained stone similar to flint or chert. Arkansas stones are available in soft or hard grades, the hard being most commonly used. Because Arkansas stones are less abrasive than oilstones, they are

The most common and most economical whetstone is a synthetic India oilstone with two grits.

used for honing dulled blades, rather than for grinding or reshaping. When blades are rubbed against the smooth, vitreous surface, they develop a burnished, polished face. This burnished edge, particularly on the edge of a flat graver, produces a shiny cut. Arkansas stones are usually much smaller and thinner than oilstones. There should be a thin layer of oil on an Arkansas stone during use.

Ruby slips and diamond blocks are made from synthetic industrial-grade materials equal in hardness to their natural gemstone counterparts. Ruby slips work best for sharpening, as the diamond cuts away steel almost too efficiently, prematurely shortening the life of gravers. For most studio jewelers, an India oilstone and a hard Arkansas stone are sufficient.

Hard Arkansas stones are a quarried natural stone that is famous for its ability to achieve a high polish on hardened steel.

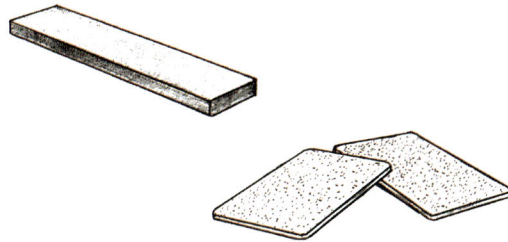

Ruby Slip Stones, or Ruby Slips, are pink and available in several shapes. Diamond blocks are made by many manufacturers, and come in several colors, sizes, and shapes.

Sharpening Jigs

In order for a graver to cut properly, it is imperative that its inclined face be sharpened to a perfectly flat plane perpendicular to the blade's lengthwise axis. If the face is rounded, curved, or sharpened at an angle, it will not produce a clean, accurate cut, if any cut at all. An improperly sharpened graver is more likely to slip, which can damage the surrounding surface and injure the individual using it. Jewelry tool suppliers offer a variety of sharpening guides or jigs in a range of prices that provide a fixed angle during sharpening. Though I own several different styles, I never use them because there is a cheaper, faster alternative. In the time it takes to adjust and secure a graver in a jig, you can sharpen a graver quite suitably by hand. Fortuitously, Mother Nature has provided you with a built-in sharpening jig.

Three of the most popular commercial sharpening jigs. While these have the benefit of providing consistent angles, even the people who use them would probably agree that they require some fussy setting up.

Sharpening a Graver by Hand

You have probably noticed that three-legged objects are reliably sturdy and wobble-free. Three-legged stools, camera tripods, soldering tripods, and the like all take advantage of this structural integrity. A graver, held in the hand in a certain way, can also be sharpened quickly, efficiently and properly using this tripodal principle.

To sharpen a graver by hand, turn the graver belly-side up. Put a few drops of light oil on the fine grit surface of your sharpening stone, and place the inclined face of the graver flat on the surface. Make sure the face is in full contact with the stone and that the blade is not tilted to one side or another. Pinch the rear side of the blade (close to the spine) with the tips of your thumb and middle finger, simultaneously sliding the tip of your index finger down the belly, pressing the blades tip to the stone. Let the tips of your thumb and middle finger rest lightly on the stone. The tip of the graver and the tips of your thumb and middle finger will create three points of contact, a tripod, on the stone. Exert just enough pressure on the tips of your thumb and middle finger to maintain the tripod without abrading your skin. Now stroke the graver tip across the stone, hold your wrist rigid, pivoting your rigid hand–wrist–forearm from your elbow only.

Some people prefer to rub the face over the stone in lengthwise strokes, and others prefer a side-to-side action (my personal preference). With a little practice, it is quite simple to properly sharpen gravers this way. To check the effectiveness of your technique, lightly touch the tip of the graver to your thumbnail. If it grabs immediately, the graver is sufficiently sharpened. If it slides or skips, more stroking is required. After the tip is sharpened, jab it into your bench pin several times to remove burrs. Use this technique to sharpen all three of your gravers, and to regrind the angle of your round graver from a 45° angle to a 60° angle. The round and anglette gravers are now ready for use, but the flat graver needs one last bit of attention.

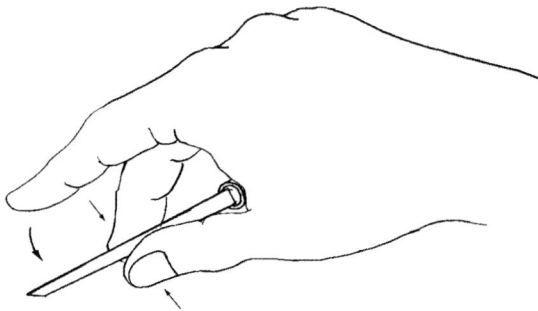

To sharpen a graver by hand, grip the graver, belly-up, and allow your fingertips to rest lightly on the stone. Use a smooth sweeping motion with the tool rigidly held in position. With a little practice, most people find they can achieve surfaces that rival those created with a jig.

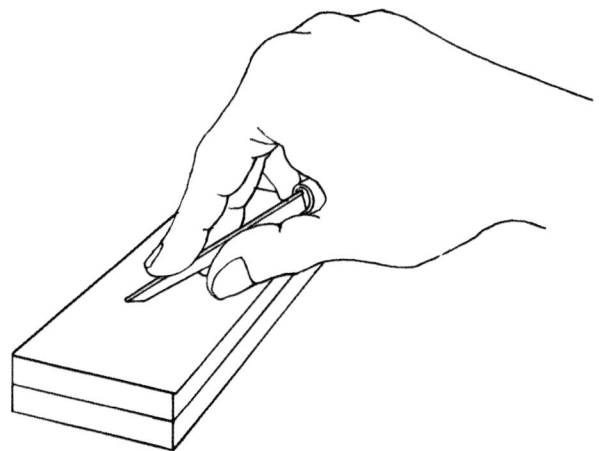

It is the belly, not the angled face, of the flat graver that is responsible for producing a bright cut. It is not necessary to polish the entire belly, but rather an area a millimeter or so in length from the cutting edge, back. To create this polished spot, after first sharpening the graver face, place the graver belly-side down on the oiled Hard Arkansas stone, then lift the handle just enough to provide clearance for your fingers. Pull the blade backwards on the

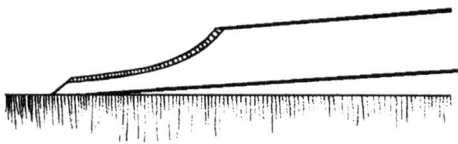

When grinding the belly, hold the graver vertical and lift it just enough to sneak a finger beneath. This will provide the lift angle, the facet on the graver that determines the angle at which the tool meets the metal.

stone several times, keeping the angle constant. Observe the path left in the film of oil on the surface. This trail should be exactly as wide as the width of the blade. If the blade leaves only a thin line, it means that you are tipping the blade to one side or another. After two or three passes, inspect the graver belly at the tip. You should see a bright, shiny flat facet. This is what you are after:

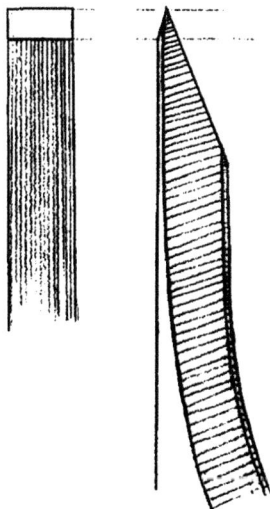

Every time you sharpen the graver, repeat this polishing on the Arkansas stone. The Arkansas stone doesn't grind away material (like the oilstone), but burnishes and hones the tip. You can also polish the face by dragging it across a piece of crocus cloth. This is a rouge-impregnated abrasive cloth. For this purpose it is important to keep it supported on a perfectly flat surface. I keep a rectangular piece of quarter-inch Plexiglas, about the size of my Arkansas stone, and a piece of worn crocus cloth in my stonesetting tool kit. When the flat graver has been sharpened, and the polished facet has been established on the belly, the graver is ready for use.

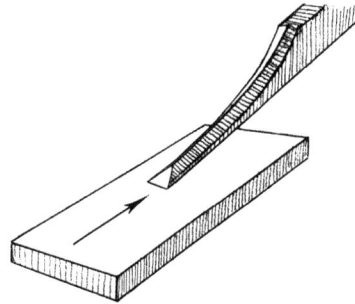

For quick touch-ups, hold a piece of crocus cloth on a flat surface and draw the graver toward yourself.

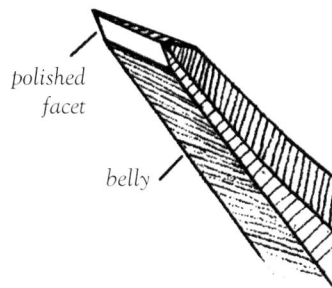

polished facet

belly

This drawing shows the intended results of the polishing operation. Polished facets are flawlessly mirror-like.

Raising Stitches

When a round graver cuts into the metal surface, its angular, wedge-shaped tip creates a sharp spur, or stitch, as the tip digs into the metal. These stitches are the fundamental means by which stones are secured in all graver settings. It is therefore incumbent on you to learn how to make a proper stitch. The best way to do so is to select a small, flat scrap of silver, and to practice, practice, practice.

Because the graver must cut down into the surface to create the stitch, this piece of metal should be at least 18 gauge thick (16 gauge is even better). If it is thinner than this, you will risk puncturing the metal. Understand that this does not mean that all pieces of jewelry that sport any of these graver settings must be made of uniformly thick (and possibly weighty) metal. Instead, the dimension at the location of the settings can be locally thickened by the addition of an appropriately sized pad or plate, soldered atop the piece (a visible design element), or on its reverse side (where it will be invisible). For your practice plate, just use a piece of 18 or 16 gauge sheet. You will also need a flat surface against which you can brace the practice plate while cutting, so that you can keep your fingers out of the graver's path. I have permanently mounted (glued and screwed) a small

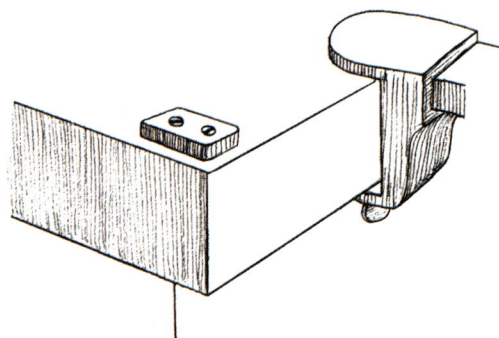

It is helpful to permanently attach a small rectangle of hardwood or plastic to a corner of the bench. This will provide something to press against when you are cutting stitches.

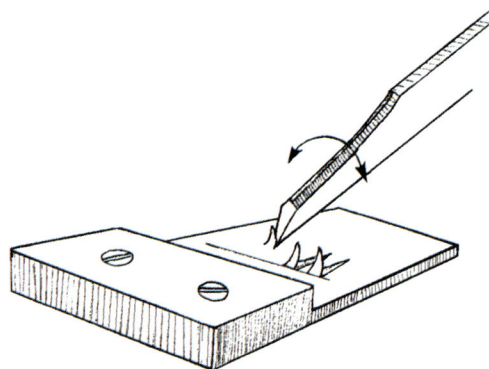

Press a sharp graver into the metal at a constant angle, press forward, and rock the tool slightly left and right.

rectangle of hardwood (rock maple) to the front left-hand corner of my bench for this purpose (I am right-handed, so the direction of my cut is from right to left. If you are left-handed, mount this bracing block in the front right corner). For a temporary bracing block, use a C-clamp to affix the wooden brace to your bench.

To make stitches, scribe a straight line on your practice plate, brace the plate against your wood block, and stick the point of the graver into the metal surface about 2 mm from the scribed line. Hold the blade at a constant angle of approximately 30° from horizontal, and, while maintaining a steady pressure, rock the blade from side to side. The combination

Jim Cotter | Ring
Aluminum, 14k, diamond.
photo: Shane McComber

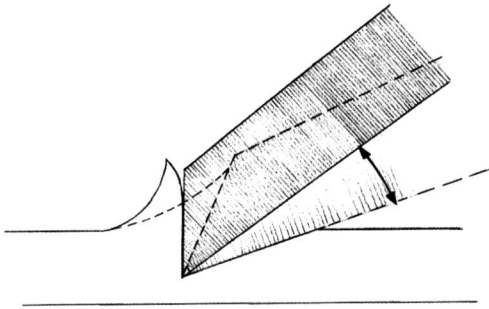

A common mistake is to think "lift" when you should be thinking "cut." The stitch will appear by itself when you are cutting properly.

of your steady pressure and the walking action of the rocking will cause the tip to cut forward and down into the surface at a uniform incline. The angled face of the graver tip will lift a slightly curved, pointed spur as it advances.

Do not attempt to push the graver forward, but let the walking advance the cut. Do not raise or lower the handle. If you lower the handle, reducing this angle, you will undercut and clip off the stitch. If you raise the handle, increasing the angle, you will not move forward, but will only bury the tip deep in the metal, possibly puncturing all the way through, or breaking off the tip of the graver.

In my experience, I have learned that the maximum height of a stitch cut with a #52 graver is about two millimeters. When I have tried to cut taller stitches, they invariably begin to curl excessively, then break off. You will never need a stitch greater than to millimeters for any of the following settings (in fact, decidedly shorter is sufficient for all but the first of these settings). When you have made a cut of the intended length, lift the handle until the graver face is vertical. This will bring the stitch into a fully upright position, perfect for a miniature prong, in which capacity it will serve. Repeat this sequence until you can consistently raise proper stitches of uniform height. Once you can do this, you are ready to try the following settings.

The Stitch Setting

This setting was developed during the Victorian era, when it was commonly used to set small flat-backed pearls and, even more extensively, tiny rose cut hematite, jet, and marcasite gems that were often set en masse on the mourning jewelry that was so popular and fashionable during that period. Because the stitches raised by a graver are relatively small, this setting is best restricted to cabochons no larger than four millimeters. Also, because it is a bit more fragile than many other settings, it is most appropriate for jewelry items not subjected to rigorous wear. I don't recommend a stitch setting for a ring or a bracelet.

Stitch setting was developed in Victorian England as an expedient way to set multiple small stones in close proximity.

The beauty of this simple style of setting lies in its simplicity and delicacy. The graver cuts that produce the stitches are covered by the stone, so only the tiny, tapered prongs around the periphery of the stone are visible. Also, because all cuts are made within the boundary of the stone, multiple stones can be easily clustered within a small area.

To make a stitch setting, you only need your stone(s), a fine-pointed scribe, a small piece of beeswax or sticky wax, and your sharpened #52 round graver. Roll the small piece of wax in your fingers until the heat of your hand warms it sufficiently to allow a bit to be rubbed on the back of the stone. Only a tiny bit is required. This wax will temporarily affix the stone in position while you trace the outline. Place the stone in the desired location and hold it down firmly with the tip of your finger. Carefully scribe a single line along the section of the girdle closest to your scribe-holding hand. Never scribe more than a single line, because you end up with multiple lines and can't tell which is the correct one. I find that I can usually trace about half of the stones circumference. My other hand, which is holding the stone in place, makes it awkward to reach the far side of the stone. It doesn't matter, because the half I can trace is sufficient to begin.

On a small round stone, a minimum of three stitches is required to hold a stone securely, but you can make any number more than that as desired. Having made a mental note as to the number and spacing of the stitches, remove the stone, exposing your partially scribed line. Starting about two millimeters inside the line, use a graver to raise two properly spaced stitches. Place the stone back in position, anchored against these two stitches, and scribe the other half of the circumference. After scribing, remove the stone and finish raising the rest of the stitches. Uniformity of both stitch spacing and overall height is important.

After all stitches are raised, rub away the wax residue, then place the stone in position inside the stitches. Push the stitches tightly up against the stone. I like to use the tip of my scribe like a burnisher to do this, working back and forth, from one side of the stone to the other, to keep the stone from shifting. Make sure that each stitch lies flat against the stone, from base to tip. Unsecured stitches can snag and pull loose. As a final step, I give each stitch one last rub with a polished burnisher to impart a bright surface. Voila! It is as simple as that.

Step-by-Step of the Stitch Setting

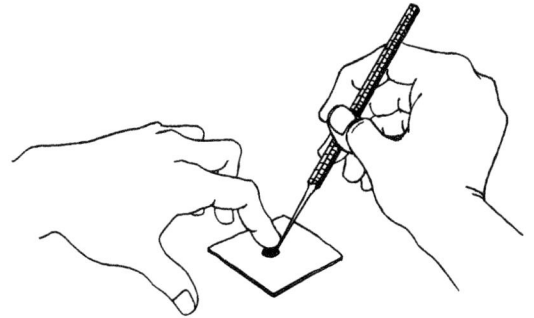

With the stone temporarily secured by sticky wax, trace a line around it.

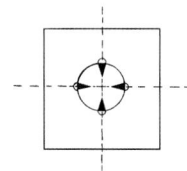

Identify the number and location of prongs.

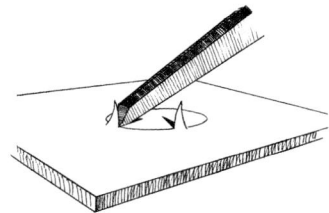

Starting inside the scribed circle, cut two stitches so they end up standing up on the line.

Set the stone in place, mark the rest of the circumference, then cut the remaining prongs.

With the stone in place, press the prongs onto the stone and smooth them down with a polished burnisher.

The next two settings entail a few additional steps. Unlike the stitch setting, where the stone simply sits on the surface, both of these settings require that the stone be recessed into the surface. Whereas the stitch setting only accommodates flat-backed stones, these settings are used almost exclusively for small faceted stones. The first step is to drill a hole and cut a seat that allows the girdle to rest slightly below the surface. This preliminary seat-cutting sequence is the same for both of the following settings.

Nicole Jacquard | Earrings
18k gold, rubies, pearls
photo: Kevin Montague

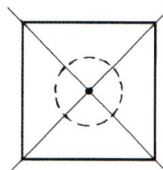

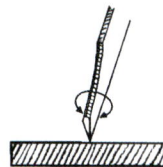

The Basic Bead Setting
Cutting a Seat
Make a shallow depression with the tip of your #52 round graver at the location where you plan to drill the hole for the seat. Stick the point in the surface and rotate the tip back and forth several times. This will create a small nick sufficient to start the tip of your drill bit without distorting the surface. Drill a guide hole with a small drill bit. Enlarge this hole to approximately three-fourths of the diameter of the stone. Opening up this hole reduces the work of the stonesetting bur, and facilitates the cutting of the seat. The conical tip of the bur is not made for drilling and enlarging holes, so use a pear, cone, or bud bur to ream the hole to size.

When using any bur, it is important to

After laying out the location of the setting with a fine-tipped scriber, make a small nick with a graver to hold the tip of the drill bit.

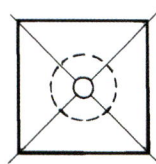

Drill a small starter hole, then enlarge as needed with a second and perhaps a third bit. It is best to proceed slowly here so you don't accidentallly take away too much.

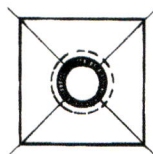

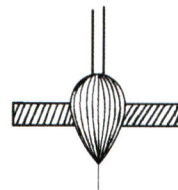

When the hole approaches the right size, use a bud bur to convert the vertical walls of the drilled hole to a sloped interior shape.

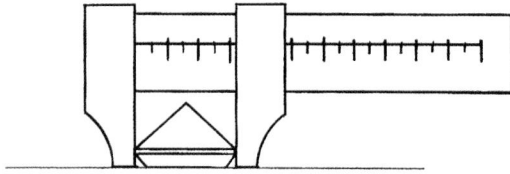

Use a sliding caliper to measure the stone, then use the same caliper to select a bur with a matching diameter.

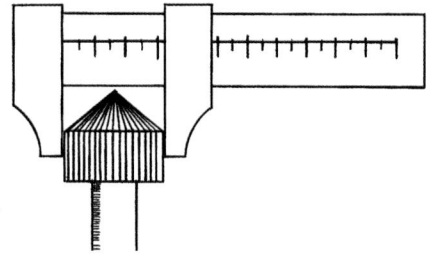

use a light oil for lubrication. This helps reduce overheating, and helps to prevent chattering (of the bur, not you...). Traditionally, oil of wintergreen is used by stonesetters because of its pleasant smell, its clear, non-staining properties, and because it is easily washed away. However, the commonly available variety is synthetic, and dissolves some types of plastics. I once had the misfortune of having a small bottle tip and leak inside my toolbox. In addition to the sticky plastic mess I discovered, the persisting smell was impossible to eliminate. A tiny amount used for lubricating has a pleasing smell, but in larger quantity, it is downright cloying. To this day, I cannot stomach the smell of oil of wintergreen. If you choose to use it, do so with caution. I now use plain old unscented mineral oil.

It is imperative that this seat is exactly the same diameter as the stone. Obviously, if the cavity is too small, the stone won't fit in. This is easily rectified by simply re-cutting the seat with a larger bur of appro-

priate size. If you cut the seat too large, the stone can never be properly secured. Either a larger stone must be substituted, or the setting must be scrapped. Use a stone gauge or a vernier caliper to measure the stone, and then use the same gauge to select the appropriate bur. If you do not have a bur exactly the same size as your stone, never use an oversize bur. Rather, use the closest smaller size. Once the seat has been cut to the proper depth, you can cut sideways, carefully moving the bur in a circular path, paring a tiny amount of metal from the inner wall of the seat. Do this judiciously, stopping as soon as the stone will fit in place with gentle pressure. When you have

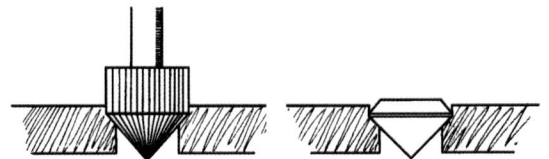

Use a setting bur to create a seat on the inside of the hole.

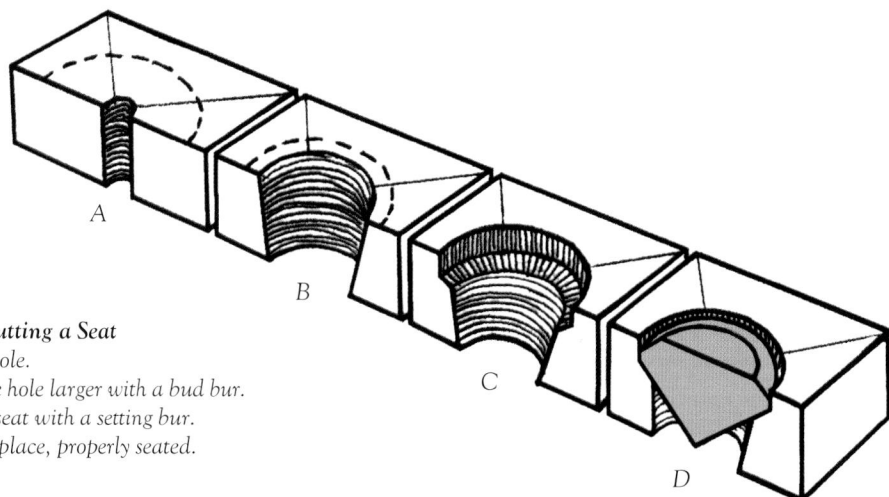

Stages in Cutting a Seat
A Drill a hole.
B Ream the hole larger with a bud bur.
C Cut the seat with a setting bur.
D Stone in place, properly seated.

cut the seat to the proper depth and diameter, the upper edge of the girdle should rest slightly below the surface. Remove the stone and use a fine grit sanding stick to smooth any rough burr created by the cutting of the seat. You are now ready to set the stone.

Raising a Bead

Using the tip of your #52 graver, lightly nick out the location of the starting point for the cuts that will ultimately produce the beads. These shallow nicks should be evenly spaced around the stone, and should be located between 0.75 mm to 1.5 mm back from the edge of the seat, (closer for smaller stones, and farther out for larger stones). You can have as few as two beads, or as many more as you prefer. Obviously, if you have only two beads, they must lie directly opposite one another.

In the preceding stitch setting, the graver tip was imbedded in the surface and wiggled forward to create a raised spur of metal that was then employed as a miniature prong. There was no danger to the stone, since it was not in place during the cutting. If you attempt to cut forward toward the cavity of the seat, you might cut all the way through, clipping away the metal needed to produce the bead, and dulling or chipping the graver tip as it hits the stone (possibly damaging the stone, as well).

Raising the bead, which probably should more properly be called establishing the bead, does not require an advancing cut or the lifting of a spur. Instead, the graver tip, once imbedded, is rocked side to side while remaining in the same spot. When raising a stitch, you may recall that I advised holding the blade at an angle of approximately 30° to the horizontal surface. The combination of the angle of approach, the inclined plane of the angular tip and the side-to-side rocking motion compelled the graver to cut forward and down into the surface. In this case, advancing forward will only prove disastrous.

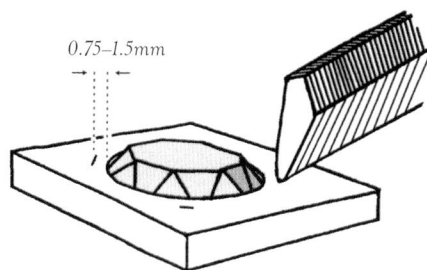

Mark the locations of the stitches with the #52 graver, approximately one millimeter outside the stone.

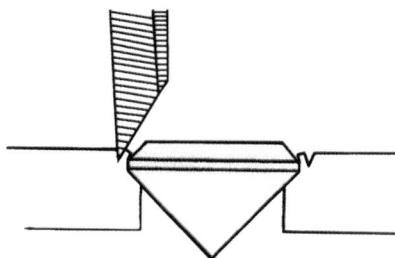

Press the tip of the graver straight down, rocking slightly from side to side.

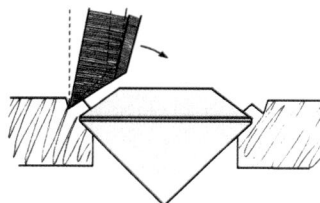

Tilt the graver toward the stone, pressing the stitch toward the stone. Do not try to tighten it at this point; instead, move from stitch to stitch for evenness.

To establish a bead, stick the graver point into the surface at the desired location, but hold the handle much higher. The V-shaped, angular tip should be perpendicular to the surface. Now, when you rock the graver side to side, the cutting action will be straight down, rather than forward. The angled tip will act as a wedge, forcing a small projection of metal out from the edge of the seat as the tip penetrates into the surface. With the point still imbedded, tilt the handle end of the graver forward, so that the face of the blade pushes this small projection over the girdle of the stone. Don't attempt to press the metal too tightly against the stone yet, or you may risk tilting the stone in the seat. Work evenly, back and forth around the stone, until you have established small projections at each desired location. Once you are sure that the stone is locked in proper position, you are ready for the final tightening.

You can accomplish the final tightening in one of two ways. The simplest is to simply reinsert the graver tip at each location and use it to lever each metal projection tight against the stone. For smaller stones (3.5 mm or smaller), this is sufficient. It is not fancy, but it's simple, unobtrusive, and effective. For larger stones, I recommend one additional, final operation: rounding off each of these projections with a beading tool to give them a smooth, hemispheric profile.

Beading Tools

Beading tools are sold in sets of a dozen or so small-diameter steel rods, tapered at one end, with concave depressions at the end of the taper. These rods can be fitted interchangeably into a single wooden handle, similar in appearance to a graver handle. The concave depressions range in size, which allows you to produce rounded beads of different sizes. To use, select a tool whose concave end just fits over the small

metal projection created by the graver. Fit it into the handle and place it on the prong. Hold the ferrule end of the handle with your thumb and middle finger, and position the tip of your index finger on the end of the handle. Simultaneously rock and rotate the tool with light pressure, being careful not to allow the rim of the concave depression to touch the stone. The tool's smooth, concave depression will reshape and burnish the metal projection into a bright bead.

Eventually, the rim of a beading tool may become chipped or roughened from accidental contact with a stones faceted surface. The same tool suppliers who

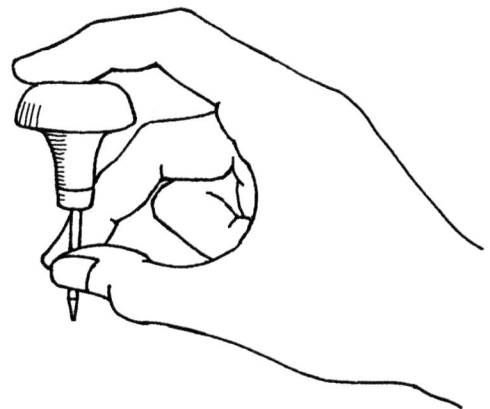

Proper position for using the beading tool.

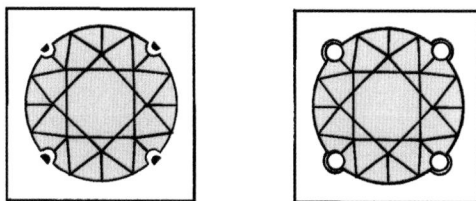

Two options for finishing the raised stitch. On the left, the stitch as made, which includes a depression where the tip of the graver was pressed into the metal. On the right, the same setting after the tips of the stitches have been shaped and burnished with a beading tool.

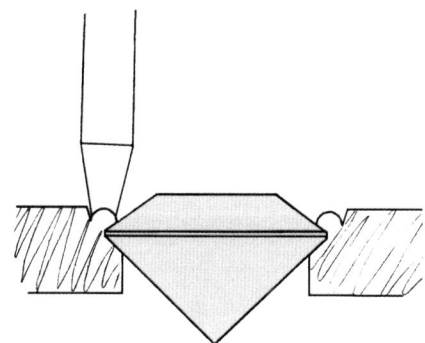

Beading tools are used to convert the pointed stitches into rounded, uniform hemispheres.

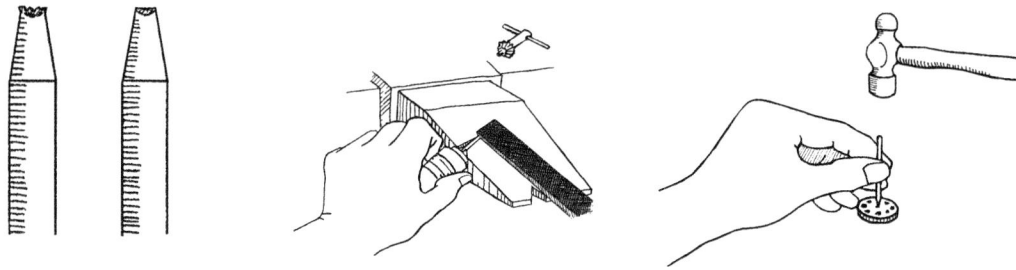

In normal use, beading tools become damaged and must be repaired. Clamp the annealed tool in a flex shaft and run it against a file or sandpaper. To restore the size and polish of the tool, stamp it into a beading block.

sell the beading tools also carry beading blocks, small brass or steel blocks with raised, hardened steel beads of different sizes. To repair your damaged tool, first anneal the end of the tool by heating it to a dull red, and allow it to air cool. Secure the rod in the handpiece of a flexible shaft. While holding the handpiece in your left hand, remove the damaged part of the rim with a fine file or a sanding stick as it spins. Remove only enough to dress the rim.

In the process of removing the damage, you will have reduced the diameter of the concave depression. To reestablish the original dimension, place the concave end of the tool on the proper steel bead and gently tap the tool with a small ball-peen hammer as you rock/rotate the tool with your fingers. As the steel bead does its job, it will swell the outer perimeter of the tool slightly, just below the rim. Put the tool back in the flex shaft and hold the taper against fine sandpaper as the tool rotates to remove this slight bulge. Your tool is now reconditioned, and ready for use. You can re-harden and re-temper, but its really not necessary because the tool is harder than the precious metal of the setting anyway. Also, should you need to re-dress the tip again, you won't have to re-anneal.

The Star Setting

A star setting is nothing more than a bead setting taken one step further. Star settings are characterized by decorative, reflective, radial cuts that emanate from the edge of the stone. The cuts themselves are produced in two stages: first, they are rough-cut with the #4 anglette graver, and then they are bright cut with the #42 flat graver. Because these cuts must be made toward, and into, the seat, they are made before the stone is secured in place.

The number, length, and spacing of the cuts are variable. Generally, a single decorative ray is sited between each pair of adjacent functional beads. Once you have determined the location for each cut, use the anglette graver to make straight

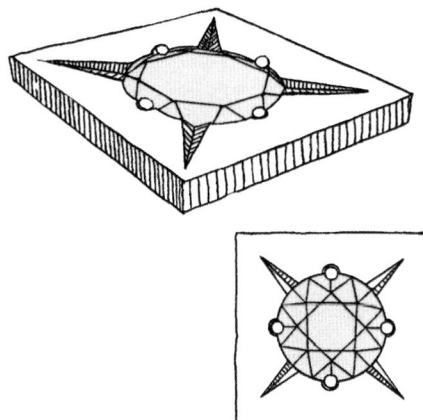

Star settings are easy to make once you get the hang of them. They offer a good bit of drama in a compact space.

shallow cuts directly toward, and into the seat. The V-shaped groove you are cutting should deepen and widen as it approaches the rim of the seat. However, if the ray is relatively long, do not attempt to cut too deeply in a single pass. Doing so will only produce a ragged cut, or worse, will bury the graver tip in the metal and break it off. Instead, cut the ray in several passes, starting each new pass in the same cut, but a little closer to the seat. I can usually cut the rays for a small setting in one or two passes. Larger, longer rays may take three or four passes.

Once all of the rays have been cut, use a flat graver to bright-cut the inner faces of each groove. Start at the shallow end of the cut and hold the graver at the same angle as the slope of the cut. Don't allow the axis of the flat belly to wobble while cutting—keep it steady as you shave away any irregularities in long, smooth strokes. When done properly, the finished ray cuts should be brightly reflective and uniformly tapered.

Using the same stonesetting bur that you used to cut the seat, remove any burs resulting from the graver cuts that protrude into the cavity. Do this de-buring by hand, not with the flex shaft. Simply rotate the bur in the seat with your fingers. Now you can put the stone in place and use your round graver to establish the beads that will actually secure it.

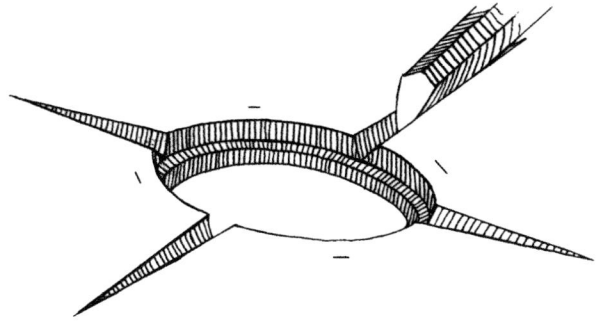

Determine the location of securing stitches and decorative rays. These can be modified to meet the design needs of each piece.

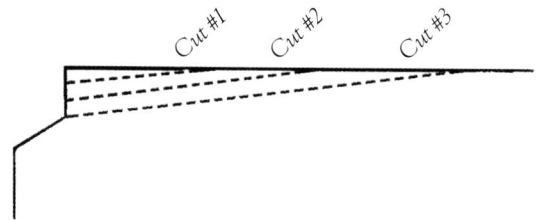

Do not attempt to cut deep rays in a single cut. Instead, use several shallow cuts.

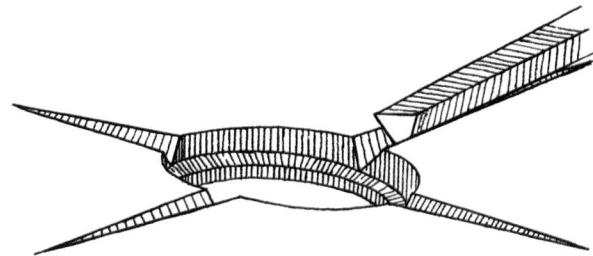

Refine and polish the rays with a highly polished graver in a process called "bright cutting."

Chapter 6
Gypsy and Flush Mount Settings

In linguistics, certain words that, at first glance, resemble other words and appear to share a common root, derivation, or meaning, but in actuality, do not, are called "false cognates." Though seemingly related, these words are often as dissimilar in meaning as they are similar in appearance. False cognates exist, in a manner of speaking, in the realm of stonesettings too. For example, many bezel settings, once customized, often appear more like prong settings. Appearances can be misleading, however. The false cognates of two other types of settings, gypsy and channel, are even more commonly mislabeled because of superficial similarities in appearance to their progenitors.

Gypsy and False-Gypsy Settings:
Similarities and Differences

True gypsy settings are, essentially, hammered settings. To gypsy set a stone, a seat is first cut or carved into thick metal (most commonly, a heavy cast ring), so that the girdle rests below the rim. This rim of

Eleanor Moty | Illusion Brooch
18k and 22k gold, sterling, limonited topaz, topaz. 3⅜" x 1½" x ⅜"

metal is then hammered down over the girdle of the stone using a flat-ended punch and a chasing hammer. Once set, and after all tool marks have been removed, the stone appears imbedded in the surface, almost as if cast in place. Visually, the finished setting is clean and simple, offering no clue as to how the stone is held. Gypsy settings can be used for both cabochons and faceted stones of any size and shape, as long as the gems are sufficiently durable to withstand the hammering. The two most identifiable features of a gypsy setting are the thick metal cross-section where the stone sits, and the domed profile of the metal surface that allows the rim to be hammered onto the stone without producing a recessed trench around the stone. It is also possible to set a stone into a flat surface by pulling metal up from the surface to hold the stone. This variant of the gypsy setting creates a recessed groove around the stone, and is known as a "roman setting."

The gypsy setting's false cognate is known by many names; often erroneously misidentified as a gypsy (which it is not), or, more commonly, a false gypsy. Let's call it by a name that more accurately describes the process and effect—burnished setting, rubbed setting, flush setting, or snap setting (so called because of the sound a stone makes when it is pressed into a tight-fitting seat). Unlike true gypsy settings, this look-alike style of setting accommodates only relatively small, round faceted stones, involves burnishing instead of hammering, and requires less metal. It is equally well suited for flat or curved surfaces.

True Gypsy Setting

A gypsy setting is sometimes described as an integral setting, technically not a structure but a process in which the piece of jewelry itself is the setting. This method requires enough metal around the stone to accommodate both a relatively deeply cut seat, and a suitably high rim that will be hammered down around the stone. Thickness equals weight, and weight is always a major consideration where jewelry items are concerned. Hence, this type of setting is almost always practiced on heavy cast rings.

The first step in gypsy setting is to make a wax model with a domed profile and adequate thickness at the location where the stone will later reside. Depending on the size of the stone, plan on a minimum of three or more millimeters of thickness, more for larger or higher profile stones. This will allow you to carve the seat deeply enough to produce an ample rim above the girdle. In my experience, it works best to begin carving the wax model by creating the seat for the stone. Once you have this cavity in the wax, the rest of the design can be symmetrically arranged around it. Be generous when estimating the thickness of the wax you will require; it is easier to file away excess wax than it is to add more if you don't have enough. Establish a flat plane slightly larger than the size of the stone. If the stone is a flat-based cabochon, simply hold it in position with a tiny bit of sticky wax, and use a fine-pointed scribe to trace the outline. If the stone is faceted, place it table-side down to trace the girdle. Remove the stone and carefully draw a second, parallel line inside the first. This second line should be evenly spaced about 1–1½ mm inside the outer line. The area between these two lines will eventually become the shelf (also called the bearing) upon which the stone will rest.

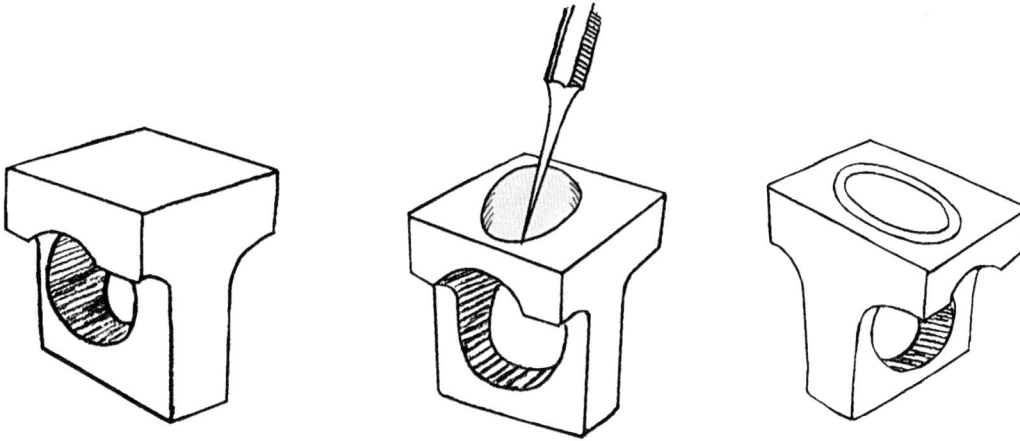

A true gypsy setting is as much a structure as an approach in which the setting is integral to the design of the piece.

Carving the Seat for the Stone

Carve the seat carefully and accurately. Like a bezel, the stone should fit very snugly. Drill a hole all the way through the wax in the center of the scribed area, then use a cone, inverted cone, or cylinder bur to cut away all of the wax up to the inner scribed line. Keep the inner wall vertical as you carve.

Now use an inverted cone or cylinder bur to create the bearing that will support the stone. This operation is critical and requires great accuracy and control. If you are setting a cabochon, the seat will be a flat ledge, about a millimeter thick, at the bottom of the cavity you have carved. If the stone is faceted, and has a tapered sloping pavilion, this ledge will be located higher up on the interior wall to accommodate the pavilion portion of the stone. For a faceted stone, this ledge can be beveled to an appropriate angle in the wax model, but

it is usually safer to make this refinement later on the metal casting.

Work slowly and methodically, carving back from the inner wall to the outer scribed line, trimming away the wax little by little. Do not try to gouge away large amounts of wax at one time, but rather pare it away with many light stokes. When I perform this operation, I like to stop just shy of the traced line, and then finish by scraping the inner wall with the end of a coarse-cut (#0) flat needle file. I hold the broad face of the tip of the file against the inner wall, and simply slide it back and forth sideways as I work around the cavity. I find that this produces a smoother, more vertical inner wall. Check the fit often and stop as soon as the stone drops into place.

Put the stone into the carved seat and make sure that it is level. Adjust if necessary by scraping away high or tight

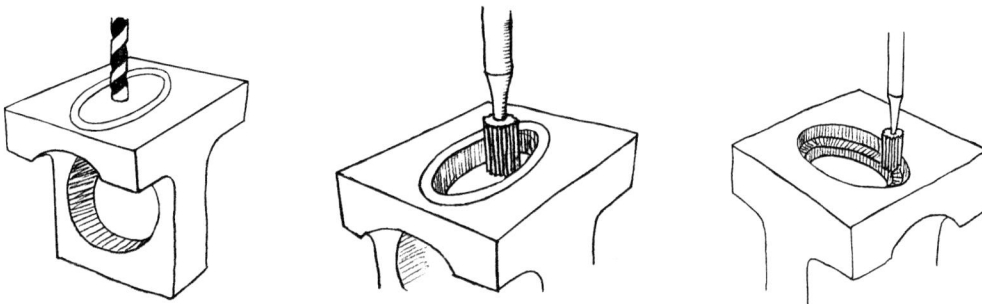

First drill a starter hole, then use cylinder burs to carve the setting for the stone. Note that the wax has been left oversized at this stage; carving the ring to final form comes later

The cavity for a cabochon has a flat floor, while the support for a faceted stone conforms to the slope of the pavilion.

height" rule of thumb. Still, a bit too high is a lot better than not quite high enough. You can always file away extra material to lower the bezel later.

Once you have adjusted the rim height to your satisfaction, you are now free to carve the rest of the ring. Leave the area in the immediate vicinity of the rim smooth and unadorned; it is going to be hammered and filed. The upper edge of the rim should be at least a millimeter wide, and the external inclined surfaces adjacent to the rim should slope away in a consistent taper. When the carving is completed, cast the wax model and clean up the casting.

Once you have cleaned up and pre-polished, check the fit of the stone again. If it fits properly, congratulations—you are ready to proceed. However, it is likely that the seat may require a bit of remedial attention. Shrinkage incurred during casting may have changed the size of the cavity. If the stone doesn't quite fit into place, use a graver (I use the sharpened edge of a #52 round graver) or a fine-cutting bur to

Andy Cooperman | Forceps Brooch
Gold, shibuichi, rubelite. 4" high
photo: Doug Yaple

spots. When the seat is fine-tuned, and the stone fits properly, make a calculated "guesstimate" as to how much wax you can file away to leave a sufficiently high rim above the stones girdle. File the wax down in stages, reinserting the stone and rechecking constantly until you reach the desired level. Because the metal you will be hammering over the edge of the stone will be substantially heavier than a bezel, you aren't bound by the "one-third the stone's

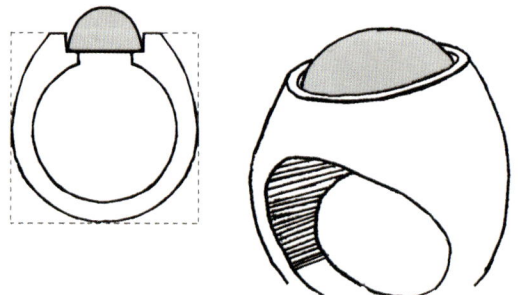

Especially in gypsy settings, it is imperative that the stone makes a tight fit. The goal is to need to move as little metal as possible.

trim the wall until the stone fits in place snugly. The success of this setting depends on a tight fit. If you overcut the seat, as in the case of an oversize bezel, you may be able to trap the stone, but it will still rattle about and eventually loosen. No amount of hammering will correct this situation.

If you are setting a faceted stone, and you did not bevel the bearing in the wax model, now is the time to do so. I like to use either the tapered end of a stonesetting bur, or an oval graver (if the bearing is not too far below the rim), to cut this bevel on the inner shelf. If you use a bur, avoid cutting sideways into the adjacent wall of the cavity.

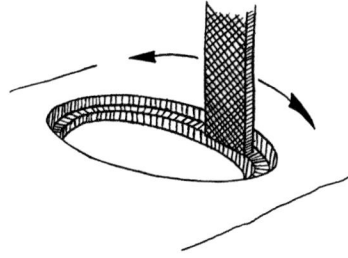

Using a needle file to gently enlarge a setting cavity. The casting process involves shrinkage, so this step is predictable.

Once the seat is properly prepared, you are ready to begin setting the stone. You will need a small chasing hammer, a setting punch, a ring mandrel, and needle files.

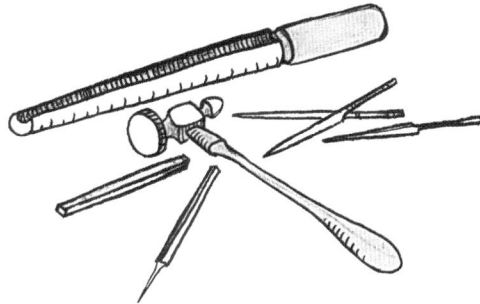

Tools used for hammer setting.

Securing The Stone

The first step in securing the stone is to isolate the portion of the rim that will actually be hammered over the edge of the stone. To do this, use a round needle file to create a groove on the outer sloping surface of the seat cavity, adjacent to, and just below, the rim. The purpose of this groove is to establish a short, stout, freestanding wall against which the punch can be positioned during the initial hammering. Be careful not to over-file or excessively thin this wall.

Slide the ring firmly onto a ring mandrel, and then secure the mandrel either in a vise or by inserting it into a hole in the front of your bench. I prefer the latter method because the punch will be positioned on the far side of the rim, and I hammer toward myself. This provides an unobstructed view as I work, while simultaneously keeping the ring anchored tightly on the taper of the mandrel. I

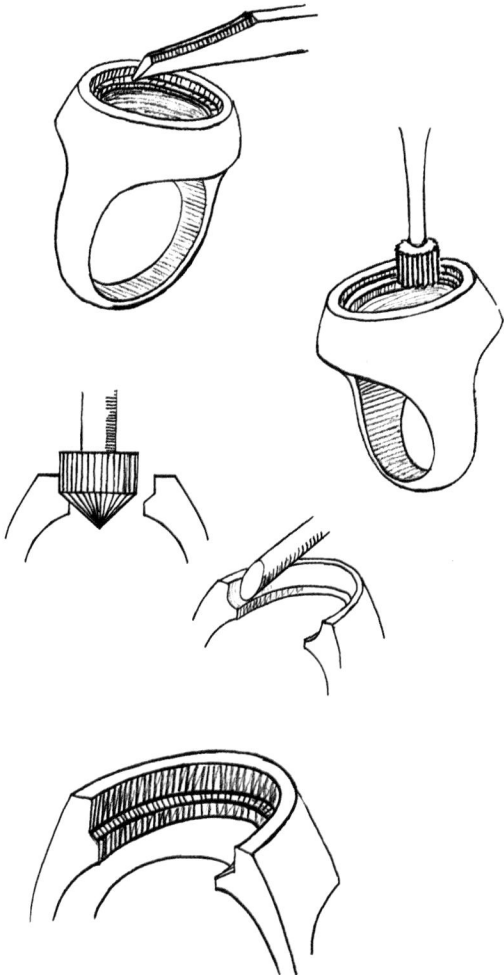

Whether you use a file, a graver, or a bur, the goal is to create a smooth even socket that fits the stone precisely.

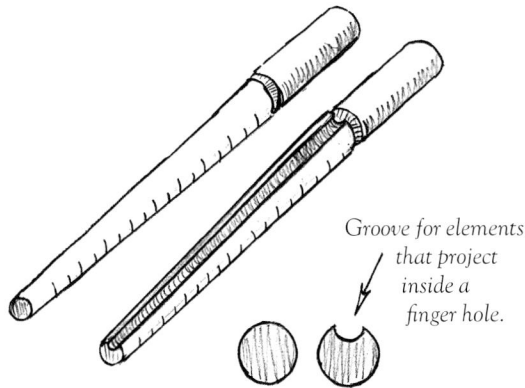

Groove for elements that project inside a finger hole.

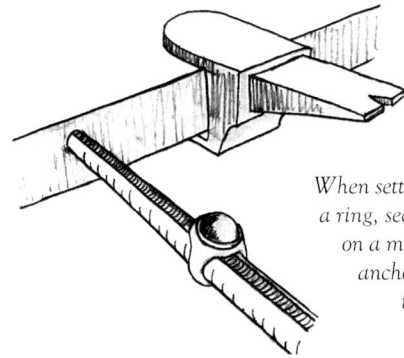

When setting a stone in a ring, secure the work on a mandrel that is anchored in a hole in the front of the bench.

reverse the ring on the mandrel frequently as I hammer to prevent the stone from shifting out of position and to insure that I hammer down the rim uniformly.

A word about ring mandrels and faceted stones: If you are setting a faceted stone, and you carved the seat properly, the pointed culet at the bottom of the tapered pavilion should be safely contained inside the seat cavity. However, what should be sometimes differs from the reality of what is. If the pointed tip of the stone projects into the finger hole, even slightly, you risk damaging the stone if you attempt to hammer set it on a steel mandrel. The soft flesh of your finger might accommodate a slight bit of protruding culet (with an emphasis on *slight*), but cold hard steel will not. If you are faced with this situation, use a mandrel that has a lengthwise groove provided for exactly this reason.

Hammering the rim down over the girdle of the stone is done in much the same manner as hammer setting a heavy bezel. First, lock the stone in position by pushing over a bit of the rim at evenly placed locations (north, south, east, west). Don't hammer too much at one time. Your intent at this point is to secure the stone so that it can't shift or tilt. When doing this preliminary operation, place the rectangular face of the punch, its wider axis held horizontally, against the rim, roughly perpendicular to the surface of the stone. As you tap with repeated light blows, gradually lift the far end of the punch as

you push the metal in against the stone. Your intent is to push the entire height of the wall, from the girdle to the top of the rim, tightly against the stone. If instead you mistakenly place the punch on the upper edge of the rim, you will only roll the edge

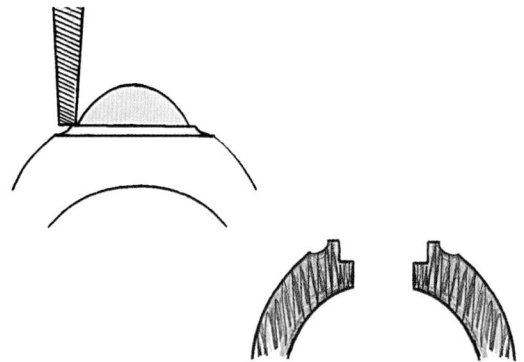

Prepare the area around the seat with files, then press the rim down using a tool held almost vertically.

over, leaving a gap between stone and rim wall. Remember to check that the stone lies level and true, reversing the ring on the mandrel repeatedly.

Once the stone is locked into position at these key points, repeat the process, bringing in the rest of the rim. Your last few passes with the punch should advance sideways along the rim, locking it smoothly against the stone. Be sure to hold the punch in the proper alignment; at no time should the punch come in contact with the stone. At this point, if the stone you are setting is a cabochon, the still slightly raised rim will look like a low bezel rising up from the surface of the ring. It you are working with a faceted stone, the rim will be substantially less pronounced because of the shallower profile of the crown of the stone. You are now ready for the second hammering operation that will compress and eliminate the raised rim.

If you are setting a cabochon, place the punch vertically on the upper edge of the rim (which, because of the stone's steep slope will be almost horizontal). Hold the tool so the wider side lies along the rim, just barely touching the stone. Tap the tool with a series of light blows, allowing the tool to float across the rim, flattening, smoothing, and compressing it. During this process, the tool will just barely touch the stone, which is what guides the action along. As long as you hold the punch vertically, and are careful not to tilt the far end of the punch away from you, the force of the blows will compress the rim down flush with the surface of the ring. If you work methodically, advancing with a smooth, continuous motion, the punch will produce a relatively flat, clean path requiring little cleanup. If, however, you allow the punch to rock side to side, or you repeatedly lift and replace it as you work around the stone, it will leave a chattered trail that will require a lot more attention.

If your stone is faceted, the positioning of the punch is a bit different. The punch is still held vertically, but should never be allowed to touch the stone. Any direct contact of hardened steel against crisp facet edges can only result in irreparable damage to the stone. Because the slope of the crown is shallower than that of a cabochon, the rim will have been hammered over at a correspondingly acute angle. This means that the plane of the rim's original flat upper edge, now lying perpendicular to the stone's surface, will be almost vertical (whereas it is almost horizontal in the case of a cabochon). Don't try to hold the punch against this steeply inclined plane. Instead, hold it atop the raised outer edge

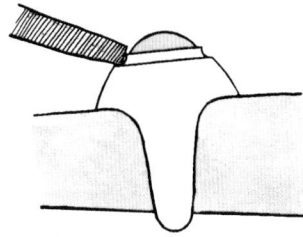

Start pressing the rim over a cab with the punch held almost horizontal.

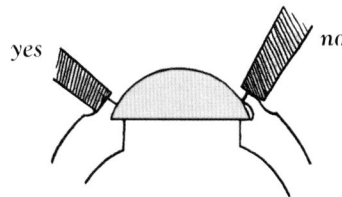

Gather material from the base of the socket so you don't create a void at the base of the stone.

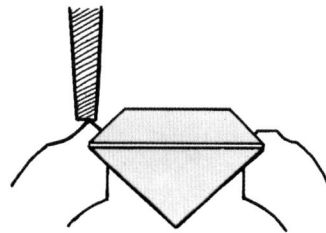

When setting a faceted stone, the tool never touches the gem. Instead, hold it along the raised outer edge of the rim.

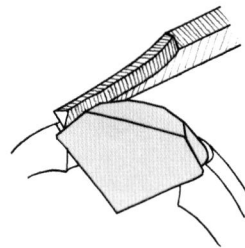

After setting, slide a flat graver gently around the stone to make a clean and bright rim immediately touching the stone.

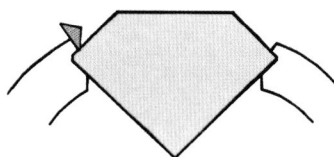

This cross section shows the proper placement of the graver for bright cutting a reflective rim.

of the rim, being careful not to let the punch come into contact with the stone. It is often safer to leave the rim raised a bit, and to use a file to blend it into the surface, rather than to try to hammer too close to the stone.

Dressing the Hammered Area

If you have hammered properly, this setting won't require much cleanup. For cabochons, I like to dress the hammered area with the fine-cut (#4/0), safe-edged barrette needle file described earlier. I can file right up to the stone, confident that the file's smooth, polished edges won't damage the stone, and the fine file marks will require only a light buffing to remove. When filing, use light, overlapping strokes. Aim for a smooth, uniform, slightly convex surface. If the filed surface is too coarse to proceed directly to buffing, you can further refine the area with the tip of a polished burnisher. I never use abrasive paper or wheels near any stone. Not only are abrasives

unnecessary, but they risk damaging the stone's surface. Even buffing and polishing compounds, including rouges, can mar the surfaces of many gemstones if used too aggressively. Whenever possible, I use only rouge with a 1" diameter miniature hard felt buff, mounted in my flex shaft, to do this polishing. By applying rouge only to the outer edge of this wheel, not to its sides, I can buff right up to the edge of the stone without having to worry about marring its surface.

Cleaning up around the perimeter of a faceted stone usually requires one additional step. After filing to refine and blend the area as close to the stone as is safely possible (remember—don't allow the teeth of files to hit facet edges), use your flat graver to trim and bright cut the inner edge of the rim. This will remove ragged edges, and give the gypsy setting a crisp, neat appearance. I usually buff the filed surface first, bright cut, and then lightly re-buff so as not to round off cut edges.

Jim Cotter | Ring
Platinum, diamond
photo: Shane McComber

Roman Settings

As mentioned earlier, there is a variant style of gypsy setting called Roman setting. The major difference lies in the manner in which the stone is hammered into place. Instead of using a flat-ended punch to compress the metal around the stone, a Roman setting uses a polished punch with a domed, rectangular face. This punch creates a shallow trench around the stone.

Rather than filing a preliminary furrow to isolate a ridge of metal, the rounded punch creates the groove and simultaneously compresses the metal against the stone. The rounded face of the punch is held just outside, and parallel to, the edge of the rim. The far end of the tool is tilted out slightly so the force of the blow pushes the inner wall against the stone. As with the gypsy setting, this operation is done in stages: first push in the strategic compass points to lock the stone in position, then work between those points to connect them and to create a continuous, shallow groove. Reverse the ring on the mandrel repeatedly.

Once a continuous groove is established, and the metal rim has been uniformly tightened against the stone, hold the punch vertically in the groove and hammer lightly along the recessed track in successive passes until the furrow is smooth and regular. If the hammering is done carefully and methodically, little clean up is required. Any stray punch marks outside the groove are simply filed away. Buff the groove with a small felt flex shaft wheel that has been contoured to fit. Final buffing should be done with a light touch to retain the crispness and definition of the ridgeline created where the outer edge of the concave groove meets the convex surface of the ring surrounding it.

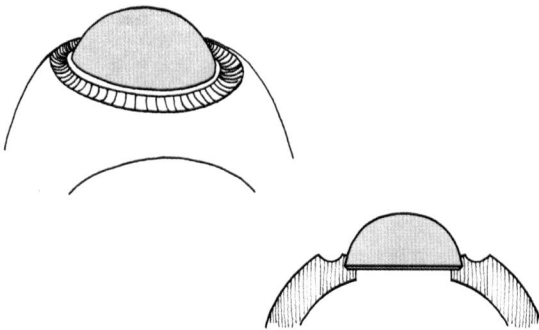

In a Roman setting, the first step is to create a trough around the stone. The inner wall of this trough (the one closest to the stone) will then be handled like a bezel.

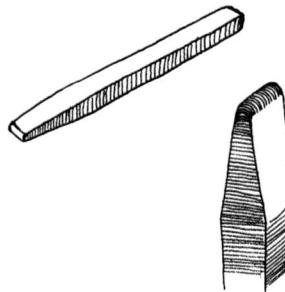

It is possible to file a trough, but more efficient and less wasteful of material to create the groove with a rounded punch

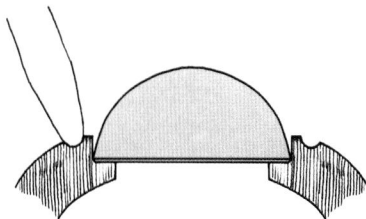

With the ring securely gripped, tap the tool around the stone, angled at first and then held vertically.

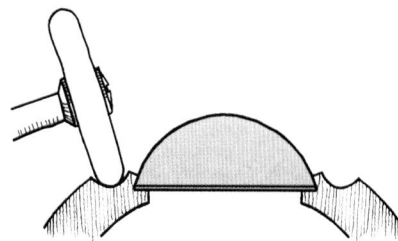

Run a polishing wheel against a file to contour the edge so it fits into the groove. Use this to smooth away hammer marks; follow with conventional buffing.

False Gypsy Setting
(also called Burnished, Flush, Flush-Mount, Rubbed, or Snap Settings)

As I pointed out earlier, the gypsy settings wannabe look-alike, though similar in appearance at first glance, is actually a totally unique, stand-alone setting with more differences than similarities to its namesake. Because the term false gypsy is so misleading, I prefer flush or flush mount, both of which more accurately describe the technique, and acknowledge its distinct character.

Unlike the true gypsy setting, flush mounts only work with faceted stones and require no hammering, which makes them ideally suited to thin gauge sheet metal constructions and many other jewelry forms besides rings. They are fast, simple, and secure and can be used singly or in groups. They are equally at home on flat or curved surfaces. Because of these many desirable qualities, flush mounts have become very popular.

Flush-Mounting a Stone

There are three major considerations that you have to take into account when you flush-mount a stone:
- Durability
- Stone Size
- Metal Thickness

Durability refers to a combination of hardness and resistance to fracture or chipping; size in this case refers to the girdle diameter of the stone; and the relevant thickness is, of course, the gauge of the metal where the stone will reside. The durability of the stone, and its ability to stand up to the rigors of being forcefully pressed into a tight fitting seat and being rubbed with a hardened steel burnisher is a primary determinant of its suitability. Generally speaking, most faceted stones are hard enough, but hardness alone is not sufficient. All the quartz family stones (amethyst, citrine, etc.) and certain other materials like peridot and garnet can be easily damaged when pressed into place too enthusiastically, or by excess pressure from a burnisher. Emeralds are very hard, but very fragile. Diamonds, sapphires, rubies, spinels, and most synthetics, on the other hand, are durable, and usually hold up very well. Once you have determined that your stones meet the durability requirement, you must now consider the other two issues.

One of the very first things you discover as you venture into the realm of stonesetting is this irrefutable fact: size really does matter. There is a very real correlation between a stone's size and the practical, realistic setting alternatives available to you. This, in great part, explains why there are so many different options. There is no one-size-fits-all solution. You would no more entertain the idea of building a four prong basket setting for a tiny, 2 mm faceted stone than you would try to stitch set a 30 mm diameter bullet-cut cabochon. If your stone is too large or too small for one kind of setting, then you choose a more appropriate alternative. This stone size limitation factor is a very important consideration with flush-mounts.

Hypothetically, you can flush-mount a faceted stone of any size, but in reality, the bigger the stone, the bigger the challenge. As the diameter of a stone increases, the girdle increases in width, and the crown gets higher. In an ideal situation, the stone's table lies flush with the surface, but with larger diameter stones, the table will end up noticeably above the surface. When the table is level with the surface, the stone is protected from exposure to the random bumps, knocks, and gradual abrasion associated with normal wear. The tiny rim of metal burnished down over its girdle is, likewise, shielded from wear, and is virtually indestructible and permanent, except, perhaps, against a purposeful assault to dig the stone out. The entire surface of the metal surrounding the stone, as well as most of the stone's own crown, would

Hughes-Bosca
Temple Rings
18k gold, platinum,
natural black diamond
crystal, white diamond
Tahitian pearl.
photo: Dean Powell

have to be abraded away in order for the stone to fall out.

A larger, higher stone, however, is a sitting duck. Every impact, no matter how minor, wears away at its surface and loosens its grip. In time, it is destined to become, first, a frosted cabochon, and then, a memory. Attempting to resolve the problem by cutting a deeper seat doesn't work, because the metal would have to be substantially thicker in order to recess the stone sufficiently, and, even were this feasible, it would be virtually impossible to burnish down the unusually high ledge above the girdle. In a case like this, it is better to pursue an alternate setting option.

In my experience, stones ranging from 1.5 mm to 4 mm can be successfully flush-mounted, with 2.5 mm to 3 mm being ideal. Stones less than 1.5 mm in diameter can barely be seen and are hardly worth the effort (I must confess that this sentiment is purely personal, a reflection of the combination of the dimming sight and stiffer fingers that have developed in my, er... mature years, and the increasing time spent crawling around on my knees, with my cheek pressed against my studio floor,

trying to find the errant little devils as they gleefully play Hide and Seek...). Stones with a four millimeter diameter are already pushing the limits, and anything larger entails the problems mentioned above.

Adjusting Local Metal Thickness

Even with stones that fall within the ideal range, you need sufficiently thick metal to create a deep seat. Usually, 20 gauge metal is sufficient for stones 2 mm or less in diameter, and 18 gauge for larger sizes. For heavier items like bracelets and rings that are fabricated of adequately thick metal, this is not a problem. However, smaller items, such as earrings, pins or pendants, constructed wholly of these gauges could be massive. Because objects like these are usually constructed of thinner gauges, it becomes necessary to thicken the metal where the seat will be cut. This can be done in several ways.

How and where to thicken the metal depends a lot on your design. This is an aesthetic as well as functional design decision. You have two options: you can add metal to the front or you can add it to the back. If you can integrate a raised pad as a decorative element into your design, simply solder it onto the surface. The gauge of this added layer should bring the local thickness to your target goal. If you deem a visible add-on to be obtrusive or distracting, add the metal thickener to the back. In this case, the easiest solution is a small jump ring, approximately 0.5 mm larger in diameter than your stone. Again, the guage of the wire should bring the total to the requisite local thickness. I usually construct with 24 gauge sheet metal, and find that a pad or ring of 22 or 24 gauge works well.

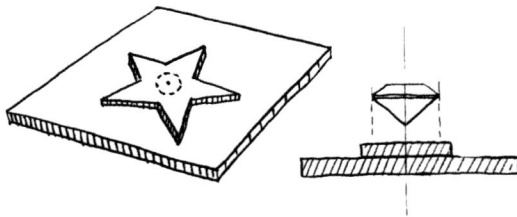

One way to thicken a piece in preparation for a Flush-Mount Setting is to solder an ornamental piece on the face of a sheet.

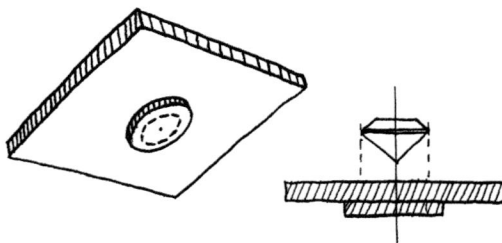

Another common device is to solder a simple piece onto the back.

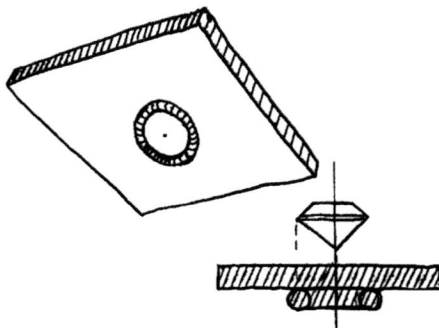

In some cases, it is possible to thicken the sheet by soldering a ring of metal that will provide support for the bearing and protect the culet.

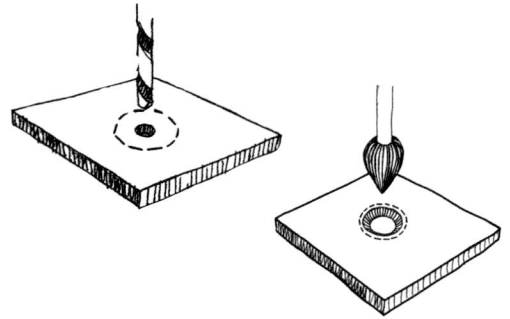

Drill a center hole, then enlarge it with a bud or flame bur, checking frequently so you don't go too far.

Cutting the Seat

At the location where you plan to set the stone, start by drilling a guide hole smaller than the diameter of your stone. I usually use a #55 or #56 bit. If you soldered a jump ring to the back surface, drill the hole from the back, centered inside the ring. Then, open up the hole with a small bud or flame bur until the tapered hole is just slightly smaller in diameter than the stone. This will facilitate the actual cutting of the seat, and eases the burden on the setting bur.

You can use a variety of burs to cut a seat. Hart, ball, and stonesetting burs will all work well, but you must remember that a tight-fitting seat is absolutely critical. If the seat is cut properly, the stone will need to be seated with light pressure. Sometimes, you will actually hear a slight click as the stone snaps into position (hence the term snap setting). If the fit is loose, it will be extremely difficult, if not outright impossible, to burnish it in place. It will tip and misalign from the pressure of the tip of the burnisher, and you may not be able to force down enough metal from the rim to go over the girdle. Remember also to select a bur very slightly smaller in diameter than the stone, because burs always cut a path slightly larger than their own diameter. You can always enlarge a seat if need be, but you can't make it smaller.

If you use a Hart bur, you can start the

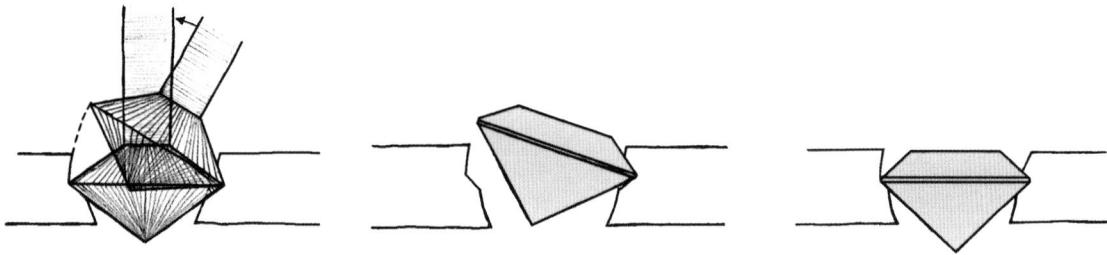

The steps in creating a seat with a Hart bur. Angle the tool as you enter the hole, then tilt the spinning bur vertical to carve the opposite side of the seat. The stone is similarly tilted into the setting, where it almost snaps into place.

cut at a slight angle, creating a shallow, undercut groove just below the surface on one side of the seat. As soon as the edge of the bur starts the undercut, simultaneously rotate the handpiece upright, perpendicular to the surface, so that the bur continues straight down into the metal to the desired depth. This takes a little practice, but helps to anchor the stone during burnishing. The stone is inserted at the same shallow angle so that part of the girdle fits into the undercut groove. This locks it in place while you burnish the other side.

If you are using a stonesetting bur, which produces an angular shelf corresponding to the profile of the pavilion, you just have to be sure that you cut the seat truly parallel to the surface so that the stone's table rests level with the surface. Also, because a stonesetting bur cuts sideways as well as straight down, be extra careful not to overcut, which will produce a loose fit.

I prefer to use a ball bur to cut the seat for several reasons. They are less expensive than either Hart or stonesetting burs, they come in a greater range of sizes, and they guarantee a seat that will accommodate most any stone. Many small stones are poorly cut and have uneven girdles, tables that are not parallel to the girdle, or are not truly round. Hart and stonesetting burs cut a specifically angled seat, and if this seat does not correspond exactly to anydiscrepancies in the stone, the table will not be plumb, and this tilt will be immediately

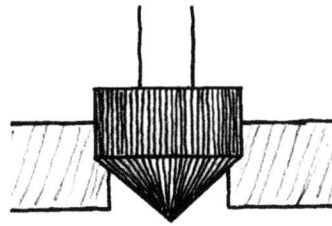

Seat cut properly.

Seat not level.

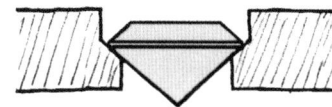

Seat cut too large and too deep.

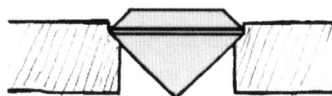

Seat cut too shallow.

You can use a stonesetting bur to cut a seat, as shown in the first drawing. The other illustrations show some common mistakes.

visible. A ball bur, on the other hand, produces a rounded seat rather than a defined shelf, which allows the stone, despite irregularities stemming from improper cutting, to be inserted at whatever angle is needed to insure that its table lies properly. Once pressed into position, it creates its own seat, and requires only the final burnishing. Regardless of which bur you use, cut the seat in stages, constantly checking the depth and the fit. Stop when the seat is sufficiently deep to permit the stone to rest at the proper level. Since the fit should be tight, you will probably find it necessary to press your wax cone firmly onto the stone and then jerk it away quickly to free it. If the stone is really tight, and the wax won't pull it free, you can, as a last resort, push it out from the back. Never do this with a steel tool, because you might chip the stone. I usually use a round toothpick with the end nipped flat with flush cutters.

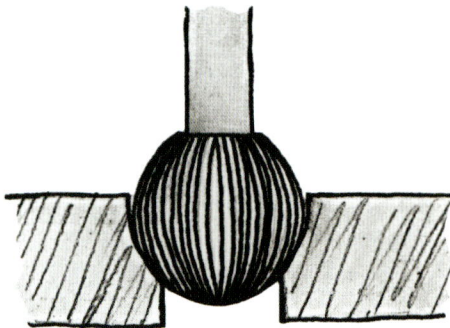

Ball burs have the advantage of low cost and wide range of sizes. In general they cut slower than Hart burs, and this can be an advantage so you don't accidentally go too far.

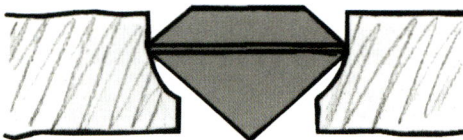

The other advantage of the generalized, rounded seat made with a ball bur is that it accommodates poorly cut and irregular stones.

Alan Perry | Man's Ring
18k, amethyst, green tourmaline.
photo: Robert Diamante

Burnishing
The Special Burnisher

Though you can burnish the stone in place with a standard burnisher, you may find this tool a bit awkward, and if it slips it will leave a nasty scratch across the surface. There is a better, homemade alternative that is fast, simple, and inexpensive. This miniature burnisher is made from the shank of a worn-out flex shaft bur. If you are like me, you probably have dozens of these dull, toothless burs lying around. I am always reluctant to throw anything away, sure that someday I'll find a use for it. And, I usually do.

Use a pair of old utility pliers to snap off the now useless head of the bur. With a small flame, heat about a quarter inch of this broken tip to a dull red, then let the shank air cool. This will anneal the steel, allowing you to reshape it. When the steel has cooled completely, chuck the shank into your flex shaft with the annealed end sticking out. Now, use an old flat file to shape the end while it spins in the handpiece. I save all of my old files as they wear out, and use them for jobs such as this, which eliminates wear and tear on my newer, sharper files.

File the tip with rounded, curving sides terminating in a slightly blunted point. The curved profile of the tip is important for proper burnishing. Once you have shaped the tip properly, you can sand it with sanding sticks. I find that a final sanding against a worn #600 grit paper surface produces a nearly polished surface. I give it a final polish, still in the handpiece, with a felt stick charged with white diamond compound. Alternatively, you can remove the burnisher from the handpiece and buff it on a polishing arbor. Using this flex shaft method to make the burnisher takes mere minutes from start to finish.

I don't usually bother to harden and temper these miniature burnishers. Even unhardened, they are substantially harder than the precious metals upon which they will be used. They do, however, require handles. I have, on occasion, simply secured the shank in a pin vise. This works, but depending on the design of the particular pin vise, and the manner in which its jaws are tightened, it can sometimes prove a bit clumsy and uncomfortable. I usually only resort to a pin vise handle when I am teaching a workshop. When I am in my studio, I prefer using a 5" (12.7 cm) section of ¼" (6 mm) or ⅜" (9.5 mm) diameter dowel. I drill a hole, slightly smaller in diameter than the shank of the burnisher, into the end of the dowel deeply enough so that when the end of the shank is imbedded into this hole, about ¾" (19 mm) of the tip is left exposed.

Burnishing the Stone In Place

Press the stone into position (Click!), and check carefully to ensure that its table, and the metal surface in which it resides, are

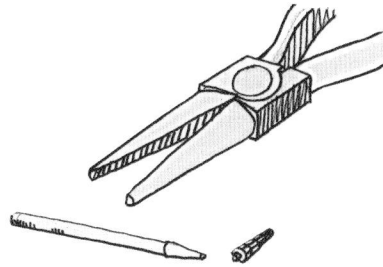

To make a miniature burnisher from a wornout bur, start by snapping off the cutting tip.

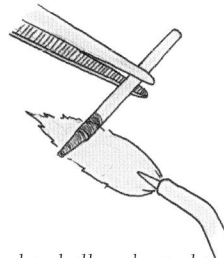

Heat the tip to red and allow the steel to cool slowly to room temperature to anneal it.

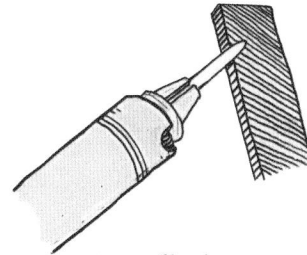

Grip the tool in a flex shaft and rotate it against a file, then on successively finer grits of abrasive paper, and eventually on a polishing stick.

After polishing, the burnisher should look like this.

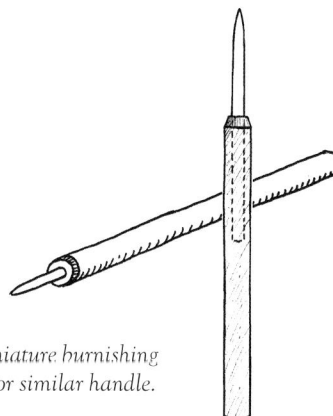

Mount the miniature burnishing tip in a dowel or similar handle.

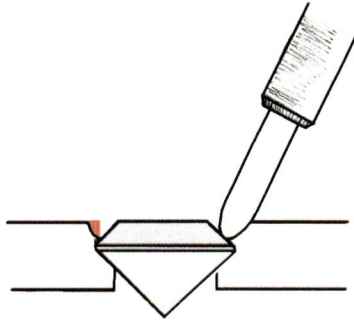

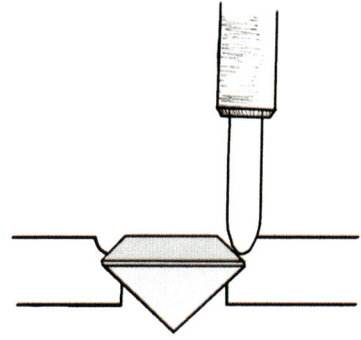

Start with the burnisher held at a 45° angle, pressing the sharp edge (in red) onto the stone. As work proceeds, raise the angle of the tool to near vertical.

true and level. Holding the burnisher at a 45° angle, begin locking the stone into position by rubbing down the edge of the metal rim at several locations around the stone. Use light pressure so as not to tip the stone. Observe closely, and you will see that the sharp rim is now beveled down and very slightly over the girdle at these points. Test to make sure the stone is locked into place by pressing the wax cone and tugging sharply. If the stone pulls free, you didn't burnish enough. Replace the stone and re-burnish. When the stone refuses to budge, complete the burnishing all the way around the stone. Be careful not to press the blunt point against the stone. The pressure as you burnish should be focused against the metal rim. Once the rim is consistently burnished all the way round, change the orientation of the burnishers handle so that it is almost vertical. Run the tip lightly in a circular path around the perimeter of the stone several times. This will produce a uniform, reflective, inward-sloping rim.

After each use, I examine the tip of my burnisher. You'll recall that I don't harden my burnisher, so it sometimes gets very slightly abraded from contact with the facets of a stone, no matter how carefully it is used. I simply give it a quick touch up on my polishing arbor, and it is set to go.

Channel Settings versus False Channel Settings

Channel setting, like gypsy setting, suffers from its own identity crisis. True channel setting, as with gypsy setting, is most commonly employed on rings, and is characterized by a row of small, same-sized stones, usually faceted, set girdle-to-girdle into a recessed trench, or channel that runs along the upper, outer surface of the ring. This channel may go all the way around the ring, or it may be partial. Individual seats are cut for each stone, and then the row of stones is secured by pushing the outer walls of the channel (the sides of the ring) over the opposing edges of the stones.

True channel setting, like plate, illusion, and pavé setting, is a very popular commercial technique used to cover a surface with diamonds and precious stones. As such, it really falls outside the purview of this book. Channel setting is more about a technical procedure for securing

In true channel setting, an individual seat is cut for each stone. This setting is most commonly used on rings.

multiple stones than it is about designing and creating unique, original metal structures with which to hold them. Like pavé, it relies on one single setting operation, repeated numerous times. The prototypical channel ring blank is usually a rather simple, featureless band, mass-produced, die-struck, or cast. Though it provides a secure receptacle for the stones it holds, it provides little or no option for creative interpretation, variation, or individualization. It's all about the stones, not about the ring itself. If you wish to learn the channel setting technique, there are many commercial diamond-setting books, manuals and videos available. In the context of this book, however, it is the channel setting's false cognate, the false channel, that is of greater interest.

False Channel Setting

False channel settings, despite a superficial resemblance to their genuine counterparts, are actually tension settings. Instead of metal being pushed over the stones to lock them in place in a rigid channel, the stones are locked into position in opposing grooves pre-cut into a U-shaped channel of springy metal. These are similar to tension settings, which will be discussed later.

Like false gypsy settings, false channel settings are best suited to relatively small faceted stones. Because the U-shaped channel must be made of metal of sufficient thickness to permit the cutting of the opposed interior grooves and to provide adequate tension, and because the depth must be deep enough to allow both clearance for the lower half of the stone, small faceted stones (round, rectangular, and square) ranging in size from about 3.5 mm to 5 mm across work best. I find 4 mm diameter stones ideal. Creating a channel for larger or smaller stones can be problematic. A channel for smaller stones may prove too small to permit the cutting of the grooves, and larger stones require an overly wide, deep and heavy channel (its depth increases in direct proportion to its width).

The production of the U-shaped channel, and the subsequent securing of the stones are in theory quite simple. The devil is in the details, however. The visual simplicity of the setting belies its technical challenge. The difficulties start when you try to bend a little piece of sheet into a parallel-sided "U" of exactly the correct dimensions and of uniform profile. Then you are faced with the challenge of filing two straight, level, evenly deep notches on the inner walls. Hmmm... perhaps it's not so simple after all.

Making the Channel

Leverage makes all the difference in the world when it comes to bending small items. If I handed you a piece of wire a mere millimeter in thickness (18 gauge), but only 3 mm in length and asked you to bend it with only your fingers, I'm certain that you'd be hard-pressed to do so even though it is thin wire. But, if that same millimeter-thick wire were a foot in length, even were it of steel, you would be able to bend it easily. The leverage provided by extra length simplifies the process.

Start with a strip of metal as wide as the combined diameter of the stones you wish to set. For example, lets say you plan to set four 4 mm diameter stones. You will need a 16 mm wide strip (4 x 4 mm = 16 mm). I always use either 20 gauge or 18 gauge sheet for false channels. Both are thick enough to permit the cutting of the seat grooves while being thin enough to bend reasonably easily. Since silver sheet comes in standard six inch width, simply cut the 16 mm strip the entire width of the sheet. This length will provide sufficient leverage, it will yield multiple channels, and any small tail end pieces will become casting scrap. This strip should be annealed.

The distance between the inner, parallel walls of the channel must be a bit smaller than the diameter of the stones

Steps in Making a False Channel Setting

Start with a strip of metal as wide as the final setting will be, or even a little wider.

Find a sturdy cylinder slightly smaller than the diameter of the stones.

Temporarily secure the rod to the strip of metal to hold it in position.

Grip the strip in a ring clamp...

... like this.

wood block

With a block of wood, lever the strip down over the cylinder.

The goal is to create a smooth bend with a uniform radius that is slightly less than the diameter of the stones.

Cut the U-shaped element off the strip. This will become the channel.

Use a sharp dividers to mark the location of the groove that will hold the girdles of the gems. Mark both sides.

Cut precisely along the scribed line with a taut sawblade.

Use a triangular needle file to create a groove for the stones.

The completed channel unit should look like this.

to allow the stones to fit into the recessed grooves. I usually estimate approximately ½ mm depth for each groove; ½ mm on each side equals a total of 1 mm, so the spacing between the walls for a 4 mm stone should be 3 mm. You'll need a cylindrical mandrel that is the exact size of the groove you are making, which is 3 mm in this example. The smooth shank of a drill bit works perfectly, and a standard drill index provides sixty different sizes. Simply use your millimeter gauge to locate the proper drill bit.

To bend the channel, temporarily tape the shank of the drill bit at one end of the strip, perpendicular to the lengthwise axis of the strip, and far enough in from the end to produce the desired height of the channel. Be generous. You can always reduce the height of the channel later, but you can't make it taller. Secure this temporary assembly into the flat end of the ring clamp, with the drill bit aligned with, and resting just below, the ring clamp edge. The long, protruding end of the strip should be sticking straight out of the clamp. You have just created a bending jig. The ring clamp serves as a handle, and all that's left now is to make the bend.

I recommend using the flat end of a small piece of wood (at least as wide as the strip), pressed flat against the metal strip where it emerges from the ring clamp, as a pushing tool to bend the strip. This insures that the strip remains flat and straight. If you try to push or pull with your fingers, the metal will curve along its length. Push the strip over until it meets the top of the opposite jaw of the ring clamp (approximately 90°). Remove the still-taped strip/drill bit and lay it, long-leg-down, flat on the bench top. Using the wooden pusher, continue bending the short, uppermost leg around the mandrel until it is parallel to the long leg. When you are satisfied with the spacing, and the legs are in proper alignment, remove the tape and the drill bit. Using the edge of the shorter leg as a

guide, carefully scribe a line along which you will now saw to separate the channel from the longer leg.

File the upper edges of the channel to level and adjust the height of the channel. Sand these edges to remove the file marks and to deburr the edges. With a small pair of dividers, mark off lines on the inner face of each leg of the channel, 1½–2 mm below, and parallel to, the edges. Use a jewelers saw to make a shallow cut, just deep enough to start the edge of a triangular needle file, at both ends of both lines. Working back and forth, gradually begin filing towards the center from both edges until the notches meet and form a single groove.

It is critical that both of these angular grooves are uniformly deep and in perfect alignment with each other when you are finished filing. If the depth of these opposing cuts is not precise and consistent, the stones cannot be uniformly compressed and locked into position when they are all inserted. If there are spots where the groove is shallower, some of the stones will act as wedges, forcing the deeper cut areas apart, making all the other stones loose. Likewise, if the grooves are not in perfect alignment, the stones will not sit level, with their tables in the same plane. It is also imperative that all of the stones be exactly the same diameter. Nominal sizes are often just that. Not all 4 mm stones are created equal. Buy a dozen 4 mm stones and they may range as much as a quarter of a millimeter larger or smaller. Measure, measure, measure!

The initial file cuts should be shallow. At the beginning, there is a tendency to start out a bit deeper at both ends, nearer the edges of the channel. This stems from the slight inclination of the needle file as you start the file in the saw cut. Once you have established a single, continuous groove, inspect it closely. It's likely that the cut will be wider at the outer ends and narrower in the middle. As you continue to deepen the cut, make sure to keep the edge of the file in full contact with the entire length of the groove. Don't seesaw back and forth, but file forward with long, straight strokes, until each groove is uniformly wide and deep, both penetrating into the wall about half its thickness. For this final filing, use the straightest edge of the file. Most triangular needle files are slightly curved near the tip, and straighter near the handle.

Test fit a stone periodically—you don't want to file away too much metal.

At this point, trial fit the stones to check the fit, and to determine if the upper edges of the channel legs need to be trimmed. The rims should be level with the tables of the stones. To press the stones into place, position one end of the channel against the front of your bench to anchor it. Start the first stone into the grooves and push it all the way to the far end. To push, use a flat-ended pusher that will not mar the setting or the stones. I use a reshaped toothbrush handle for this. The flexible plastic is soft enough to be safe, but resilient enough to do the job.

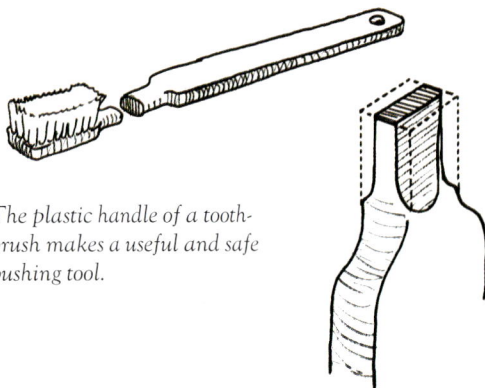

The plastic handle of a toothbrush makes a useful and safe pushing tool.

Insert all the stones and check each one with a pair of pointed tweezers to make sure it is tight. A loose stone means one of two things: either the grooves are true, but the stones are not the same diameter, or the stones are the same diameter, but the grooves are not true. If you measured carefully, it means a little remedial filing is in order. Remove the stones to make any adjustments. Never try to file or sand the upper edges of the setting with the stones in place! Hardened file teeth and abrasive grits can chip, scratch, or abrade most stones in the blink of an eye.

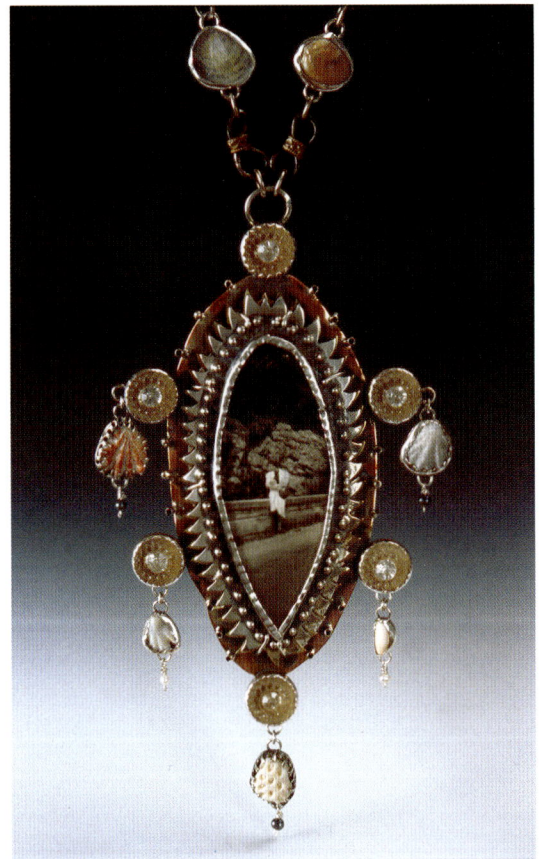

Kristin Diener | Cotton Plant
Sterling, fine silver, brass, buttons, mica, shells, pearls, road atlas, plexiglas
9" x 5" x 5"
photo: Margot Geist

Design Applications

When the setting meets your approval, but before the stones are ready to press into final position, it's time to attach findings or install the channel into a jewelry piece. I personally find these false channel settings ideal as small pendants or earrings. For use as pendants, I often drill a small hole (below the bottoms of the stones!) through which I can thread a chain or neck wire. For earrings, I solder posts on the back. Obviously, it goes without saying that you should consider, and determine, exactly how you plan to use the settings before you make them. Doing so affords you the opportunity to allow extra height, thickness, etc., so that your modifications won't structurally weaken the setting. Don't worry about annealing a false channel if you solder. You will still be able to reestablish sufficient spring tension when you are ready to secure the stones. Pre-polish at this point.

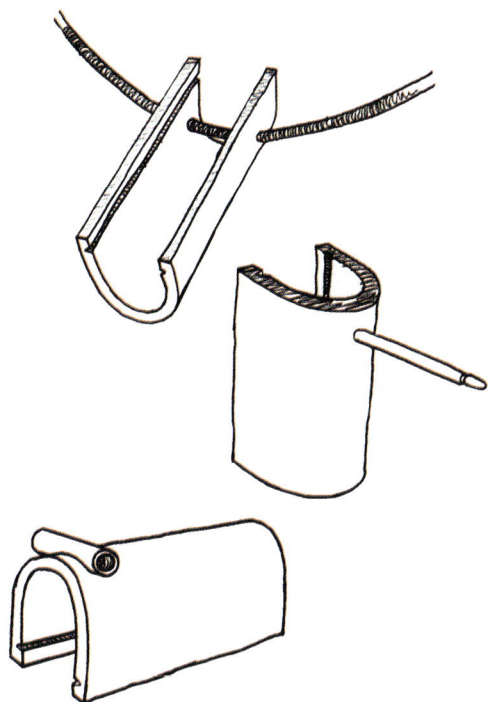

The Final Setting of the Stones

Lay the setting on its side and, with your wooden pusher, press to close the "U" just a bit. Flip the setting over, and do the same thing from the other side. This will establish sufficient spring tension to secure the stones.

In the same manner that you inserted the stones when you were trial fitting, press them into final position. Particularly in the case of earrings and pendants, neither of which is subjected to heavy wear and tear, the spring tension alone would probably be sufficient. However, there is one last step that, in addition to the tension, makes the setting even more secure. With a #50 round graver, raise a stitch in one of the grooves at each end of the row of stones. It is only necessary to raise one single small stitch at each end. These stitches will wedge against the girdles of the end stones, preventing the row of stones from moving in the grooves. Because they are small, and hidden down in the notches, they will not be visible. Give the finished setting its final polish (or tumble, which I find works quite well), and you are finished.

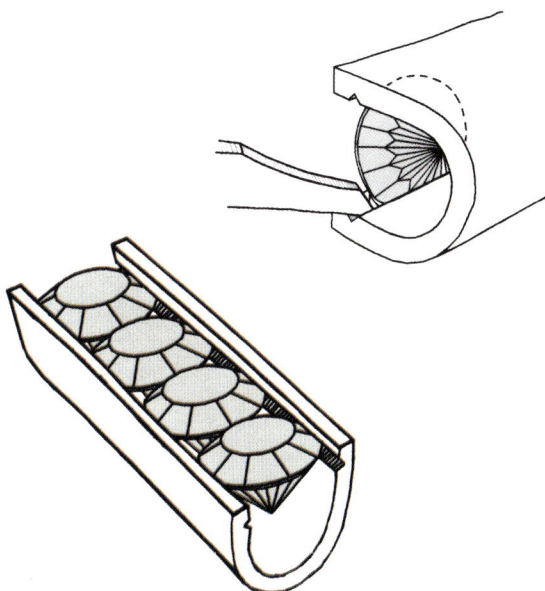

The false channel settings lend themselves to earrings, pendants, and other familiar jewelry items.

Once the stones are properly positioned, lock them in place by raising a stitch at each end of the grooves with a round graver.

Michael Boyd | Green Beryl Ring
18k and 22k gold, emeralsd, black sapphire, tourmaline, citrine

photo: Seve Bigley

Chapter 7
Beads, Pearls, and Gem Balls

Let me begin this chapter with some definitions, exclusions, and a clarification of the specific topics that I will be addressing. Let's start with beads. Beads are commonly fashioned from many materials, including natural and manmade varieties. Natural beads can be made from precious, semiprecious or ornamental gemstones, or from organic materials such as amber, coral, ivory, bone, wood, nut, or shell. Pearls, technically beads when drilled all the way through, fall into the organic category as well. Manmade beads are typically created from glass, ceramic, plastic, paper, or metal. Regardless of source, all beads share one very important common denominator—they all have a hole.

All true beads are drilled all the way through, usually at their midsections. This through-drilled hole is the universal, and most identifiable, characteristic defining "bead-ness." This hole, of course, is what allows beads to be strung. This hole

usually makes it difficult or unappealing to set beads in the kinds of setting discussed in this book for cabs and faceted stones. Even if you are successful in concealing one hole, the other often ends up in full view. This tiny little tunnel excludes all beads from further consideration here, placing them outside the purview of the stonesetter, and, more appropriately, in the realm of the stringer.

Our focus, rather, is on undrilled, or, more often, partially drilled pearls and gem balls. Further, I am limiting our consideration specifically to spherical pearls and gem balls because baroques, free forms, tumbled irregulars, and the like are the anomalies of stonesetting. Each represents a unique, one-of-a-kind challenge, and, basically, we simply have to figure out some manner of securing them as best we can. Spherical pearls and gem balls, on the other hand, are a standard part of the jewelry world, widely available in calibrated sizes from many sources.

Because spherical pearls and gem balls are, in a sense, fraternal twins, similar in form, handling and application, differing mainly in color and composition, from this point on, I am going to refer to pearls only for the balance of the chapter. This is for simplicity's sake only—anything I say about pearls is true for gem balls as well, unless specifically noted otherwise.

Setting Challenges and Considerations

Pearls pose unique setting challenges. Their smooth, spherical surfaces afford little or no grip for prong and bezel settings. A prong setting could hold a pearl, but the pearl could turn like a ball bearing in its socket, damaging the surface as it chafes against the metal. Bezels are an equally unsuitable solution because they would require excessive wall height to extend above the equator of the pearl. Not only would this look visually massive, but it would hide more than half of the pearl, which is hardly the definition of a successful setting.

Attempting to simply epoxy a pearl to a surface is an equally poor solution. Epoxy alone, no matter how good the quality, would never hold the pearl securely. A pearl's relative mass with respect to its limited contact to a background surface, combined with the poor adhesion offered by both non-porous surfaces (pearl / metal) is a formula for certain disaster. Like a golf ball on a tee, it only takes one good sideways blow to send the ill-fated orb sailing off into the void.

Pearls are relatively soft and fragile. They scratch and abrade easily, and are often unsuited to the rigors of daily wear jewelry applications like rings and bracelets. The same is true of many ornamental gem balls, particularly those of organic composition. They are too soft to be cut, set or classified as true gem material, but possess pleasing color or pattern. Consider very carefully the physical environ-ment to which they will be exposed. Will they be subjected to excessive knocking and banging about? As with any kind of setting, think carefully about the best and safest way to secure the pearl.

There are three simple and time-honored solutions that have been used to hold pearls for generations. These are a cup, a peg, and a marriage of the two. When used in conjunction with a high-quality epoxy, these options produce a stable, reliable means of affixing a pearl in place. The determination of which to use depends on two major considerations: (1) is the pearl partially drilled? (2) In what environment will the pearl reside? To answer the first question, simply examine the pearl.

Many, but not all, pearls are partially drilled. The hole penetrates only half to three-quarters of the sphere's diameter. This hole allows the pearl to be fitted onto a small wire post, or peg that has been soldered to a background surface. If the pearl or gem ball is undrilled, it will not, quite obviously, permit the introduction of a peg. This automatically eliminates two possibilities, leaving the cup as the sole choice. If it is drilled, you have two choices, and it is then a question of deciding which is most appropriate.

Gem balls and pearls are available in three varieties: drilled-through, undrilled, and half-drilled.

Susan Jo Klein | Black and White and Red
18k, sterling, cuprite, hematite, pearls.

photo: Peter Groesbeck

Three Possible Solutions

Option One: The Cup

If your pearl is undrilled, the cup is your sole viable solution. The idea here is to create sufficient surface area to allow a strong epoxy bond—more than would be possible at a tangent point. Make a cup from a small disk by forming it in a dapping block so the curve of the cup precisely matches the curve of the pearl. The cup should be big enough to provide sufficient surface contact for the epoxy, but not so large that it overwhelms the pearl. As a general rule of thumb, a flat disk measuring approximately one-half to two-thirds of the diameter of your pearl, when dapped, will be the right size.

In some designs, the cup is hidden, so a plain surface is all that is needed. If the design calls for the cup to be more visible (for example, if the pearl will hang as a pendant), consider embellishing the

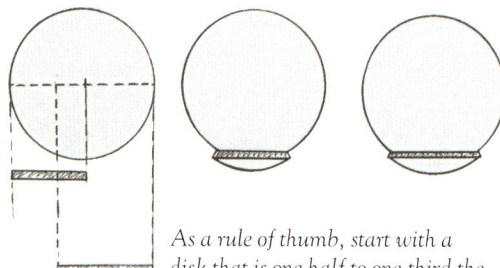

As a rule of thumb, start with a disk that is one half to one-third the diameter of the bead. Dap to match the radius for a perfect fit.

surface, for instance, by piercing, engraving, or roll printing. Another alternative is to create a decorative edge by filing scallops, points, or other ornaments. If you choose this option, make the initial disk a bit larger since some of it will be cut away.

If you do choose to sculpt the perimeter of the cup, do as much sawing and filing as possible while the disk is still flat. It's much easier than trying to do so after it is dapped. Also, when you dap, be careful not to stretch or mar the disk with

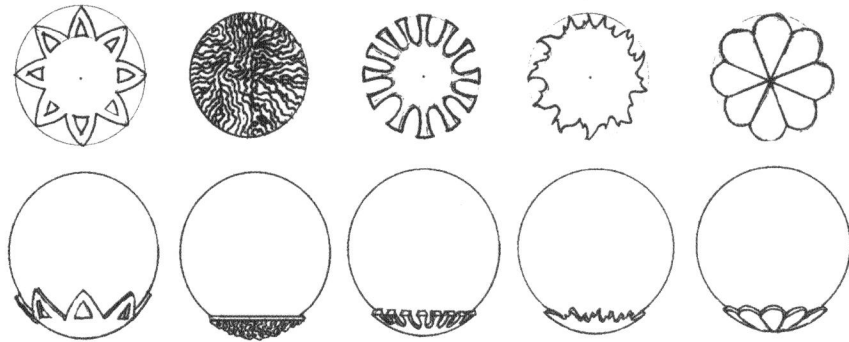

Bead cups offer a great opportunity for creative embellishment. Here are a few of the hundreds of possibilities using only a saw and files.

the punch. I always use a rubber mallet to strike my dapping punches. This prevents mashing the disk from undue force, and keeps the blunt end of the punch from developing a sharp, mushroomed edge. Your intent should be to form the disk, not forge it. Once the cup is properly formed, I scratch the interior surface with the tip of a scriber. This roughened surface provides better grip for the epoxy.

Option Two: The Peg

If your pearl is drilled, you have two additional options for securing it, a peg, or a cup and peg combination. Pegs are, obviously, the simpler of these two solutions,

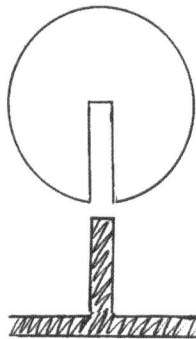

The peg method is simplicity itself, but as with everything that is simple, special care is needed to yield an elegant result.

but have somewhat limited applications when used alone. The location on the body, and the rigors to which the piece of jewelry will be subjected, should be carefully considered. Pins, pendants, and earrings are usually not subject to wear and tear, and are therefore usually good candidates for peg-only attachments.

A peg is simply a short wire that anchors the pearl in position, used in conjunction with epoxy. The gauge of wire you will use for your peg depends on the pearl's drilled hole size. Generally, I'd advise at least 18 or 20 gauge, but the size of the pearl will be the deciding factor. Use the largest gauge the pearl can accommodate. If the hole is too small for the size wire you'd like to use, enlarge it with a drill bit or cylinder bur. A diamond drill will be needed to enlarge the hole in a gem ball. Use a moderately slow speed and use water as a lubricant for both.

I like to roughen or notch a peg before soldering it in place to provide a better grip for the epoxy. Use a small triangular needle file to make shallow notches, thread the wire with a die, or use a twisted square wire. An alternative is to use a pair of dull clippers to gently and repeatedly squeeze the wire to notch the surface. Regardless of what means you choose, I highly recom-

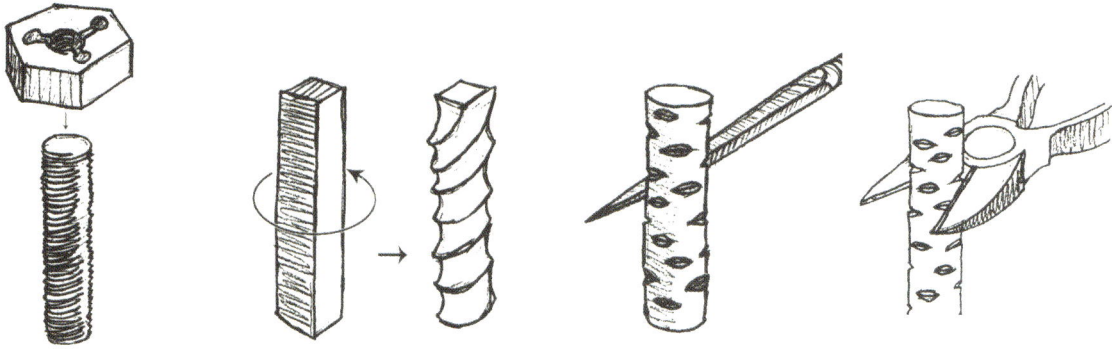

To insure a strong grip for the epoxy, provide a texture on the post in one of these ways.

mend texturing the piece of wire before you solder it in position. Epoxying the pearl is usually the final operation.

When the peg is ready to be soldered into position, drill a small hole to locate and secure the wire. If this is not feasible, make a small, shallow crater with a drill bit or ball bur at the spot where the peg will be attached. This hole or slight depression helps position the base of the peg when soldering, creates more surface contact, and exposes bare metal, which encourages a stronger solder joint. Like steel rebar in a concrete structure, this little peg is going to provide the invisible reinforcement for your epoxied joint so you want it to be as strong as possible.

Option Three: Cup & Peg

As I mentioned earlier, the combined cup and peg system of securing a pearl is simply a marriage of the two preceding methodologies. It encompasses the best features of both, and is the very best solution whenever applicable. The peg provides an anchor inside the pearl, and the cup provides additional surface contact for enhanced epoxy adhesion. Both parts are prepared as described earlier, and are then soldered together. As with all fabricated settings of any sort, always assemble the parts with Hard solder, and then attach to the workpiece with a lower grade of solder.

It won't matter how strong the glue is if the post breaks off. To insure a strong joint, either drill a hole for the wire or use a ball bur to make a rounded depression. Both of these methods increases the contact area between parts.

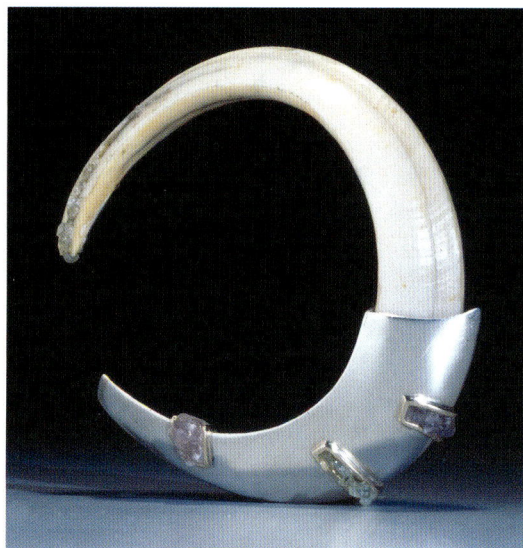

Nicole Jacquard | Bone Bracelet
Sterling, 14k gold, crushed amethyst, blue topaz, bone
photo: Kevin Montague

Split Peg with Wedge

High quality polymer epoxy is a relative newcomer to the jeweler's bench. Before it became widely available, many alternative cements, mastics, gums, natural resins, and glues were used. None of these ever came close to matching the strength and reliability of today's epoxies. Because the early adhesives were too weak to be depended upon, some clever soul invented an ingenious solution, a split peg with a wedge that permanently locked the peg inside the pearl as it was pressed into position.

In theory, this is the peg of pegs, but alas, theories don't always match the reality. Sometimes this wedged peg works,

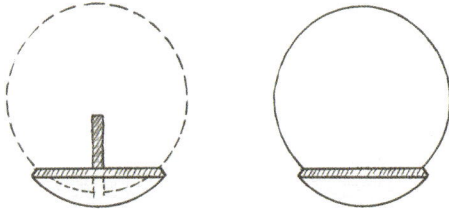

This is a combination of a peg and cup that has the advantages of both. When done, the peg is hidden, of course.

and when it works, it works very well. But, sometimes it doesn't work, and when it doesn't work, it's an absolute nightmare. I speak from experience. The potential problem isn't the peg, or the wedge, or the pearl. It is all three in combination, as I will explain in a moment.

Splitting the Peg

The production of the peg and wedge are actually pretty simple. Determine the depth of the hole and clamp a piece of 16 gauge wire into a pin vise with this amount projecting out. Using a very fine sawblade (#8/0–#12/0), split the wire down the middle, about two-thirds of the exposed length. When splitting, keep turning the wire back and forth, sawing little by little from opposite sides, to keep the cut straight down the middle (this is described more fully in A Simple Prong Setting Made from Square Wire in Chapter 4). Leave the peg attached to the length of wire for the time being.

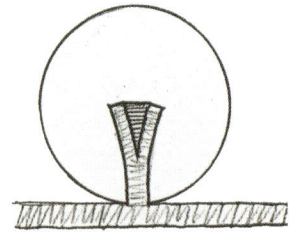

In a split peg mounting, the pressure of the bead onto a prepared peg presses the legs of the pin to create a mechanical grip.

Daphne Krinos | Ring
18k, sterling, beryl.
photo: Joel Degen

Making the Wedge

To make the wedge, hammer a piece of the same gauge wire to a smooth taper. This wedge shouldn't be too thick, or it will cause the peg to spread too much. All you need is a thin taper that is as long as the cut, and no wider than the peg. When you are satisfied with the wedge, cut it off and set it aside where it won't be lost. You can also saw the peg free and solder it in position.

Enlarging the Hole Inside the Pearl

Since the hole in the pearl is cylindrical (i.e., uniform diameter its entire length), you will need to ream the hole inside the pearl larger to permit the wedged peg to spread open. This needs to be done carefully, so as to produce a tapered conical cavity, wider at its farthest end, tapering to the original diameter of the hole at its entry. Select a cylinder bur that is slightly smaller than the diameter of the hole and, clamped into a flex shaft, insert it all the way into the hole. Hold it at a slight angle so that its far end is against the side of the wall, and run it slowly using light pressure. I keep a small bowl of water nearby, dipping the pearl in occasionally to keep it cool and rinse out the dust produced by the bur. Keep the image of the taper you are creating in mind as you excavate a conical cavity, decreasing in diameter smoothly as it approaches the outer surface. Once you have hollowed out the hole to your satisfaction, you are ready for final assembly.

The Assembly: Delight or Distress

The conundrum built into this split peg connection is this: this is a one-shot assembly. There is no trial run, no test and re-test until you get it right. You only get one chance. If all goes well, it is the strongest of pegged connections.

Insert the tip of the wedge into the split, just enough to hold it, but not so far as to prematurely spread the peg. Apply epoxy to the peg and put a bit in the pearl

Steps in Making a Split Wedge Post

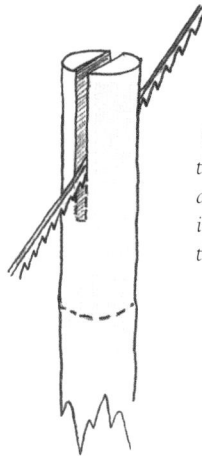

Use a fine sawblade to slide down the center of a round wire. Leave about a third of the finished length intact, but don't cut the peg from the wire until making the slot.

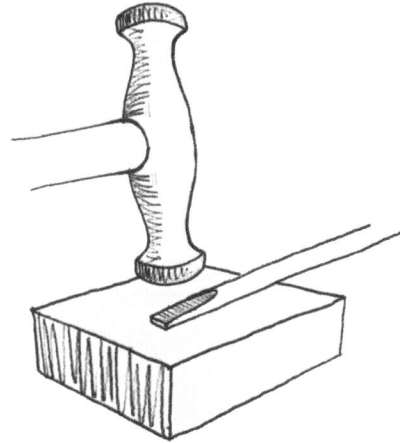

Planish a small piece of wire to make a taper.

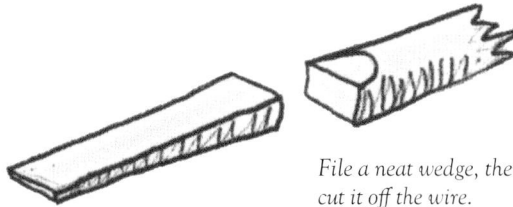

File a neat wedge, then cut it off the wire.

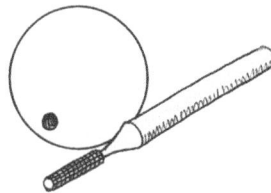

Use a cylinder bur to enlarge the interior of the hole. The system depends on having a hole that is larger at the top than the bottom.

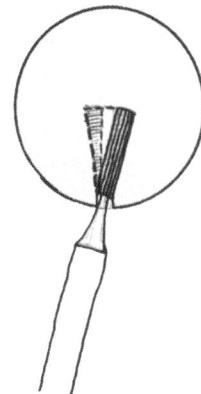

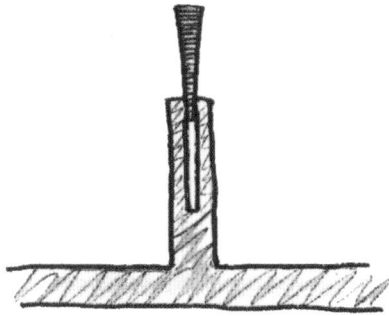

When all construction and finishing is complete, prepare to mount the bead by sliding the wedge into position.

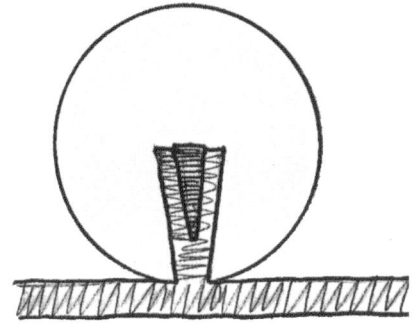

Press the bead or pearl onto the post, where the action will push the wedge down and spread the arms outward.

hole too. Carefully position the pearl onto the wedge-and-peg, taking care not to dislodge it. As you press the pearl down on the wedge, the rear wall of the hole presses against the wedge, driving it into the split, where it spreads the peg and locks it permanently inside the pearl. If you have done everything right, the pearl should fit all the way down to the base of the peg. Set it aside to allow the epoxy to set. Once the epoxy has cured, the pearl is solidly and permanently locked in place. Reach over your shoulder and give yourself a pat on the back for a job well done.

If, however, you were unfortunate enough to have unwittingly made the wedge or peg even the tiniest bit too long, or if it is a smidgen too thick, or if the wedge shifts out of position and prevents the peg from fitting all the way in, or if you didnt excavate the hole sufficiently, or if you forgot to apply the epoxy, or if the pearl cracks because the wedged peg is too tight and it can't stand up to the pressure, or if anything at all goes awry, the sky will darken and so too will your mood. Short of breaking off the peg and drilling it out, there is absolutely no other way to get it back out, short of destroying the pearl. To make matters even worse, if you are unable to dig out the peg before the epoxy you applied sets, the task is even more difficult. Like I said, I speak from experience.

If you really feel up to the challenge, by all means, try this split peg and wedge

setting. I think you will find that it is one of those processes you undertake once, and then say to yourself, "There, I've done it, and I will never do it again." I suggest that you try it on an inexpensive pearl, so that if the worst-case scenario does play out, you haven't lost anything but a little time. For what it's worth, I feel that a dependable epoxy used in conjunction with a sturdy peg renders the split peg and wedge system outdated and unnecessary.

Epoxy

There are two aspects of setting pearls—the metal structure and the adhesive that secures the sphere into that structure. Let's start with the glue, then turn attention to the metalwork that will be used in conjunction with it.

Epoxy is a thermosetting polymer which, when mixed with a hardener, also called a catalyst, produces a structural, adhesive resin. Whew! That's a mouthful. The important thing to know is that epoxy is more—much, much more—than plain old glue. Epoxy adhesives create exceptionally strong bonds, and they have been developed for many diverse applications. They are used in the construction of airplanes, automobiles, skis, and many other applications requiring bonds of great strength, flexibility, and resistance to chemicals and heat. Epoxies come in many varieties, and are exceptional adhesives for wood, metal, glass, stone, and plastics.

Michael Boyd | Necklace

photo: Steve Bigley

18k and 22k gold, lavender jadeite, black nephrite jade, maw sit-sit,
gem silica, lapis, coral, opal, sapphire, emerald, purple chalcedony, peridot.

Avoid generic, all-purpose epoxies sold in grocery, hardware, or building supply stores. These are usually utility or industrial grade, unsuited to jewelry applications. Many are tinted, or tend to yellow and discolor with age. Some come in "convenient" syringe applicators, which, once opened, can never be properly resealed, and continue to ooze and create a horrible gooey mess until finally discarded. Refrain, also, from resorting to one drop, instant-bonding cyanoacrylates. These were developed during the Korean war to temporarily seal wounds closed until injured soldiers could be transported to field hospitals for surgery. Though they certainly work well on flesh (many is the poor soul who inadvertently glued his fingers together while attempting a quick repair), and promise a temptingly simple and fast bond, they have no shear strength (resistance to sideways pressure), degrade over a relatively short time and are generally unreliable. I always keep a small tube in my studio to seal small cuts (your body produces a natural form of acetone, which breaks it down gradually, allowing it to be harmlessly absorbed). Its also handy for gluing small parts together for soldering. It holds units in place until your solder flows, and burns away without residue. It doesn't work for everything, but is worth trying for small elements that are too small or delicate to bind with wire. I do not, however, use it in place of epoxy.

Creating an epoxy bond upon which you can rely depends on five factors:

- proper epoxy
- proper preparation of surfaces
- proper mixing of epoxy and catalyst
- proper application
- proper curing

Epoxy will always be sold as a two-part kit, polymer and catalyst. Equal parts of each are mixed together, applied, and then allowed to cure. When fully cured, the epoxy is colorless, waterproof, and produces an extremely strong, long-lived, dependable bond. My personal favorite is "Epoxy 330" manufactured by Hughes Associates, available from most jewelry and craft suppliers. It has an initial set time of ten to fifteen minutes, and cures in about two hours at room temperature. The cure time can be shortened to about fifteen minutes with low heat, such as that provided by a swing arm lamp with a 75W bulb positioned about four or five inches above the epoxied item. I avoid this practice, preferring instead to let the item cure slowly, undisturbed, overnight. Microscopic gas bubbles created as a by-product of the interaction of resin and catalyst outgas during the curing process, and it seems to me better to allow as much time as possible to allow this process to play out.

Mixing Epoxy

Always follow the manufacturers instructions when you are mixing epoxy. Mismatched, poorly measured portions of resin and catalyst, or purposeful attempt to speed cure time by increasing the percentage of catalyst will produce sticky, semi-set results.

When I am preparing a small quantity of epoxy, I first cover the lid of a small jar with aluminum foil. Onto this, I squeeze out equal size drops of resin and catalyst, which I mix thoroughly with a wooden toothpick. I mix until the blend is uniformly homogeneous and slightly translucent. It appears a bit grayish at this point, but will cure water-clear. I apply the epoxy as needed, and after I am finished, I simply fold up the foil, toothpick and all, into a neat little packet and discard.

Michael Boyd | Necklace
18k and 22k gold, sterling, magnasite, shale, opal, jasper, lapis, tourmaline, dinosaur bone, maw sit-sit, citrine, fossil palm, emerald.

photo: Tim Brown

Applying Epoxy

To get the full benefit of the strength of the adhesive, it is imperative that all contact surfaces are absolutely clean and free of any oils or grease. Wherever possible, I roughen the surface by crosshatching with a scriber, then I clean everything with denatured or isopropyl alcohol. I wear disposable rubber gloves to prevent contamination from fingerprints and to keep epoxy off my fingers.

My favorite epoxy applicator is the untoothed end of a broken saw blade, stuck into the eraser of a pencil that serves as the handle. I collect these broken blade ends from my lap tray with a magnet, and store them in a small container. Since the blades come many different sizes, I can simply select one that suits the particular job. If I am epoxying a pearl onto a peg, for example, I choose a blade shank that just fits the hole in the pearl. I find that the flat shank of the blade picks up a perfect amount of epoxy—much better than the cylindrical shaft of a common pin. When I am finished, I wrap up the blade shaft with the toothpick in the foil packet.

Determining exactly how much epoxy to apply is a tricky skill, and like most every other skill, gets better with practice and experience. If you don't use enough, you risk an incomplete, unreliable bond. Use too much and the excess epoxy oozes out, producing an unsightly fillet at the edge of the interface between metal and the pearl. It usually doesn't take much epoxy to make a good bond, but it always takes enough. Generally, a thin, uniform coating over the interior surface of a cup, on a peg or inside the hole of a pearl is sufficient. Epoxy 330 has an initial set time of about 10 minutes, so if you work quickly, you can separate the parts and add a bit more if necessary.

To produce the tightest and least visible bond, clamp the pearl in place while the epoxy cures. Any means of applying moderate pressure without damaging the pearl will work. I have used cross-lock tweezers

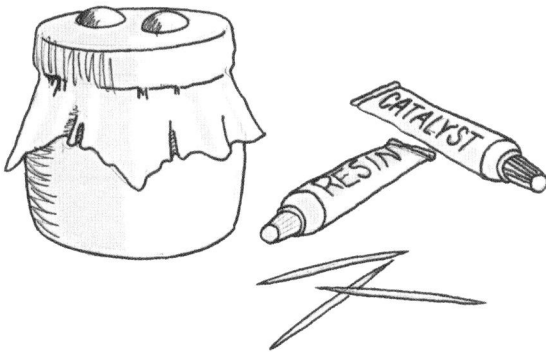

My system is to work on a small piece of aluminum foil stretched over a jar. This puts it up off the table and makes it easy to discard the excess when I'm through.

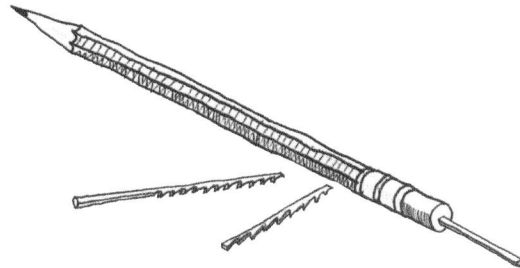

If you have a pencil and some bits of broken sawblade, you have all the makings for a convenient and disposable epoxy applicator.

(with tips wrapped with masking tape to protect the pearl), clothes pins, pairs of popsicle sticks secured at both ends with rubber bands, scotch tape, and miniature plastic clips.

Particularly when the pearl is clamped, it is perfectly normal for a tiny bit of epoxy to ooze out of the joint. If this happens, immediately wipe away the excess epoxy with a little isopropyl alcohol on a wiping pad. Do not use cotton swabs, or you'll give your piece an unexpected beard! I find a small folded pad of toilet paper works well.

I know some jewelers use acetone instead of rubbing alcohol, but I have also heard reports that acetone can dull the luster of a pearl. Since the alcohol works well, poses the lesser health hazard of the two, and has no effect on pearls, I prefer to stick with that. If you accidentally apply too much epoxy, and its not possible to remove the residue with the pearl in place, quickly pull the pearl off before the epoxy has the chance to set, clean it up and start over. Remember, whenever working with any chemicals, no matter how purportedly innocuous, wear protective eyewear, have adequate exhaust ventilation, and wear suitable rubber gloves to limit exposure to your skin.

Once you have applied the epoxy and positioned the pearl, it is important to let it cure undisturbed for the length of time suggested by the manufacturer. Any attempt to twist or re-orient the pearl during the setting phase will only interrupt the curing process, producing, at best, a poor bond, or at worst, no bond at all.

Removing Cured Epoxy

Removing fresh epoxy is relatively simple, but separating pearls from their seats after epoxy has cured is a much more complicated procedure. Cured epoxy resin is far more chemically resistant than fresh epoxy, and is impervious to relatively mild solvents like isopropyl alcohol or acetone.

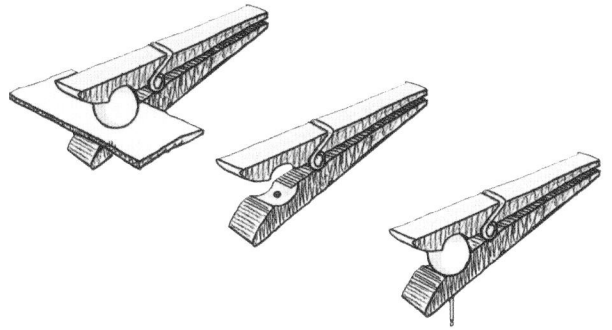

To insure a tight and attractive glue joint, it is important to keep the parts in tight proximity as the epoxy sets. Here are a couple favorite methods.

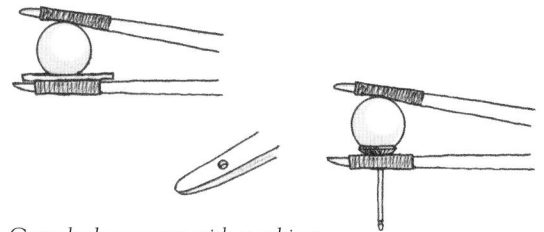

Cross-lock tweezers with masking tape are especially good for small items. Drill one tip if needed to accommodate an earring post.

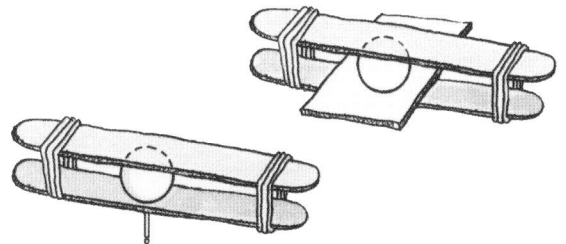

For larger items, try this approach, which uses popsicle sticks and small rubber bands.

Always try the least damaging alternative first, and move on to other, more dramatic options only if that doesn't work.

Before resorting to any chemical solutions, first try prying the pearl or gem ball loose. On occasion, I have successfully dislodged the pearl by wedging it free from its backing using a pair of flush cutters with thin, sharp edges. I positioned the jaws of the cutters at the base of the pearl, on opposite sides, then gently squeezed. I was careful not to squeeze so hard that I clipped off the peg. The wedging action of the jaws popped the pearl free from its epoxy bond, and I was able to pull it free. Any adhering epoxy left on the pearl was easily peeled off with my fingernail—don't use anything that will scratch the pearl. I used a scriber and a graver to remove the epoxy from the metal article (this is where most of the epoxy was after the pearl popped free). If you try this, be very careful to monitor the progress of the wedging. Use your eyes and your sense of feel. If it doesn't look or feel like the pearl will separate easily, or if it looks like the pearl is being damaged in any way, stop and try the next method.

I have also had some success freeing pearls by soaking them in hot water. Put several inches of water in a small saucepan and bring it to a boil. Remove the pan from the heat and put the epoxied article in the water. Allow it to soak in the hot water for about a minute, then remove it with tweezers and try to twist the pearl gently. After one or two consecutive cycles of soaking and twisting, the epoxy often softens enough to allow the pearl to twist off. The metal gets pretty warm on bare fingers, so use a paper towel to hold the item if you try this.

There is a commercial epoxy solvent called ATTACK, that softens and dissolves epoxy. The main ingredient is methylene chloride, a chlorinated hydrocarbon that is highly flammable, evaporates quickly, and releases toxic fumes. The solvent

Sarah Nelson
Trees, Fall
18k, sterling, coral, moonstone.
3½ inches tall.
photo: Sarah Nelson

is easily absorbed through the skin, dissolving fatty subcutaneous tissue, causing dermatitis, and damage to internal organs including the liver and kidneys. Use good exhaust ventilation and wear protective gloves made of chemically resistant material like neoprene, polyvinyl chloride (PVC), nitrile, or butyl. Disposable latex gloves do not provide sufficient protection.

Using ATTACK to remove epoxy usually entails an overnight soak in the solvent. Place the item in a jar with a tight-fitting lid, away from excessive heat or flame. Add sufficient ATTACK to submerge the article and secure the lid. The solvent will gradually soften the epoxy until the pearl can be pulled free. Any residual softened epoxy on the pearl can usually simply be rubbed off with a small pad of toilet paper; use a toothpick to scrape off any epoxy on the metal. Wash the parts with isopropyl alcohol, and let it air dry, as a final step. Once everything is epoxy-free and clean, you can proceed.

Important: You must also be very careful when using ATTACK, on certain gem materials and "assembled" pearls. Though genuine pearls (natural or cultured) may be safely immersed in this solvent, many softer gem or ornamental materials, such as turquoise, are often stabilized by being soaked in epoxy-like resins. Mabe pearls and certain faux pearls (which have a nacre-like coating affixed to a glass core) are assembled with epoxy or similar polymer resins. Any of these can be damaged by immersion in this solvent. If you have any doubts about the quality of the pearl, don't use the solvent.

If, in a worst-case scenario, you should break off the peg inside the pearl while attempting any of these procedures, the only solution is to drill or bur it out. Select a drill bit or ball bur smaller than the diameter of the peg. Work slowly, up the center of the peg, to avoid enlarging the hole in the pearl or accidentally drilling right on through. Persistence and patience will pay off here.

Sam Shaw
Brooch/Pendant
22k gold, lapis lazuli, emerald
2" x 2"

Chapter 8
Tension Settings

I suppose for a beginner (or if you are the nervous type), almost any setting could be viewed as a tension setting. I have observed countless students chewing their tongues, beads of sweat dotting their brows, hands trembling, as they attempt the settings discussed in prior chapters. I wouldn't be surprised if some of them even developed tension headaches. However, these are not the tension settings to which I refer.

Tension settings, as the name implies, are those that trap a stone by means of spring tension. It's important to understand that tension setting is decidedly more concept than step-by-step fabrication technique. All tension settings are simple cold-connections. There is no soldering involved (I will explain in a moment). There is no formal, standardized system of assembling components. There is just spring tension. The stone is secured solely by compression.

Because springiness is an integral, req-uisite factor for tension setting, heating to annealing temperatures (and this includes soldering), should be minimized, or better yet, avoided altogether. If you absolutely must solder, do so before you work-harden the piece. However, consider very carefully whether or not your soldered applications are absolutely necessary. Work-harden-ing a surface while attempting to avoid appliqués can be a real nuisance, and at worst, can prevent access for satisfactory hardening of a surface. I recommend that objects on which you intend to use tension settings be designed so they can be con-structed without heating.

Tension Set Applications
The most common use of tension settings is in rings—other jewelry forms are not candidates for this system of stone setting for several reasons. Larger-scale jewelry forms, like bracelets and neckpieces would need to be excessively thick and heavy to

deliver the springiness and compression needed to secure the stone. They would also have to be large enough to fit loosely over the head or the hand, since they couldn't be flexed open. This could entail a marketing problem as well, since wearing something the size of a toilet seat around your neck doesn't appeal to a whole lot of people. The restrictions of mass and weight are even more pertinent with regards to earrings. Rings simply provide the ideal structural format for tension setting.

A well-designed, well-made tension-set ring has many positive points: it's wearable, strong, requires no solder construction (which means less clean-up, since there's no solder or firescale to remove), and it secures the stone with minimal coverage. However, there are also limitations that must be carefully weighed. Tension-set rings cannot be resized and the range of stone size is limited in direct correlation to the mass of the ring and the degree to which it is hardened. Comfort usually dictates restricted scale and mass, which additionally harkens back to stone size. The type of stone is also restricted, since only stones that can withstand the considerable compression are suited to the application.

Work-Hardening

The most commonly used precious metals—high karat gold and sterling—are malleable (in practice, what we call soft), so they must be treated in some way that will render them hard and springy. Most of us learn early in our careers that many of the things we do to metal makes it harder, springier, and often, more difficult to work with. Hammering, rolling, bending, twisting and stretching all produce work-hardening. Usually, when this happens, we restore the metal's malleability by annealing. Sometimes, however, we find that this hardened state serves us well, and we take advantage of this condition to produce strength, rigidity, and springiness. Tension setting exploits work-hardening this way.

Refiners have developed a few specialty alloys that can be heat-treated to produce springiness, but most jewelry is still made with traditional silver and gold alloys. Sterling can be heat-hardened by soaking it at 500°F to 600°F (260°–315° C) for several hours, and while this increases resistance to denting somewhat, the degree of hardening is far less than what we need for tension setting. The more exotic heat-treatable alloys, which do become suitably

Daphne Krinos
Oxidized Silver Brooch
Sterling, tourmalinated quartz.
2 inches tall.
photo: Joel Degen

hard and springy require sophisticated
equipment that place them outside the
scope of small studios.

The two most notable exceptions are
the studios of Steven Kretchmer in the US,
and Niessing in Germany. Both studios
have, independently, devised sophisticated heat-treatment processes and have
developed special alloys that are extremely
hard and exhibit high-compression characteristics. Understandably, both studios
also rely heavily on patents, secrecy, and
litigation, for obvious reasons, and neither
is ever likely to share the fruits of their research. This leaves the rest of us to fend for
ourselves, trying to come up with alternate,
workable solutions in our own somewhat
less lavishly equipped studios and with our
slightly more conventional repertoire of
tools and techniques. There are, as I mentioned a moment ago, a number of suitable
possibilities for generating work-hardening
or springiness sufficient for our purposes.

Methods for Work-hardening and Developing Springiness

Hammering

Hammering (planishing, forging, peening,
etc.) is probably the simplest and most
direct means of work-hardening. As
the crystalline structure of the metal is
compressed and densified, the metal gets
harder and springier. All you require by
way of technology are a hammer and a
steel surface like an anvil, a bench plate, or
a section of railroad track. This is certainly
the simplest, fastest, least labor and equipment intensive means of work-hardening a
piece of metal.

The major drawbacks to this method
are overall deformation, thinning of the
metal cross section, and the risk of over-
working and subsequent stressing of the
metal to the point of fracture. A little
practice goes a long way here, and if you
listen to your metal, you will quickly learn
its limits.

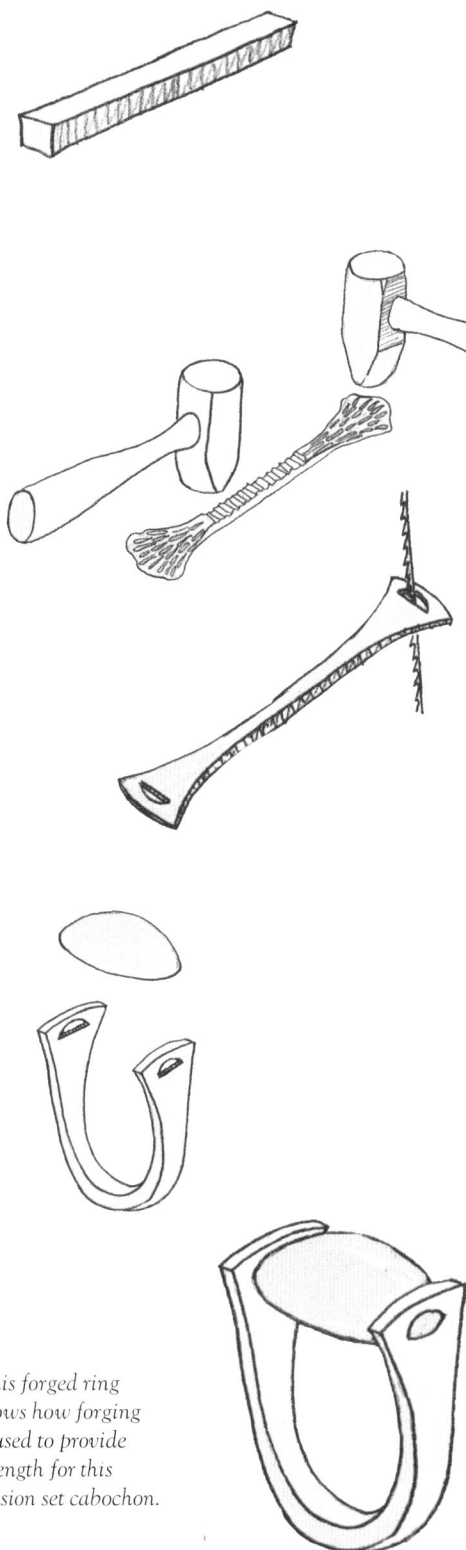

This forged ring shows how forging is used to provide strength for this tension set cabochon.

Hammering is the only technique for work hardening that allows you to selectively control the direction in which the metal moves as it is reduced in thickness. You can make it wider, longer, or just plain thinner, and thinner it will definitely become. When selecting a piece of metal for hammer hardening, plan on a reduction of at least 50% to produce the necessary springiness and strength.

Rolling

Sometimes a rolling mill can replace hammering for work hardening. Instead of swinging a heavy hammer, you simply let the mill's gear reduction and the consistent force of the rollers do the work. There are three basic types of mills: sheet, wire, and combination mills (which offer both in a single machine). Sheet rollers reduce the gauge of flat metal stock (sheet, flat strip, plate), making it longer with minimal sideways widening. This is referred to as directional stretching.

A wire mill reduces the gauge of wire and rod stock as it is forced through the rollers, usually producing a diamond-shaped cross-section. By "stepping down" (rolling short sections of stock through increasingly smaller grooves in the rollers), the wire can be tapered. As the wire thins and lengthens, it also hardens. Planishing the angular edges will round out a squared taper. As in the case of hammering, maximum hardening will depend on significant reduction in cross-sectional dimension.

Twisting

Twisting a piece of rod or wire quickly hardens it. When round wire is twisted, the effect is almost invisible. Because the round cross section has no corners, a round wire looks the same after twisting as before. This is not the case with square wires, or anything other than round, where the edges produce a screw-like threaded appearance. Though perhaps attractive, the exposed outer edges are delicate and easily marred, making it difficult to form, for instance, to bend into a ring shape.

When I am twisting a piece of wire, I make a small L-shaped bend at both ends. This prevents it from turning as it is twisted. I clamp one end in a vise and the other in a pair of vise grips. I like to make a stripe down its length with an indelible marker, so that I can monitor the progress of my twist. As I rotate the wire, the inked line creates a lengthwise, barber-pole candy stripe. I always twist slowly, and keep tension on the wire to keep it straight. If the wire is slack, it will snarl, and if I twist too quickly, the wire twists more at both ends than in the middle, and will often fatigue and break prematurely. Slow twisting allows the wire to twist evenly along its length. I keep twisting slowly, watching the candy stripe develop uniformly, until the wire finally breaks off at the vise or the vise grips. It is now as uniformly hard and springy along its entire length as I can make it. The inked line is easily removed with a quick rub of a nylon scouring pad, or with a little denatured alcohol.

I use this method of work-hardening to produce the shanks for simple tension set rings for small stones. I find that 10 gauge round sterling silver wire works very well for this. Gold would work equally well, and because karat golds are tougher, a slightly smaller gauge could be used. Because the rod is significantly hard and springy after twisting, you'll want a fairly long piece to supply leverage for bending. Removal of the damaged, clamped ends from the twisting operation, coupled with the excess removed while trimming the ring to size, together represent substantial waste, usually more of an issue when working with gold because of the initial investment.

To make the ring shank, wrap the wire around a ring mandrel at a point about a size smaller than the desired finger size (the stone, when inserted later, will open

Making a Tension Ring from Twisted Round Wire

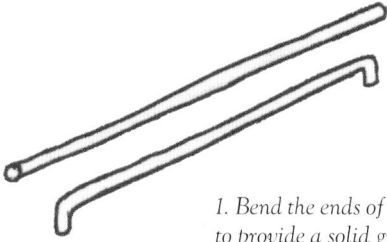

1. Bend the ends of a wire down to provide a solid grip.

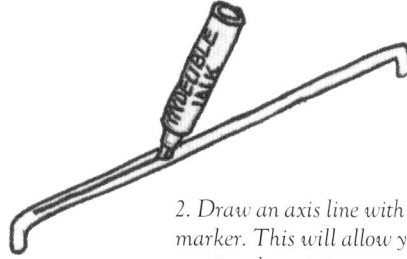

2. Draw an axis line with a marker. This will allow you to monitor the twisting.

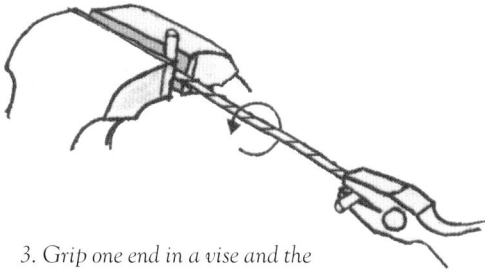

3. Grip one end in a vise and the other in stout pliers. Maintain a backward pressure on the wire throughout the twisting operation.

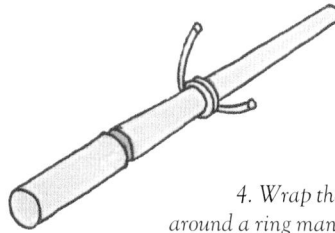

4. Wrap the hardened wire around a ring mandrel to create a ring shank. Note that you will need a good bit of extra wire to provide leverage.

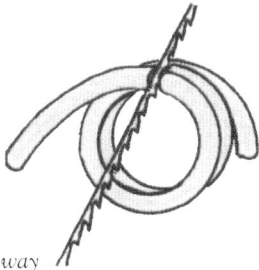

5. Cut the coil in the same way that jump ring coils are cut.

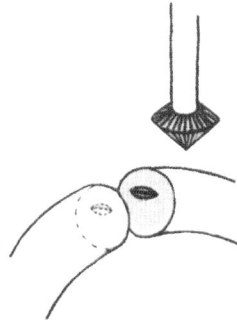

6. Use a Hart bur to cut notches into the smoothed and polished faces of the cut wire.

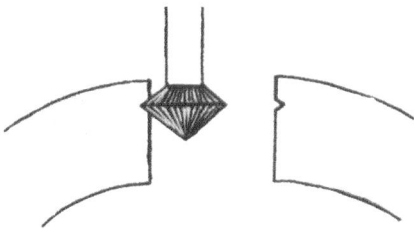

7. Be certain to hold the bur vertically so the notches are perfectly located. You really only get one chance at this.

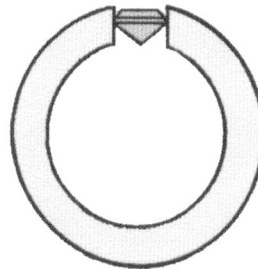

8. The finished ring.

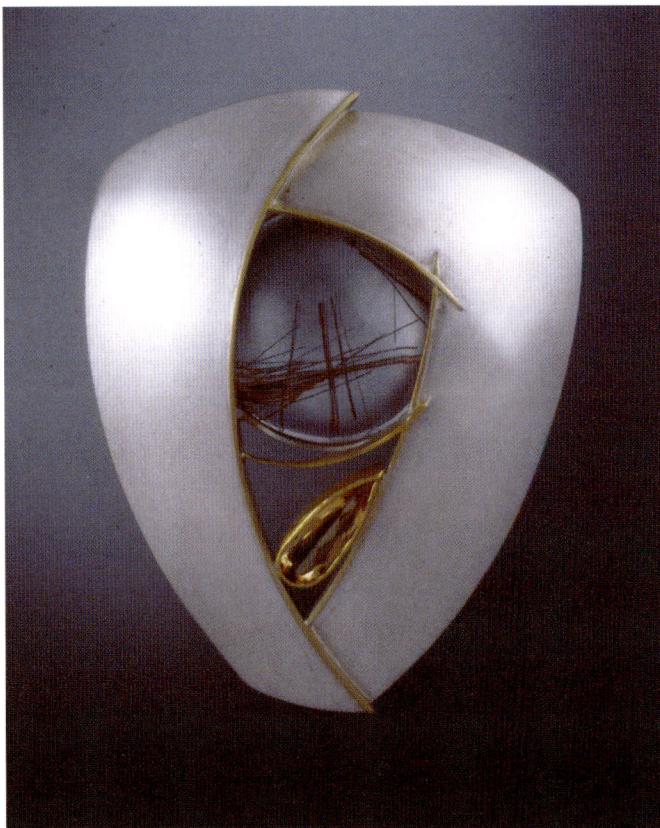

the ring to the correct size). In appearance, this might look like a larger version of the coil you create when making a jump ring. The important point is to start with an oversize length of wire, and bend what amounts to a loop and a half, or one and a half times around the mandrel. This will insure a uniform curvature throughout the ring. Slide the coil off the mandrel, cut the ring free and open the ends sideways, just as you would do when opening a standard jump ring. In this case, we need access to cut seats for the stone in both ends of the wire. If I am setting a faceted stone, I use a small Hart bur to cut a shallow notch in each end. If its a small gem ball, I use a ball bur. I then close the ends (sideways, the same way we close a jump ring), slide the ring up a ring mandrel, wedging the ends just far enough apart to pop the stone into the notches, and then slide it back off, compression-fitting the stone in place. A second set of hands comes in handy at this time. Niessing and Kretchmer both produce rings with a somewhat similar overall final appearance, but that similarity is purely superficial. In both cases, their rings are fashioned from cast, heat-hardened special gold or platinum alloys of their own secret recipe. (They are also almost always set with diamonds, not something most of us would consider in sterling silver).

Drawing

Drawing entails pulling wire through successively smaller holes in a drawplate to reduce its cross-sectional dimension while making it longer. In the process, it also gets harder. Unfortunately, there are two drawbacks to this method. Producing a piece of wire of sufficient gauge, hardness, and springiness requires starting with a substantially thicker wire or rod. This, in turn, usually requires the use of a draw bench.

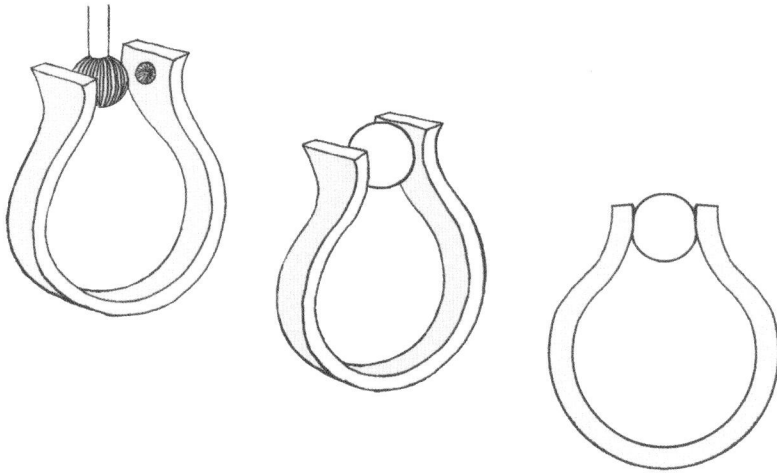

Here is another example of a tension mounted ring. In this case a gem ball is trapped in rounded depressions cut into the inner faces of a workhardened ring shank.

Commercial models are expensive, take up a lot of space, and, because they only do one thing, are not economically feasible in many small studios. I have a portable, homemade drawbench that requires little space, stores easily, and is capable of drawing pretty thick stock. If you do not have access to a drawbench, it will probably be more cost-effective to produce the hardened stock you need by hammering, rolling, or twisting.

As I mentioned at the beginning, tension setting is more a concept than an organized, systematic approach. There is no prototypical tension setting. Put on your thinking cap—every stone and every design will demand its own one-of-a kind solution. Inspect the stone you wish to set, and sketch out possible ways by which you might trap it by compression.

Alternative Materials

Sometimes, thinking outside the box, so to speak, expands our options. Many years ago, I worked for a commercial manufacturing jeweler, where we worked almost exclusively in precious metals and stones, mostly gold and diamonds. When I entered graduate school, I found myself in a far more conceptual, far less material-oriented environment. My instructors and my fellow students were fashioning things from paper, crushed eggshell, rubber, plastic. We learned that value came from what we did with otherwise valueless materials. We discovered that we were idea-generating conceptualists, designers and craftsmen all rolled up in one. Everything is a potential material with which to work. Currencies come and go and precious metals are unstable stock market commodities, jockeyed by financial marketeers. Market value is both highly variable and unreliable. Cost price is not an accurate indicator of the real value of silver or gold. I quickly came to realize that the real value of the things I make has less to do with market bullion value, than what I do with them. The intangibles with which we imbue our work, those unique things that issue from our hearts, our hands, and our minds, are the things that truly give value to what we do.

Beginner jewelers and traditionally trained metalsmiths can be intimidated by the expense of precious metal, and this tends to have a restrictive, inhibiting effect on their work. I always try to make them understand that gold and silver are precious for their working characteristics (color, luster, malleability, etc), not because of perceived market value. They are simply the materials with which we work. The price we pay to procure them is simply the cost of doing business. At the same time, I encourage all designers to look at alternative materials.

There are many other metals and materials that provide the hardness and springiness we need. Titanium, stainless steels, spring steels, even certain plastics are potential candidates and I'll bet there are others. Most are easily tooled, durable and are readily and widely available. They also offer one additional thing: novelty. Jewelry created from alternate materials stands apart from more commonly employed silver and gold. I repeatedly tell students (in my best worst English), "More different is often more better!" When you create something that makes passers-by look twice, that can be a good thing. Dare to stand apart and try new things. You may be pleasantly surprised. At the very least, allow yourself to consider alternative materials.

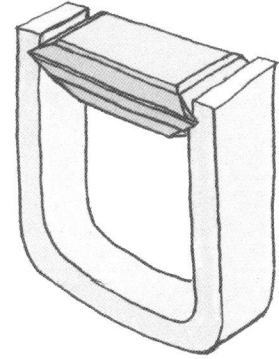

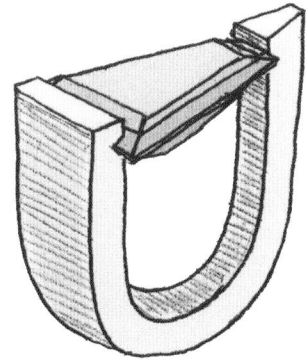

These two examples show a tension setting in which the seats for the gems were probably made with a combination of Hart burs and needle files. The shanks should be hardened by forging or rolling.

This classic channel set earring is a poster child for tension settings. Start by hardening a piece of sheet, bend it around to form a trough, solder an earpost on the back, and cut channels that make a tight fit for the stones. Maybe not quite as easy as it looks, but a terrific exercise to teach measurement, filing, and setting.

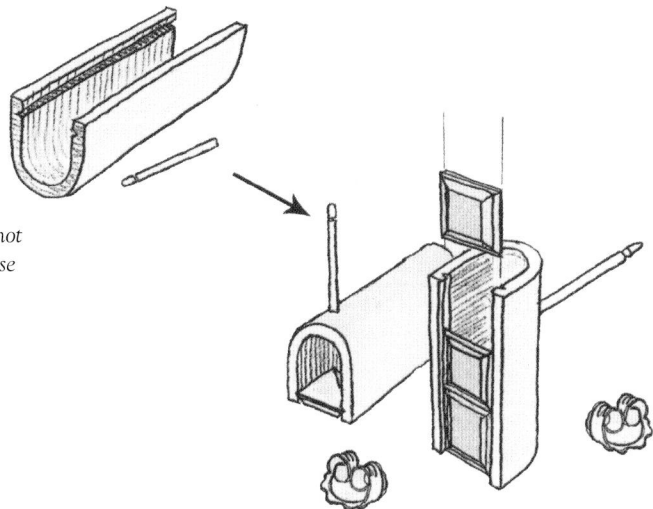

Appendix

Sam Shaw
Big Ring
18k cast twig. rutilated quartz
2½ inches tall.
photo: Robert Diamante

COMMON GEMSTONES AND MATERIALS

Mineral Family	Mohs Hardness	Common Varietes	Common Colors
Amber	2 – 2.5	Amber	Light Yellow to dark brown; orange; red
Coal	2.5 – 4	Jet	Velvet-black
Coral	3.5 – 4	Coral	White; pink; orange; red; golden; black
Beryl	7.5 – 8	Aquamarine	Greenish-blue or light blue
		Emerald	Deep green
		Goshenite	Colorless; yellow-green, brown
		Heliodore	Golden yellow to golden green
		Morganite	Pink; purple-pink; peach
		Red beryl	Raspberry red
Chrysoberyl	8.5	Alexandrite	Red in incandescent light / green in daylight
		Cat's Eye	Yellowish to greenish
		Chrysoberyl	Yellowish green to pale brown
Corundum	9	Ruby	Intense red
		Sapphire	Blue; grey; yellow; green; pink; lavender; orange
Diamond	10	Diamond	Colorless to faint yellowish tinge (variable)
Feldspar	6 – 6.5	Amazonite	Yellow-green to greenish blue
		Labradorite	Iridescent stones in yellow, orange, red, green
		Moonstone	Colorless; white; yellowish; reddish-bluish gray
		Orthoclase	Pale yellow; flesh red
		Peristerite	Blue-white iridescence
		Sunstone	Gold spangles from inclusions of hematite
Garnet	6.5 – 7	Almandine	Orange-red to purplish red
		Almandine–Spessartine	Reddish orange / Yellow-green; orange-yellow; black
		Andradite	Green to yellow-green
		Demantoid	Yellow orange to red
		Topazolite	Orange-red
		Grossular	Colorless; orange; pink; yellow; brown
		Tsavorite	Green to yellowish green
		Hessonite	Yellow-orange to red
		Pyrope	Colorless; also pink to red
		Chrome pyrope	Orange-red
		Pyrope-Almandine	Reddish orange to red-purple
		Pyrope-Spessartine	Greenish-yellow to purple
		Rhodite	Purple-red to red-purple
		Spesartine	Yellow-orange
		Uvarovite	Emerald green
Iron	5	Hematite	Steely gray
Jade	6 – 7	Jadeite	White; blue; green; lavender; blue-green; black
		Nephrite	White deep green, creamy brown, black

COMMON GEMSTONES AND MATERIALS

Mineral Family	Mohs Hardness	Common Varieties	Common Colors
Lapis lazuli	5 – 5.5	Lapis lazuli	Azure blue; greenish blue with flecks of gold
Olivine	7	Peridot	Olive to lime green
Pearl	2.5 – 4.5	Pearl	White; cream; rose; black; gray; bronze; blue; dark blue; blue-green; red; purple; yellow; violet
Quartz	7	Agate	Variable patterns and colors
		Amethyst	Purple
		Black opal	Flashes and speckles agains black background
		Bloodstone	Green with red spots (a.k.a. heliotrope)
		Carnelian	Reddish orange
		Chalcedony	Blue; gray
		Chrysoprase	Green
		Citrine	Yellow to amber
		Fire opal	Reddish or orange opal
		Green quartz	Green
		Jasper	Green
		Morion	Black
		Onyx	Black
		Rock crystal	Colorless
		Rose quartz	Transluscent pink
		Sardonyx	Reddish orange
		Smoky quartz	Smoky gray to brown (a.k.a. cairngorm)
		Water opal	Colorless with brilliant flashes of color
		White opal	Opaque; porcelain-like white material; colors resemble slashes or speckles
Spinel	8	Almandine spinel	Purple-red
		Balas ruby	Red
		Chlorspinel	Green
		Rubicelle: orange	Blue
		Sapphire spinel	Blue
		Spinel	Colorless pale brown; golden
Topaz	8	Topaz	Yellow; pale blue; deep blue; green; violet; red
Tourmaline	7 – 7.5	Achorite	Colorless
		Brazilian emerald	Green
		Dravite	Brown
		Indicolite	Dark blue
		Rubellite	Pink to red
		Siberite	Violet
		Verdilite	Green
Turquoise	6 – 6	Turquoise	Sky blue; greenish blue
Zircon	7.5	Hyacinth	Yellow; orange; red; brown
		White zircon	Colorless

Weight & Measurement Comparisons

Troy / Metric
1 grain = 0.0648 grams
1 pennyweight = 1.5552 grams
1 troy ounce = 31.1035 grams
1 troy pound - 373.24 grams

Avoirdupois / Troy
1 grain = 1 grain
1 ounce Avoir. = 0.914
1 pound Avoir. = 14.5833 troy ounces

Avoirdupois / Metric
1 grain = 0.0648 grams
1 ounce Avoir. = 28.3495 grams
i pound Avoir. = 453.59 grams
2.2 pounds Avoir. = 1 kilogram

Carat / Metric
1 grain = 0.648 grams
1 point = 2 milligrams
1 carat = 200 milligrams

Metric to English
1 millimeter = 0.03937 inches
1 centimeter = 0.3937
1 meter = 39.37 inches
1 meter = 3.2808 feet

English to Metric
1 mil = 0.0254 millimeters
1 inch = 2.54 centimeters
1 foot = 0.3048 meters
1 yard = 0.9144 meters

B&S	Inches	Millimeters
0	0.325	8.26
2	0.257	6.54
4	0.204	5.19
6	0.162	4.12
8	0.128	3.26
10	0.102	2.59
12	0.081	2.05
14	0.064	1.63
16	0.051	1.29
18	0.040	1.02
20	0.032	0.813
22	0.025	0.644
24	0.020	0.511
26	0.016	0.405
28	0.013	0.321
30	0.010	0.255
32	0.0080	0.202
34	0.0063	0.160
36	0.005	0.127

Equivalents

1 meter (m) = 10 decimeters (dm) = 100 centimeters (cm) = 1000 millimeters (mm)

1 meter (m) = 0.1 decameter (dkm) = 0.01 hectometer (hm) = 0.001 kilometer (km)

1 millimeter (mm) = 1000 microns (μ) = 0.03937 inches (") = 3937 mils

To convert from	to	multiply by:
Avoirdupois ounces	troy ounces	0.911460
	grams	28.3495
	pennyweights	18.2292
Carats	grains	3.0865
	pennyweights	0.1286
	grams	0.2000
Pennyweights (dwt)	carats	7.7760
	grams	1.5552
	troy ounces	0.0500
Grains	carats	0.3240
	grams	0.0648
	troy ounces	0.0021
	pennyweights	0.0417
Inches	millimeters	25.40
	meters	0.0254
Millimeters	inches	0.0394
Kilograms	Avoir. ounces	35.274
	troy ounces	32.151
	pennyweights	643.015
	Avoir. pounds	2.2000
Troy ounces	grams	31.1035
	Avoir. ounces	1.097
	pennyweights	20
	Avoir. pounds	0.06857

Tools & Supplies

Allcraft Tool & Supply
135 West 29th Street, Room 205
New York, NY 10001
800-645-7124 or 212-279-7077
allcraftonline.com

Contenti Company
123 Stewart Street
Providence, RI 02903
800-343-3364 or 401-421-4040
contenti.com

Otto Frei
126 Second Street
Oakland, CA 94604
800-772-3456 or 510-835-0355
ofrei.com

Gesswein
255 Hancock Avenue
Bridgeport, CT 06605
800-243-4466 or 203-366-5400
gesswein.com

Indian Jewelry Supply
601 East Coal Street
Gallup, NM 87301
800-545-6540 or 505-722-4451
IJSinc.com

Metalliferous
34 West 46th Street
New York, NY 10036
888-944-0909 or 212-944-0909
metalliferous.com

Rio Grande Albuquerque
7500 Bluewater Road NW
Albuquerque, NM 87121
800-545-6566 or 505-839-3300
riogrande.com

T. B. Hagstoz & Son
709 Sansom Street
Philadelphia, PA 19106
800-922-1006 or 215-922-1627
www.hagstoz.com

Gemstones

Gary Abbott
PO Box 1311
Roswell, GA 30077
gabbott@hotmail.com

Dikra Gems
56 W. 45th Street, Suite 1005
New York, NY 10036
800-873-4572
212-869-6332
dikragem.net

Raymond Gabriel
1469 Rosena Avenue
Madison, OH 44057

A. F. Greenwood
10 W. 47th Street
New York, NY 10036
800-882-9908
212-719-4243
afggems.com

Lucien L. Stern, Inc.
230 Fifth Avenue
New York, NY 10001
212- 532-5760

Leo Wolleman, Inc.
1156 Avenue of the Americas
New York, NY 10035
800-223-5667
212-840-1881
leowolleman.com

Precious Metals

Hauser & Miller
10950 Lin-Valle Drive
St. Louis, MO 63123
800-462-7447
314-487-1311
hauserandmiller.com

Hoover & Strong Refiners
10700 Trade Road
Richmond, VA 23236
800-759-9997

INDEX

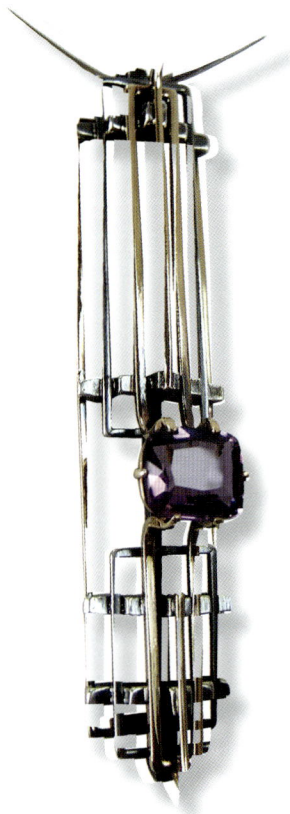

John Cogswell | Pendant
Sterling, 14k gold, amethyst
photo: John Cogswell

COLOPHON

This book was composed on a Macintosh G5 computer using Adobe InDesign layout software. The text and headings are set in LTC Goudy Oldstyle Pro, a font designed by Frederick W. Goudy in 1916. It is known for its readability and understated elegance.

Creative Stonesetting was printed in Hong Kong
by Elegance Printing and Bookbinding.